BRUEGEL

BRVE

An Artabras Book

R.H. MARIJNISSEN · M. SEIDEL

GEL

HARRISON HOUSE · NEW YORK

Text, catalog and notes by Roger H. Marijnissen,
Institut Royal du Patrimonie Artistique, Brussels.
Photographs and picture research by Max Seidel.

For their cooperation in the production of this book gratitude is expressed
to the following museums and collections: Antwerp, Musée Mayer
van den Bergh; Brussels, Musées royaux des Beaux-Arts; Darmstadt,
Hessisches Landesmuseum; London, National Gallery; Madrid, Prado;
Naples, Museo Nazionale; Paris, Louvre; Rome, Galleria Doria; Winter-
thur, Collection Dr. O. Reinhart. Special appreciation is due Dr. Delporte,
Brussels. Thanks are also extended to: Berlin, Staatliche Museen; Buda-
pest, Országos Magyar Szépmüvészeti Muzeum; Detroit, Institute of
Arts; Hampton Court, Collections of Her Majesty the Queen of England;
London, Collection A. GrafSeilern; Munich, Pinakothek; New York,
The Metropolitan Museum of Art; Prague, Národní Galerie; Rotter-
dam, Museum Boymans-van Beuningen; Vienna, Kunsthistorisches
Museum.

Originally published in German by Chr. Belser Verlag, Stuttgart.
English translation © G.P. Putnam's Sons, New York.

Front cover: Detail from *The Fall of the Rebel Angels*, see p. 142.
Back cover: *The Massacre of the Innocents*, see p. 249.

Library of Congress Cataloging in Publication Data

Marijnissen, Roger H.
  Bruegel.

  Translation of: Bruegel.
  1. Bruegel, Pieter, c. 1525–1569.   I. Seidel,
Max.   II. Title.
ND673.B73S413   1984   759.9493   84-4562
ISBN 0-517-44772X

CONTENTS

ILLUSTRATIONS

FOREWORD

Books printed in the Netherlands in Pieter Bruegel's time are often introduced by a foreword addressed *"totten goetwilligen leser"* (to the gracious reader). This foreword is addressed to the gracious viewer whose curiosity has been aroused by Max Seidel's splendid photographs.

The works of the old masters admirably lend themselves to photographic examination, to analysis by the insatiable eye of the camera. Often an unhurried study of details brings fuller understanding of the original. And Bruegel's paintings are well suited to sectional reproduction. Any area we single out, however small, is full of interest—a perfect little picture complete in itself.

Besides bringing us closer to the works of the old masters, photography has also lengthened our perspective. It both distorts and corrects our vision. As André Malraux says in *The Voices of Silence*: "Reproduction has created fictive arts by systematically distorting the scale of its subjects." As art historians turn increasingly to photographic reproductions as a tool of research, they may tend to neglect what one scholar has fretfully referred to as "those damned originals."

The camera has become an accessory organ of sight, exposing minute details which were hitherto overlooked. Familiar objects reveal unsuspected facets. The detail is no longer part of the whole; rather, the whole is now the sum of the details. There is no denying the parallel between this way of seeing and the tendency of modern science to disregard the totality of an object in order to dissect and analyze its components.

Photography teaches us to see the works of the old masters through the eyes of Bruegel's contemporaries and thus to understand them better. The long titles of books published in those days often end with the words *"ende is seer genoechlijck om te lesen"* (and [this work] offers very pleasant reading). The same can be said of Bruegel's paintings. Even more important, his paintings contain a meaning which was obvious to his contemporaries but which we have to rediscover.

Present-day critics see many old masters such as Bosch, Bruegel, Archimboldo, and Piranesi as forerunners of the Surrealists. These photographic reproductions of Bruegel's works certainly prove that he had his surrealistic side. The terrifying hallucinations revealed in the details from the Madrid "Triumph of Death" (plates pp.110–35) are far more macabre than any modern work. But is Bruegel's art truly surrealistic? Before we can answer this, we must define the term. In the act of creation the artist transforms his daily reality, heightening it to sublimity or distorting it into something horrifying. The closer his statement comes to either of these two poles, the more "surreal" it will be. The surrealistic nature of the visual arts is easily demonstrated. From this viewpoint Bruegel is indisputably surrealistic, particularly as he sometimes succeeds in heightening reality into sublimity and horror simultaneously.

But the term "Surrealism" is too closely linked with the artistic and literary movement of the 1920's which grew out of the Dadaist revolution, and too rich in confusing implications, to be applied to Bruegel. It inevitably suggests the works of Max Ernst, Salvador Dali, Victor Brauner, René Magritte, Paul Delvaux, and many other supporters of a movement still alive today. Obviously the Surrealism of our time is not to be equated with the spirit of Bosch' and Bruegel's works.

Bruegel in truth defies categorization; he cannot be identified with any movement to which a specific name was later assigned. Was he a Mannerist or not? Before this can even be discussed, there must be some definition of terms. The Bruegel of "The Triumph of Death" is not surrealistic, though he was certainly giving his visionary impulses free rein. The monsters he borrowed from his famous predecessor, Hieronymus Bosch—in "The Fall of the Rebel Angels" (plates pp. 138–51), for instance, and in his engravings—might more accurately be described as fantasies.

Can anyone look at these plates and not be enthralled? Those encountering Pieter Bruegel the Elder for the first time will discover a unique genius. A similar surprise even awaits Bruegel connoisseurs who will make new discoveries on every page. All will appreciate the unusual opportunity this book offers of comparing paintings displayed in museums all over the world.

Pieter Bruegel the Elder ranks among the great masters of Western painting—indeed, of the world. Without doubt these photographs will stimulate experts and art lovers to closer examination and analysis of his artistic legacy. Scholars, historians, folklorists, and art experts agree that the work of this painter, once nicknamed Pieter the Droll, is a world to itself. Many see him as a misanthropist; for others his drawings and paintings ring with the laughter of the people of Brabant—a people said to be afflicted with a harmless form of madness which gets worse with age. Let us for the moment set aside the question of his *Weltanschauung* and enjoy the colorful spectacle of his tempestuous world.

The plates are accompanied by brief notes and excerpts from contemporary texts. Of course Bruegel himself never read Marcus von Vaernewijck's chronicle. Yet these texts reflect the mentality of sixteenth-century man, and this has been the basis of their selection.

Pieter Bruegel lived in a turbulent age marked by struggles for power and religious strife. Much of what he wanted to say had to be communicated in a sort of secret code. Thanks to their Humanistic education, his contemporaries were well able to understand and delight in his cryptic symbolism. The rich allusional content of his work has inspired the most diverse interpretations and misconceptions. The surest way to a proper understanding of Bruegel's art is careful scrutiny supplemented by the widest possible knowledge of the intellectual climate that produced it.

This book contains a comprehensive documentation of Bruegel's paintings and selected details from them, together with references to the most important literature and sources. It is hoped that this hard core of factual information may produce a fresh and timely understanding of his work. Four hundred years have passed since the death of this great painter. His art lives on. Our eyes must rediscover it.

BRUEGEL

THE LIFE OF PIETER BRUEGEL THE ELDER

Little is known of Bruegel's life. Apart from some handwritten notes on sketches indicating the colors of the figures' clothing,[1] no original text attributable to him survives.[2] We possess no contracts, no correspondence, little more than ten contemporary documents. Our only source of information is the chapter dealing with him in Carel van Mander's famous *Schilderboeck*, and even this biography is to be taken with reserve, since it was published only in 1604, more than thirty years after the painter's death.[3] Besides, Van Mander, like all chroniclers of his time, had nothing against hearsay, as his account of Bruegel shows. Nevertheless, scholars readily admit that many of his facts are corroborated by documents in the archives.

This is what Van Mander[4] tells us (the translation is that of Constant van de Wall):

Nature was wonderfully felicitous in her choice when, in an obscure village in Brabant, she selected the gifted and witty Pieter Breughel to paint her and her peasants, and to contribute to the everlasting fame of painting in the Netherlands.

Pieter was born not far from Breda, in a village called Breughel, a name he took for himself and his descendants. He learned his craft from Pieter Koeck van Aelst, whose daughter he later married. He often carried her in his arms when she was little, and when he lived with Aelst. From Aelst he went to work with Jeroon Kock, and then he went to France and to Italy.

He practiced a good deal in the manner of Jeroon van den Bosch, and made many similar, weird scenes and drolleries. For this reason, he was often called Pier den Droll. Indeed, there are very few works from his hand that the beholder can look at seriously, without laughing. However stiff, serious, and morose one may be, one cannot help laughing, or smiling.

Pieter painted many pictures from life on his journey, so that it was said of him that while he visited the Alps, he had swallowed all the mountains and cliffs, and, upon coming home, he had spit them forth upon his canvas and panels; so remarkably was he able to follow these and other works of nature.

He settled down, selecting Antwerp as his residence, and there he entered the guild of the painters in 1551. He did a great amount of work for a merchant by the name of Hans Franckert,[5] a noble and worthy man who liked to chat with Breughel. He was with him every day. With this Franckert, Breughel often went on trips among the peasants, to their weddings and fairs. The two dressed like peasants, brought presents like the other guests, and acted as if they belonged to the families or acquaintances of the bride or of the groom. Here Breughel delighted in observing the manners of the peasants in eating, drinking, dancing, jumping, making love, and engaging in various drolleries, all of which he knew how to copy in color very comically and skillfully, and equally well with water color and oils; for he was exceptionally skilled in both processes. He knew well the characteristics of the peasant men and women of the Kampine and elsewhere. He knew how to dress them naturally and how to portray their rural, uncouth bearing while dancing, walking, standing, or moving in different ways. He was astonishingly sure of his composition and drew most ably and beautifully with the pen. He made many little sketches from nature.

As long as he remained in Antwerp, he lived with a servant girl whom indeed he would have married, had it not been for the unfortunate fact that she used to lie all the time, which was repugnant to his love of truth. He made a contract or agreement with her that he would check off all her lies upon a stick. For this purpose he took a fairly long one, and he said that if the stick became full of notches in the course of time it would prevent the wedding. This happened before much time had elapsed.

At last, since Pieter Koeck's widow had finally settled in Brussels, he fell in love with her daughter, whom, as we have said, he had often carried in his arms, and he married her; but her mother requested that Breughel leave Antwerp and make his residence in Brussels, in order that he might get his former girl out of sight and out of mind. This also happened.

Breughel was a quiet and able man who did not talk much, but was jovial in company, and he loved to frighten people, often his own pupils,[6] with all kinds of ghostly sounds and pranks that he played.

Some of Breughel's most significant works are at present in the possession of the Emperor; for example, a great "Tower of Babel" with many beautiful details. One can look into it from above. Furthermore, there is a smaller representation of the same subject. There are, besides, two "Carrying of the Cross" paintings, very natural-looking, always with a few drolleries in them somewhere. Again, there is a "Massacre of the Innocents," in which there is much to see that is done true to life, of which I have spoken elsewhere[7]—a whole family, for instance, begging for the life of a peasant child whom a murderous soldier has seized in order to kill it; the grief and the swooning of the mother and other events appear realistic.

Finally, there is a "Conversion of Saint Paul," also representing some very beautiful cliffs. It would be very hard to enumerate every thing Breughel did—fantasies, representation of hell, peasant scenes, and many other things.

He painted a "Temptation of Christ,"[8] in which one looks down from above, as from the Alps, upon cities and country borne up by clouds, through the rents in which one looks out.

He made a *"Dulle Griet,"* who is stealing something to take to hell,[9] and who wears a vacant stare and is strangely dressed.[10] I believe this and other pictures are also in the possession of the emperor.

Herman Pilgrims, art lover in Amsterdam, has a "Peasant Wedding" done in oils, which is very beautiful. The faces and bare limbs of the peasants in it are yellow and brown as if they were sunburned, and they show ugly skins, different from those of city dwellers.

He painted a picture in which Lent and Carnival are fighting; another, where all kinds of remedies are used against death;[11] and one with all kinds of children at games; and innumerable other little, clever things.

Two canvases painted in watercolor can be seen in the home of Willem Jacobsz., who lives near the new church in Amsterdam. They represent [a "Peasant Fair"[12] and] a "Peasant Wedding," where many amusing episodes together with the true character of the peasant may be seen. Among the group giving presents to the bride is an old peasant who has his little money bag hanging around his neck and who is busy counting the gold into his hand.[13] These are unusual paintings.

Shortly before his death, the townsmen of Brussels commanded Breughel to represent in pictures the digging of the canal from Brussels to Antwerp.[14] These pictures were not completed because of his death.

Many of Breughel's strange compositions and comical subjects one may see in his copper engravings. But he has made many skillful and beautiful drawings; he supplied them with inscriptions which, at the time, were too biting and too sharp, and which he had burned by his wife during his last illness, because of remorse, or fear that most disagreeable consequences might grow out of them. In his will[15] he left his wife a picture of "A Magpie on a Gallows." By the magpie, he meant the gossips whom he delivered to the gallows.[16] In addition, he had painted a picture in which Truth triumphs.[17] According to his own statement, this was the best thing painted by him.

He left behind two sons who were able painters. One was called Pieter[18] and studied with Gillis van Conincxloo and painted portraits from life;[19] the other, Jan,[20] learned watercolor painting from his grandmother, the mother of Pieter van Aelst. Jan studied the process of oil painting with a certain Pieter Goekindt,[21] who had many beautiful things in his house. He went to Cologne and then to Italy, where he made a great name as a landscape painter; he also made other subjects, very small in size, a type of work in which he excelled. Lampsonius speaks of Pieter Breughel in the following lines, with the question:

Who may be this other Jeroon Bos,

Who came in this world again,

Who pictures to us the fantastic conceptions of his own master again,

Who is most able with the brush,

Who is even surpassing his master?

Ye, Pieter, ye work in the artistic style of your old master.

But you rise still higher:

For reason that you select

Pleasant topics to laugh about.

Through these you deserve great merit

And with your master you must be praised for being a great artist.

A few details from later sources supplement Van Mander's biography. Bruegel's birthplace is still uncertain. Rather surprisingly, Van Mander's statement that he was born "not far from Breda in a village called Breughel" is not specific enough, since this might mean any one of three villages: a Breugel north of Eindhoven about thirty-four miles from Breda in northern Brabant in present-day Holland[22] and Grote Brogel and Kleine Brogel near the little town of Brée in the province of Limbourg in present-day Belgium. In his *Descrittione di tutti i Paesi Bassi* published two years before Bruegel's death, Guicciardini speaks of "Pietro Brueghel di Breda."[23] The question is further complicated by the fact that in those days the name "Brée" was commonly Latinized as "Breda" or "Brida."[24] Some scholars have opted for one village, some for another—and some for Breda itself. To us Breda seems the most likely, and in our opinion Bruegel's family probably came from Breugel near Eindhoven. The fact that Guicciardini's account, summary as it is, was published during Bruegel's lifetime makes it more plausible than Van Mander's. The little town of Brée was probably less well known than Breda; besides, it is not in Brabant but in Looz, which in Bruegel's time belonged to the prince-bishopric of Liège. And Van Mander speaks specifically of a village in Brabant. His statement that Bruegel assumed the name of his native village has been legitimately challenged. He is entered on the rolls of the Saint Luke's Guild of Painters in Antwerp as "Peeter Brueghels, painter," that is to say, "Peter, son of Brueghel, painter."

The dispute about Bruegel's exact birthplace is in our opinion of minor importance. In the absence of conclusive proof, we may provisionally assume that he came from northern Brabant.[25] It is much more important to note that the world of ideas he was born into was that of Hieronymus Bosch. Bruegel's work bears unmistakable traces of the "devilry" of that great predecessor, whose genius was as prodigious as his imagination.

The date of Bruegel's birth is equally uncertain. Since he became a free master of his guild in 1551,[34] he must have then been at least twenty-one and might have been as old as twenty-five. This would mean that he was born between 1525 and 1530. But it seems that many painters became free masters quite late in life. Some scholars, believing this to have been the case with Bruegel, set 1522 as his birth date.[26] In any case he was born before 1530. More than that the documents do not tell us.

It is doubtful whether Bruegel really learned his craft from Pieter Koeck d'Alost, also known as Pieter Coeck van Aelst.[27] Van Mander's statement that he did is justifiably questioned by art historians on stylistic evidence. In any age an artist's work usually bears some relationship to that of his master; yet Bruegel's style seems quite different from Coeck's—unless, as Marlier suggests, we are misled by "the immediate contrast between Bruegel's peasant scenes and Coeck's sophisticated, Italianate compositions."[28] Perhaps this question can only be answered by analyzing Bruegel's total oeuvre. Unlike many of his colleagues, he was not much influenced by Italian art. Such elements as he did borrow from Italian Renaissance masters he adapted and transformed in his own way.[29] If he remained uninfluenced by the greatest works of the Renaissance, why should he have taken the Romanizing style of a painter like Pieter Coeck as a model? Nevertheless, Bruegel's connection with Pieter Coeck is a matter of record, for he later married Coeck's daughter, Mayken.[43] So we must accept Van Mander's statement at its face value until it is refuted, particularly as it has been shown that Bruegel did adopt some of Coeck's principles of composition.[30]

A few dates can be documented. Between September, 1550, and October, 1551, Bruegel was working on an altarpiece for the Glovers' Guild in Malines. A legal document dated 1608[31] mentions a certain Claude Dorisi in whose workshop "the most eminent masters worked, among them the famous Breugel the Elder, who painted the side panels of the glovers' altarpiece for him [Dorisi] while Pieter Balten painted the center panel in the same workshop." Dorisi's commission[32] specified that the center panel was to depict the legend of Saint Gummarus, patron saint of the guild, and the side panels, when closed, were to show two large figures of Saint Gummarus and Saint Rombaut, with a heraldic tree in the center. It was also stipulated that the outside of the panels "should be in black and white only," that is to say, in grisaille. Probably Pieter Balten painted the inside of the triptych,[33] while Bruegel's contribution was confined to the painting and possibly the composition of the grisaille panels. Since the altarpiece no longer exists, the question will never be resolved unless documents still to be discovered yield new information. The commission is dated August 30, 1550, so Bruegel probably painted his panels in 1551. His subordinate role in the painting of the Malines altarpiece may be explained by the fact that he had only just become a free master. In any case the *Liggeren* (membership rolls) of Saint Luke's Guild in Antwerp support what Van Mander says.[34] Bruegel's name was entered at approximately the same time as that of the engraver Giorgio Ghisi of Mantua,[34] who was then also working for Hieronymus Cock.

Pieter Bruegel's interest in landscape painting was greatly stimulated by a long visit to Italy. We do not know the exact date of this, but it was probably 1552, the year of his earliest surviving drawings.[35] He probably traveled by way of Lyons, as the only extant document concerning his later visit to Rome suggests. In Rome he apparently became friendly with the famous miniaturist Giorgio Glovicic (1498–1578), a Croatian who changed his name to the more Italian-sounding Giulio Clovio.[36] When Clovio died, his effects included "*un quadro di Leon di Francia a guazzo di mano di Mro Pietro Brugole*" (a view of Lyons in gouache); a gouache depicting a tree: "*un quadro di un albero a guazzo di Mro Pietro Brugole*"; and a "Tower of Babel": "*una torre di Babilonia fatta di avolio [avorio?] di mano di Mro Pietro Brugole.*" Another interesting item in Clovio's estate was a miniature painted by Clovio and Bruegel in collaboration: "*un quadretto di miniatura la metà fatto per mano sua l'altra di Mro Pietro Brugole.*" Clovio must have set great store by these works, since he mentions them in his will dated December 27, 1577: "*quadro babilonie et tribus aliis quadrettis Petri Brugel.*"[36]

Did Bruegel also see Naples and the Straits of Messina? Everything indicates that he did, although there is no conclusive proof. A "View of Naples" (plates pp.182–89) is attributed to him, but unfortunately this painting is neither dated nor signed. The engraving "Sea Battle in the Straits of Messina"[37] is dated 1561—several years after his return. He probably made his way home by way of the western Alps and the Rhine valley, possibly passing through Geneva.[38] Rubens owned a painting by Bruegel of the Saint Gotthard massif.[39]

The date of his return to the Netherlands is unknown. In 1556 he was at work in Antwerp on drawings for engravings to be made in Hieronymus Cock's workshop, "The Four Winds."[40] His collaboration with Cock continued until Bruegel's death. The years between 1556 and 1563 are documented only by dated drawings, engravings and paintings. Bruegel's most important paintings date from 1559; he created an oeuvre, which constitutes a world to itself, within a mere ten years before his death in 1569. In 1559 he changed the spelling of his name; from then on, his drawings and paintings are signed "Bruegel," not "Brueghel."[41] A number of dated drawings suggest that he went to Amsterdam in 1562, but this is not certain.[42] Van Mander does not mention when Bruegel married Pieter Coeck's daughter, but the archives of Notre Dame de la Chapelle in Brussels[43] show that the marriage of "Peeter brùgel" and "Mayken cocks" took place in 1563. This supports Van Mander's statement that Bruegel left Antwerp and went to live in Brussels. Since the little picture of "Two Monkeys" with the city of Antwerp in the background is signed and dated "Bruegel MDLXII," scholars conclude that he moved to Brussels in 1563, the year of his marriage.

Information about the last six years of his life is equally scanty, and consists chiefly of dates on the paintings, references in the works of Guicciardini[23] and Vasari,[44] two letters from Italy,[45] and finally the date of his death, presumably September 5, 1569.[46] One document, however, deserves particular attention.[47] On February 21, 1566, that is to say, while Bruegel was still living, an Antwerp merchant called Nicolas Jongelinck pledged his collection of paintings to the city as security for a tax debt of 16,000 guilders owed by one Daniel de Bruyne. The document mentions thirty-nine "pieces" (i.e., paintings). Unfortunately of the sixteen Bruegels in the collection only three are mentioned by name: a "Tower of Babel," a "Christ Carrying the Cross" and "The Twelve Months."[48] Their estimated value, 410 guilders per picture, seems very high. One wonders whether Bruegel knew of this transaction.

Bruegel was buried in Notre Dame de la Chapelle, the church where he was married. He left a widow and two young sons, Pieter,[18] born in 1564, and Jan,[20] born in 1568. He is commemorated in the epigram of Lampsonius[49] which we have already quoted and in an epitaph by his friend Abraham Ortelius, the eminent geographer (1527–98).[50] His name is mentioned in many later documents[51] and in several printed texts.[52] While this documentary information is of great importance in determining the origin and sequence of his paintings, it sheds no light on their more cryptic side.

That is the extent of the positive data; everything else is merely conjecture or personal opinion. The known facts yield a biographical outline, but they can never provide a coherent picture of Bruegel's life. Perhaps someday research will discover more precise data in the archives, but the chances of this are slim. Bruegel seems never to have worked on a regular basis for any institution such as Church, guild, city or court. (His subjects alone prove this.) It therefore seems unlikely that manuscripts in libraries or unpublished documents from the archives will yield any significant data.

THE AGE OF PIETER BRUEGEL

Few periods in history are as fascinating as the sixteenth century.[53] This was a terrible yet exciting age which defies assessment, for both its positive and its negative sides are characterized by disconcertingly conflicting phenomena. It was a golden age of great minds: Erasmus, Montaigne, Copernicus, Mercator, Vesalius, Brahe, Galileo. The earth was finally being explored. Across the Atlantic, Spain and Portugal were conquering great empires. For the first time history was being played out on a world scale. Trade with distant lands flourished—while the native populations of America were being exterminated, together with their culture. This was the age of Humanism and of inhuman religious wars illuminated by scholarship yet overshadowed by intolerance and hate. Later ages have been impressed by the "modernity" of the sixteenth century; to some the time of Rabelais and Bruegel seems more modern than later periods. On the other hand, as Henri Hauser remarks in his fine account of this century: "One marvels how much of the Middle Ages still survives in the age to which we have given the glorious name of Renaissance ... In the sixteenth century, as in all ages, the innovators were fated to walk alone, opposed by all the forces of the past."[54] Copernicus' famous work of 1543 on the heliocentric orbits of the planets *De revolutionibus orbium coelestium* had no revolutionary impact in its own time. In fact, seventy-five years after its author's death it was placed on the Index. To quote another historian: "To represent and glorify the sixteenth century as an age of skepticism, license and rationalism is completely false—sheer illusion. Judged by the aspirations of its best representatives, it was rather a century of enlightenment which sought a reflection of the divine in everything."[55]

The tragic events that determined the fate of the Netherlands in the sixteenth century are well known; only the major ones need to be recalled. Since religion and politics were closely linked, the heretical movements inspired by Luther, Calvin and Zwingli's protests and demands for reform posed a serious threat to the state, for religion penetrated deeply into men's daily life and even their work. To put it simply, the Church was for one man an instrument of power, for another a refuge; ordinary people found comfort in it. Popular religious fervor was easily aroused. Marcus van Vaernewijck, a patrician of Ghent, wrote an astounding chronicle of this "*rasenden curtsigen tijt,*" this frenzied, feverish age. In his commentary on the outbreak of the iconoclasts' revolt he says: "*Want als men tghemeen volck eenighe liberteijt gheeft, zij en hauden gheen mate, zij tenderen altijt voort ende voort.*" (If the common people are permitted any freedom, they quickly lose all sense of porportion and demand more and more.)[56] Any suggestion that the Reformation was anti-Church or even antireligious in nature must be regarded with skepticism. Although many other factors such as social conditions undoubtedly played an important role, it was essentially a religious movement: a struggle for renewal of the Church.

The Holy Roman Emperor Charles V had instituted repressive measures amounting to organized persecution of heretics. His famous *plakkaten* were edicts couched in unambiguous language. The edict of 1550 decrees that heretics are to be treated as "*séditieuse personen ende perturbateurs van onsen staet ende der gemeyne ruste*" (seditious persons, disturbers of our state and of the public peace) who are to be executed "*te weten de mans metten sweerde ende de vrouwen gedolven*" (the men by the sword and the women by burial alive). This penalty, however, applied only to those who renounced their heresy. Anyone who held fast to the new faith faced death at the stake. When this ruthless edict was promulgated, Bruegel had just completed his apprenticeship.

The young Prince Philip of Spain had not succeeded in winning over his future subjects, despite his travels through the Netherlands and Germany between 1549 and 1551. According to a letter of the Bishop of Arras, Antoine Perrenot de Granvelle of the Franche-Comté, "People deplore our noble prince's conduct and accuse him of being haughty and aloof." No doubt Philip's character and his Spanish upbringing were responsible for this lack of understanding and coldness, which were to lead to tragedy. At that time he spoke no Dutch and not enough French to communicate with the representatives of his "provinces beyond the Pyrenees." At Charles V's formal abdication in Brussels on October 25, 1555, he admitted as much: "Gentlemen, while I have some understanding of the French language, I do not know it well enough to speak it. You will hear what the Bishop of Arras has to say to you on my behalf."

"El Rey" Philip spent four reluctant years in the Netherlands. On August 25, 1559, he took ship at Vlissingen after a leave-taking which offered no prospect of a return. A fortnight before he left the Netherlands he ordered the council of Brabant to enforce the edicts against the Protestant faith with all due rigor.

Despite merciless persecution, the Reformation, particularly Calvinism, continued to spread; its proselytizing fervor gained support from all segments of society. No doubt it was fed by a universal spirit of discontent, especially over the crushing tax burden. Year by year the situation grew more serious. The Count of Egmont's mission to Spain was a failure. The inexorable Philip reproved his sister, Margaret of Parma, regent of the Netherlands, for a policy which he considered too lenient. On April 2, 1566, a delegation of the nobility drew up a petition, which the regent promised to sponsor. The privy council made concessions promising a certain degree of tolerance, but the open profession of Protestantism was still prohibited. Yet no official prohibition could prevent itinerant preachers from spreading the new religion in *hagepreken*, outdoor, or rather extramural, services.[57] These clandestine gatherings became more and more common. Van Vaernewijck compares them to "a fire which flares up suddenly in the straw, driven in all directions by the wind, always finding fuel enough to spread." Before long, people were flocking to them "by thousands rather than hundreds," to quote Van Vaernewijck again. He notes, however, that they were chiefly "common people, folk who have not much to lose" and that "some of them used foul language on the streets."[58] Psalms were sung at these services, but attacks were also made on the clergy, alleging, for instance, that "the only religious thing about them is their dress."[59] The people were told that to revere the statues of the saints was idolatry, and this seed fell on fertile ground. Van Vaernewijck describes the execution of one Ghyselbrecht Cools, a plumber aged about thirty-six, who lived in the Schepenhuustraetkin, a little street which still exists opposite the Ghent city hall. Before he died, the condemned man naïvely said that he "had been awakened at night and dragged out to plunder churches. He did not realize that he was doing wrong in joining in, and he bitterly resented having to die when he was innocent."[60]

The iconoclasts' revolt spread like wildfire. It broke out on August 10, 1566, in Steenvorde, Hondschoote, Armentières, and Valenciennes and spread to Poperinge, Ypres, and Oudenaarde, then to Antwerp and Ghent, and finally to the northern provinces. Within three weeks the rioters had looted more than four hundred churches, smashing statues, altarpieces and stained-glass windows, burning ritual objects and desecrating graves.

On August 22, 1567, a year after these riots, the Duke of Alba entered Brussels at the head of a Spanish army and established a merciless regime. The rising was put down by brute force. A tribunal popularly known as the Bloed-raad, the Council of Blood, served as the instrument of government and as a symbol of terror. Pieter Bruegel died while these repressive measures were in full swing. One document among many equally horrifying ones gives some idea of the Council of Blood's ruthlessness. On May 5, 1571, it pronounced the following sentence on a number of condemned heretics: "If the aforementioned condemned are not willing to die a Catholic death, we direct Juan de Bolia, captain of justice, in his capacity as His Majesty's provost general, to have the tips of their tongues burned before they are taken from the prison for execution."[61]

Bruegel lived through the uprising and the iconoclasts' revolt and their suppression. Being a man of the people and living among them, he must have had a close view of these events. It is easy to see why certain scholars have found direct allusions in many of his pictures to the terroristic regime of the unsympathetic and fanatical Philip II.[62] Their findings are supported by Van Mander's statement that before he died, Bruegel ordered many of his drawings with particularly biting captions to be destroyed.

We in our affluent society can hardly imagine the conditions in which men lived four hundred years ago. To try to evoke a true impression from documents of the age would be a bold undertaking, for everything would hinge upon which quotations one included and which one rejected. While we should not try to derive the quintessence of an entire age from any one text, we may well ponder an account whose authenticity is beyond doubt. In 1573, four years after Bruegel's death, beggars from distant provinces appeared before the city of Troyes and in its streets, starving and ragged, scabby and verminous, like the miserable wretches in some of Bruegel's pictures.[63] The citizens of Troyes were afraid of an uprising, and in order to get rid of them "the rich and powerful men of the said city of Troyes met in council to seek a solution." The council decided that the beggars must be driven out of the city. "To accomplish this, bread was to be baked for distribution among the said beggars, who were to be rounded up at one of the city gates without being initiated into the secret. Each of them was to be given a loaf of bread and a coin, and they were to be driven out of the city through the aforementioned gate, which would be closed behind the last of them. People would shout over the wall after them, telling them for the love of God to seek their food elsewhere and not to return to Troyes before the new grain of the next harvest. Those who were most horrified after receiving the alms were the poor people who were driven out of the city of Troyes."

A strange kind of charity! Yet we have no right to condemn it. Fernand Braudel, to whom we owe this text, continues: "For centuries famine recurred with such crushing regularity that it pervaded man's biological existence and became part of his daily life. High prices and shortages were universal and became almost the normal state of affairs, even in Europe, which was relatively well off. A few rich men living in luxury do not change the picture. Yet how could it have been otherwise? Grain yield was only moderate. Two bad harvests in succession meant disaster. Farming was badly organized, and farm produce was unevenly distributed."[64] On the first page of a series of woodcuts entitled "The Customs and Life-style of the Turks"[65] by Pieter Koeck d'Alost, Bruegel's supposed master, appears the following legend: "These are the mountains in the land of Slavonia, where there is nothing to eat for man or beast, except what travelers may happen to bring with them. To find or beg a little bowl of milk there is a triumph." Looking at magnificent sixteenth-century Brussels tapestries in museums, we tend to forget that they reflect only the splendor of the court and a few noble families. Above all we forget that for the common people simply getting enough to eat was a heavy daily burden.

In a play written in 1561, which was part of the repertoire of a *Rederijkerskamer* or school of rhetoric, an allegorical figure called Behoeflijcke nature, een arm man (Indigence, a Poor Man) complains that he cannot get wine, beer or bread when he wants them and asks: "How am I ever to own gold ingots / lands / rich feasts / delectable preserves / precious stones / silks and cloth of gold / pearls and rings / if I have to devote all my strength to earning my daily bread?"[66]

A rhymed chronicle of 1565 says: "Soon after Easter early in May / the whole people began to complain bitterly / The poor were in dire need / The only thing they talked about was that the seed had not sprouted / Many were afraid of bad times and cried Alas / we shall have to spend all we have."[67]

Only the usurers welcomed a poor harvest. The common people muttered angrily against the "*corenbijters*" (corn weevils), grain profiteers "who rove through towns and villages / buying up all the grain / and hoarding it / and locking their granaries / and refusing to sell anything until every bushel is worth its weight in gold." These scoundrels should be banished from the land, sighed the peasant. But he added bitterly: "Alas, alack! They are too rich, and the man who has money can always arrange things the way he wants them."[68]

We recall what the Flemish Till Eulenspiegel said to his mother when he brought her the stolen bread: "*Eet nu als ghijt hebt, ende vastet als ghijs niet en hebt.*" (Eat now while you have something to eat. You can fast when there's nothing left.)[106] Chronic malnutrition was probably one source of the old legend of the Land of Cockaigne. According to modern psychoanalytical theory, popular imagination must have invented this life of ease and plenty as a form of compensation. The licentiousness of Carnival, Rabelais' works,[115] the success of some of the farces performed by the schools of rhetoric, and the popularity of chapbooks such as *Le voyage et navigation que fist Panurge*[91] show that breadwinning was the most pressing of everyone's daily burdens.

Even worse than hunger were the deadly epidemics it brought with it: typhus, scarlet fever, diphtheria, smallpox, leprosy, and many other diseases. Since the return of Christopher Columbus in 1493, Europe had been afflicted by a new scourge: syphilis, variously known in those days as *le mal napolitain*, the French disease, and *lo mal francioso*. Erasmus mentions it several times, referring to it as *scabies gallica*. Worst of all, bubonic plague caused indescribable devastation. Medical knowledge was negligible and hygiene practically unknown. Erasmus complained bitterly of the lack of cleanliness among his contemporaries.

All this helps explain certain aspects of Bruegel's work: the feasts, kermesses and popular festivals, where everyone ate and drank his fill. Carousing and dancing were no more than a momentary escape from a grim, constantly threatened existence. The legend on the engraving "Wedding Dance"[133] calls upon the bagpiper to keep the merriment going "*want ten is vrij met haer gheen bruijloft alden dach*" (because it's not every day the peasants go to a wedding). In a contemporary play the character representing Carnival says: "And if we didn't celebrate Shrovetide according to custom, we'd melt away like snow in the sun."[69] Life expectancy was much shorter than it is today. Few people lived long enough to get to know their grandchildren. Death came quickly, so every moment had to be lived to the full.

One does not need to be a Marxist or a specialist in economic history to realize that the poor were mercilessly exploited. The stage was one outlet for popular discontent. There was grumbling about usurers and dishonesty, selfishness and poverty in general, yet surprisingly, instead of laying these evils at the door of the rich or the upper classes, the common people abjectly held themselves to blame for them. One of the popular morality plays known as the *Spelen van Sinne* attacks laziness: "Sad to say, man fritters away his time in idleness / often he is the one who suffers for it / until he finally falls into dire poverty."[66] The behavior of the *varende luyden* (vagabonds) is censured. The *Aernoutsbroeders*,[70] the *ghesellen van Sint Reynuyt*[71] ("reyn uyt" means: empty), the *ghildekens*[72]—the gluttons and tipplers, cheats and spongers, in brief, carousers and all those afraid of work "heavy or light"—are sharply reproved. "Like the bird which has to seek its food, man is born to work" and "Idleness is the source of all vice" were universally accepted axioms.

Behind this criticism a typical characteristic of the Netherlanders is clearly recognizable: their willingness to work and their inexhaustible energy. No painter ever portrayed these toiling, drudging people better than Bruegel. For them the worst misfortune was to wind up in the poorhouse. The *Book of Vagabonds* gives detailed directions to "the shortcut to the poorhouse," citing a whole list of candidates for it—and there seems to have been no shortage of them. It includes "the man who has little but spends a lot; the merchants who buy at high prices and sell their wares dirt cheap; the man who plays dice or bowls and loses all his money at it; the man who recites poems or sings in taverns; the man and wife who quarrel and fight, separate and go their own ways, he as a swindler, she as a whore; the skirt-chasers who run after pretty girls, squandering their goods and property; all those who say, 'Let us be merry, for wine was not meant for pigs or beer for geese'," and so on. Today we find it hard to believe that masters who treat their employees kindly are well on the way to the poorhouse. But the list includes "masters who give their workers fresh, hot bread; masters whose wives set the servants' table with bread, meat, beer, and such things."[73]

Leafing through the history of the sixteenth century, we come upon horrifying details on nearly every page. Yet we should not make the mistake of judging this age by the standards of modern man, who is no longer exposed to many of the vicissitudes of life that his forefathers had to confront. We should accept the facts as the documents present them—though this need not deter us from comparing our own time with that of Bruegel. In many respects the attitude of his contemporaries is confusing: toward the problem of beggars, for instance. We marvel at their aloof indifference to the grimmest poverty, which they accepted as a matter of course. What we would today call the scum of society then—and for centuries to come—comprised quite a large part of the population. Beggars were a common sight throughout the countryside and in the towns, as Bruegel's work testifies. The beggars were the dregs of the masses: the naturally handicapped, the victims of congenital diseases, those crippled by inadequate care, plagued by chronic ills, mutilated by barbaric legal penalties, and incapable of any useful occupation. Their only resources for eking out a living were guile, trickery and cunning. The *Book of Vagabonds* enumerates some forty different types of begging, each with its own name: "*biegeren, stabulieren, loseneren, kammesieren, dutseren, vopperen, bultdragherinnen, kandieren, momsen, zeeperen, sweygheren, burckaerten, sefelgravers*" and so on.[73]

Some people, of course, lived carefree lives of almost princely luxury. If a man could make a fortune anywhere, it was in the city of Antwerp, which within a few decades had become the world's leading port.[74] Rhymesters sang the praises of this town, which had "grown tremendously and renewed itself" in so short a time. The merchants brought vigorous trades and crafts and prosperity to the metropolis. "Portuguese, Spaniards, Genoese, Castilians, Frenchmen, Scotsmen, Englishmen, Venetians, Orientals, Luccanese, Italians, Germans, and many other foreigners opened counting houses there. And all were convinced that in Antwerp money rained from the sky."[66]

In 1561 a rhymester made the naïve but legitimately proud boast: "About a hundred years ago all we knew was the cloth trade / today Italy and even India come to us / thanks to its circumspection and its diligence / Antwerp has become so powerful / that neither Cairo in Egypt / nor Alexandria / nor any city in Asia / or in Africa / or in Asia Minor / not even Venice in Italy / or Lyons in France / or Paris / or London in England can be compared with it."[66]

When the theatre-festival known as the Landjuweel[143] was held in Antwerp in 1561, the port was at the height of its glory. One of the set themes of the contest was "The Benefits of Trade." The rhetoricians outdid one another in tributes to the merchants, who built "fine residences" in the city and thanks to whom "anyone who wants to work can earn a living." Yet we should not draw the conclusion that the people of Antwerp or even Brabant and the whole of the Netherlands lived in affluence. To be sure, Guicciardini tells us that the citizens of Antwerp feasted and drank, danced, sang, and dressed fashionably to the point of excess,[23] but this was not true of the vast majority of people. The merchants were not a middle class in our sense of the term; an abyss separated the rich from the poor. There were fewer intermediate gradations than today between the broad masses who did little but vegetate and the privileged few who lived in luxury. The peasants, artisans, employees, shopkeepers, and all those who lived on the margin of society had no share in the profits to be earned in mercantile trade, not to speak of speculation and other financial dealings.[75]

The rhetoricians stress the "loyal behavior" of those merchants "who do not mix with the profiteers and rich men who would like to devour the common folk through the power of money." They make so much of this that we begin to wonder whether all these shippers, wholesale traders and importers really were "the great comfort of the poor"[66] after all. In a play performed at the Landjuweel by the Berchem Chamber of Rhetoric an allegorical figure called Ghoet ghevoelen (Good Feeling) urges the rich for the love of God and Christian charity to give to the poor in their dire need: "*om Gods wille en uyt liefden den Armen nootdruft toe te worpen.*" Another character, Volmaeckte Christenheid (Perfect Christian), admonishes the needy not to complain but to show their gratitude by praying for humanity: "*gheen murmureerder te zijn maer danckbaerlijck te bidden veur den mensche.*"[66]

Five years after these rhetorical exhortations the iconoclasts' revolt engulfed the Netherlands.

THE WORK OF PIETER BRUEGEL

Pieter Bruegel the Elder is world famous, but what was he really like? In fact contradictory images of the man exist. Some see him as a peasant and buffoon, others as a skeptic, an enlightened and critical universal Humanist or even a misanthropic philosopher. The contradiction should warn us against hasty judgments. Bruegel's work does indeed lend itself to conflicting interpretations. Everyone seems to find in it whatever he may be looking for. Our critical method should therefore aim primarily at discovering what message his work held for his own contemporaries.

The theme of "The Triumph of Death" (plates pp. 110–35) is obvious: on the one hand individual man's inescapable fate; on the other, the attempts of the ordinary mortal to evade it. Paintings like the "*Dulle Griet*" (plates pp. 152–77) and "The Land of Cockaigne" (plates pp. 274–77) are much more difficult to interpret. As for the small picture of "The Cripples" (plate p. 329) and "The Magpie on the Gallow" (plates pp. 314–27), we are forced to admit that their message remains obscure.

A careful study of Bruegel's paintings and engravings reveals one indisputable fact: He is always close to the common people from whom he stems. No matter to what heights his genius carried him, his work remains closely linked to his time.[76] The troubles of his contemporaries were his troubles. A knowledge of this background may not solve the mystery of Bruegel, but at least it will restrain us from too fanciful interpretations.

Many scholars believe—in our opinion rightly—that many of the scenes in Hieronymus Bosch whose meaning eludes us today can be satisfactorily explained by idioms in the Dutch language as it was spoken in the late fifteenth and early sixteenth centuries, that is to say, by expressions which have now fallen into disuse.[77] Bosch often rendered idiomatic expressions literally, and it seems that Pieter Bruegel the Elder adopted this trick. Sometimes his allusions have no symbolic meaning; he is simply giving a pictorial illustration of popular sayings. This form of wit was apparently popular in his day, and everybody understood it. Till Eulenspiegel's humor and the plays of the *Rederijkers* (rhetoricians) are further examples of it.

The Bruegel literature is ridden with mistranslations and false interpretations stemming from insufficient knowledge of the language, literature and dramatic art of the sixteenth-century Netherlands. This has to some extent prevented a proper evaluation of his work. Before inventing scholarly explanations of subjects which today suggest a rebus or code message, we should ask whether the solution is not actually much simpler than we think. We must go back to the sources, and there is good reason to believe that the philologists and linguists can show us the way.[78] To expect them to clear up all the problems that confront us would be unrealistic, but there is no doubt that their research can resolve many contradictions. Bruegel's work cannot be understood without a knowledge of the traditional sixteenth-century emblems and symbols which the rhetoricians had helped popularize.

Let us take as an example Bruegel's drawing "*Elck*" ("Everyman"), dated 1558 (plate p. 60), and the engraving based on it.[79] Lantern in hand, "Everyman looks out for himself" and "pulls so as to get the longest end." The symbolic figure of this bearded, bent old man, with a pince-nez before his myopic eyes, rummaging through bundles, sacks, baskets, tubs, and barrels suggests Shylock, the merchant of Venice. On the wall in the background hangs a picture of a fool looking at himself in a convex mirror. The legend reads: "*Nymant en ckent sy[n]seluen*" (No one knows himself), a saying which occurs in Villon's "*Ballade des menus propos*"; "*Je cognois tout, fors que moy mesmes*" (I know everything except myself). This sentence appears so frequently in sixteenth-century morality plays and farces that we can take it as a commonplace. The fools were especially fond of quoting it.[80] "*Elck*" satirizes avarice. If we look more closely, however, we see that it is not merely attacking the profiteers and speculators whose activities Bruegel must have often observed in the port of Antwerp. In the foreground the attributes of gambling are clearly distinguishable, proving that the drawing is also meant as a castigation of grasping *tuyschers*—gamblers and cheats.

Bruegel's contemporaries were always complaining bitterly about *giericheyt* (avarice). Among the suggested themes for the Landjuweel[143] of 1561 *giericheyt* is mentioned four times.[81] An engraving by Remigius Hogenberg (ca. 1536–88), a contemporary of Bruegel, makes an important contribution to the interpretation of "*Elck*." Its title is "*De Wagen met rapen*" (literally, "the cart with turnips"). But "*rapen*" is a pun. Besides meaning "turnips," it can also be a verb meaning "to grab." The legend dispels all doubt about what the scene represents. It reads: "Day and night everyone keeps trying to grab (turnips); clergy and laymen, men and women—they all try to snatch (turnips) out of the cart, and the one who grabs the most (turnips) is sure to win universal approbation."[82] Bruegel reverted to this theme in the engraving of "The Battle Between the Money Banks and the Strongboxes" (plate p. 60).[83] Again the legend leaves no room for doubt; what he is attacking is avarice.[84] A point worth noting is that the money banks are just as belligerent as the strongboxes.

It is not difficult to prove by specious reasoning, using *Utopia* as evidence, that Thomas More was a Communist before his time. The mercantile trade of Antwerp certainly contributed to the emergence of capitalism by promoting international trade relations, speculation and agreements concerning exchange and banking. But we should not forget that capitalism as an economic system was unknown to Bruegel even by name. Hence the contention of some scholars that he was attacking capitalism seems untenable.

Another curious and cryptic engraving is "The Alchemist" of 1558 (plate p. 61). It depicts a tragic figure enslaved by passion and false beliefs. He is sitting at his furnace, surrounded by flasks, retorts and crucibles, absorbed in the pursuit of chimeras, alone in the world. His wife is pointing out that the money bag is empty and the family in need. The scene in the background suggests that his children are dependent on public charity. On one of the manuscripts on the lectern the words "*ALGHE MIST*" are clearly legible. Their meaning is ambiguous: it can be read either as "Alchemist" or in the literal sense of "everything [has gone] wrong." Is Bruegel ridiculing an age that is dead and gone?[85] We should not forget that alchemy was still assiduously practiced in the sixteenth and seventeenth centuries by charlatans as well as by those seeking the philosophers' stone. Perhaps Bruegel was not attacking men who stubbornly persisted in seeking a process for transmuting metals; his target was not necessarily alchemists as such. It seems more likely that he was satirizing those whose passion overrides their common sense by depicting a man who is ready to endure terrible poverty to satisfy his *auri sacra fames*, his hunger for gold. The alchemist is an excellent illustration of this didactic theme. It was probably not alchemists as such that prompted Bruegel to make this drawing and publish it to a wide audience as a print—although this hardly makes it any less insulting to the adepts of the Great Art. The drawing's unmistakably satirical tone makes one skeptical of the hypothesis that Bruegel was a follower of hermetic philosophy.[86]

Here again literature offers parallels which can serve as a touchstone in interpreting this print. The *Rederijkers* also make fun of alchemy and its adepts. In a play performed at the Landjuweel of 1561, alchemy is represented by a figure named Vlieghenden gheest, een lichtverdich manspersoon (Flighty Mind, a frivolous male character) who says that he has tried many trades but never found exactly what is right for the flighty mind. Now, however, he has dedicated himself to alchemy, which has no peer among all the arts.[87] In another passage alchemy is referred to as fraud and compared to counterfeiting. All this is condemned as dishonest, and the alchemist is warned that he will live to regret his trickery.[88]

Other literary sources offer illuminating sidelights on Bruegel's favorite theme of good living and carousing. Several contemporary Carnival plays contain scenes like the ones depicted in "The Fight Between Carnival and Lent" and give us a good idea of the boisterousness of popular celebrations. An allegorical figure representing Shrove Tuesday welcomes the audience: "Be cheerful and merry. Celebrate Carnival, you pure spirits with untroubled heads. I greet you all, great and small. Be gay. Celebrate Carnival ... As you love me, give free rein to your nature. Bake your pancakes and waffles in the streets. Fry your sausages and eat! Carnival comes but once a year!" Twice already Lent has signaled her approach with her rattle, and Carnival exhorts his followers: "Hurry, hurry. Time is pressing. Eat all you can. Drink beer and wine. Everything must be eaten up today, because on Ash Wednesday all food is spoiled." He makes fun of Lent's followers: "They pull a long face and have hollow cheeks. They are as thin as hop poles. You can hear their ribs rattling, because they live on fish and oil. They don't drink brandy or wine—not even sour wine. They are timid, shabbily dressed and ill-tempered." Carnival licks his lips when he describes the pancakes and waffles: "You've never tasted better in your life. Twelve eggs to one bowl of flour. Spread thick with butter and sprinkled with sugar. And what does it matter if you haven't got a penny left tomorrow? Let us do honor to Carnival." He distributes golden waffles dripping with fat and flavored with cloves, cinnammon, pepper, saffron, and many other spices.[89] But Lent replies: "All that is nothing but hay," meaning that it will not last.[90]

Over the years Bruegel came to typify feasting and carousing. In Flanders gluttons are still often referred to as Breughelians, as though Bruegel himself had been a drinker, a bon vivant and a gourmand. It is true that the Flemings have always been accused of setting too much store by the pleasures of the table. Emperor Charles V, a native of Ghent, was reputed to be a great gourmet and suffered terribly from gout. In the thirteenth chapter of *Le voyage et navigation que fist Panurge*, published in 1538, Panurge describes the Land of Cockaigne, where there is "a tremendous mountain of fresh butter, the finest and best anyone has ever tasted."[91] Everyone can eat as much as he likes, but, says Panurge, "I wouldn't show it to the Flemings, for big as it is, I believe they would eat it up."

Bruegel did not invent the details of the Land of Cockaigne. Many of them are found in a Dutch description of it printed in 1546, twenty-one years before he painted his picture.[92] The description includes the porridge mountain through which one had to eat his way, the roofs tiled with cakes and pies, the fence of linked sausages, the river of milk, and the broiled pigeons. But these details occur in an unexpected context. Instead of singing the praises of a life of ease and plenty, the anonymous author has harsh things to say about laziness and vice. According to this text, the Land of Cockaigne was discovered by good-for-nothings. It is very overpopulated, chiefly by scoundrels and people who do not believe in propriety and virtue. Virtuous, reasonable, honorable, well-bred, hard working people are unwelcome and are driven out of the country.

26

Bruegel's contemporaries also expressed indirectly their disapproval of gluttony in their literature and plays. At the Landjuweel of 1561 the Turnhout School of Rhetoric performed *Die Heybloeme (The Heather)*, a Breughelian farce. A captain is recruiting soldiers for the Count of Schocklandt, and the recruits have names such as Langderm, Hoolbuyck, Slickbrock, Schoonteughe (Long Guts, Hollow Belly, Tidbit Swallower, Handsome Gullet). Each enumerates the feats he is capable of: fifteen plates of beans, a whole sheep with fifteen one-pound loaves of bread. Handsome Gullet could never fall asleep without his eighteen pints of beer. As soon as they have been enlisted, they swear an oath on porridge, milk gruel, roast ox, ragout, and tripe.[66]

But we really do not need such parallels to prove that Bruegel, like his contemporaries, was critical of gluttony and drunkenness.[93] All we have to do is look at his work. To call Pieter Bruegel a Breughelian shows the same lack of understanding as to take *Gulliver's Travels* for a foolish fairy tale.

An examination of "The Procession to Calvary" (plates pp. 200–11) shows that Bruegel was in a sense the heir of the fourteenth- and fifteenth-century wood-carvers. Like those masters, who created so many magnificent altar-pieces, he is a wonderful storyteller. But his descriptions are more modern; Bruegel observes the world as a psychologist. One never tires of looking at this picture. Although the principal motif, Christ stumbling under the cross, is in the center of the picture, it is almost lost in the teeming activity of the scene he portrays. The cart bearing the two thieves, their faces as pale as death from fear, is surrounded by curious onlookers. Simon of Cyrene is resisting the soldiers who want him to help carry the cross. His wife, her rosary hanging from her girdle, defies their halberds and violently drags him back, not wanting him to get involved. A crowd of idlers is cold-bloodedly enjoying the violent anger of this mannish woman.

Many scholars, believing that Bruegel's Biblical scenes show a lack of reverence, have questioned his faith. Are they right? Does not the form in which his religious feeling expresses itself mark the end of a long iconographical development? The Romanesque Madonna stepped down from her unapproachable throne to become in the Gothic a human being, a mother playing with her child. In Bruegel the sacred is completely secularized. The parallel with our own time is, however, a limited one—although it certainly exists.

Bruegel's great achievement was to observe minutely the common people and to paint a scrupulously faithful picture of them, feature by feature. We might even say that he devoted his whole lifework to the scoundrels and boorish peasants whom medieval art banished to the margins of illuminated manuscripts or to obscure corners of the churches. Bruegel transposes Biblical scenes to his own familiar setting, the landscape of Brabant. His Madonna is more than a mother; she has become a woman of the people. In the London "Adoration of the Kings" (plates pp. 212–17) someone is whispering in Saint Joseph's ear—but is there any reason to suppose that his words are insinuative?

Secularization in Bruegel is in no way remarkable, for the Reformation was, after all, a popular movement, as the translations of the Bible prove. These literary parallels support the theory that Bruegel sympathized with the cause of the Gueux (Beggars), as the malcontents were called. Whether he was a Protestant or not, the religious element is certainly of primary importance in his Biblical scenes. Why should we read into "The Fall of the Rebel Angels" (plates pp. 138–51) any theme besides the Biblical one? The subject is part of Christian iconography and was traditionally used in Netherlandish art as a warning against pride and arrogance. Can a valid case be made for the theory that "The Resurrection" (plates pp. 136–37) represents anything besides the story of the Resurrection?

Does the famous engraving of "*Fides*"[94] ("Faith," plate p. 68) prove that Bruegel was a skeptic or even an atheist? No doubt he realized that devout men practiced their religion in a herdlike manner; like Erasmus, he was critical of the religious feeling of his time.[76] But that is no reason to conclude that he was a freethinker.

In "The Numbering of the People at Bethlehem" (plates pp. 250–67) Bruegel depicts the Holy Family with the utmost simplicity: a carpenter arriving in the village with his pregnant wife. Saint Joseph, carrying his gimlet stuck in his belt and his saw on his shoulder and dragging his ox and his ass after him, merges into the crowd. The secularization is complete. Yet the longer one looks at the painting, the more one wonders whether it is not really an expression of devout belief. It takes no great literary talent to prove that it is actually the most moving confession of faith that exists in Dutch painting of the sixteenth century.

Let us pause for a moment to look at the drawing "*Justitia*"[95] ("Justice," plate p. 68) in the series of engravings of "The Seven Virtues."[141] We may be surprised to find Bruegel confining himself to justice as it was practiced by the society of his day. The entire picture deals with methods of torture and execution: death at the stake, by hanging, by beheading, by the strappado and the lash. One poor devil in the foreground is being submitted to the ordeal by water. Off in a corner the clerks of the court go about their work with bent heads: public servants performing their function, which was merely to record. Our twentieth-century minds are quick to interpret "*Justitia*" as courageous, bitter criticism. But we should not jump to the conclusion that Bruegel was protesting against corporal punishment. How much of the Middle Ages survives into the sixteenth century! In those days to torture a suspect while interrogating him was accepted practice. The cutting off of a hand was considered a fair sentence. Not until the seventeenth century did the United Provinces of the northern Netherlands stop burning witches at the stake—a humanitarian innovation which set an example for the whole of Europe. So it is questionable whether we can assume on the basis of this engraving that Bruegel was an advocate of more humane justice.

Another picture that has aroused the scholars' interest and curiosity is the famous small painting now in the Louvre called "The Cripples" or sometimes "The Beggars" (plate p. 329). Yet all their learned explanations leave the meaning of this sinister, clandestine gathering as obscure as it ever was. The headdress of the figure on the extreme right, which looks like a bishop's miter made of paper, has been taken for a gibe at some eminent member of the clergy. The foxtails are a complete enigma to the scholars. What do they represent? Foxtails were used in a masquerade given by the Count of Mansfeldt on June 19, 1564, when a figure representing Cardinal Granvelle was whipped by a devil with the tails of a fox. This satirical farce dealt with the intrigues of Ambassador Simon Renard (i.e., Fox), one of the Cardinal's opponents,[97] and Granvelle is known to have made a strong protest against it.[98] Is there a connection between this performance and Bruegel's painting? Probably not. A beggar wearing a coat trimmed with foxtails appears in the earlier "Fight Between Carnival and Lent,"[99] but this painting is signed and dated 1559—long before the Count of Mansfeldt's masquerade. There is good evidence that "The Cripples," painted in 1568, was a new treatment of a motif from the bigger painting of 1559. Van Bastelaer believes that the foxtail was "one of the most important identifying badges of the dissidents."[100] Others cite the popular contemporary German expression "to stroke the foxtail," meaning "to sham, put on an act, prevaricate, flatter" or "fawn."[101] J. S. Gudlaugsson claims that the foxtail was the identifying sign of the leper.[102] There is much to be said for and against all these explanations.

Van Vaernewijck's chronicle suggests that the foxtail could stand for many different things in Bruegel's time, but the passages mentioning it shed no light on the problem.[96] One of them concerns a Spanish soldier sentenced to death by hanging for the murder of a citizen of Ghent. The military authorities tried to appease the widow with an indemnity of fifty guilders, the usual compensation for a personal injury. The chronicler says that for the murderer "the gallows would thus be turned into a foxtail." In another passage Van Vaernewijck elucidates the symbolic meaning of the foxtail somewhat more clearly. In February, 1567, he tells us, Calvinist knights appeared in the streets of Brussels with tin bowls stuck on their lances, which were decorated with foxtails. The latter represented a challenge to the catholic clergy who had made fun of the Calvinists, saying that they would now have to creep into their foxholes. "*Willende betooghen duer de vossensteerten dat zij niet als vossen emmertoes in haer holen ghaen duucken waren, ghelijc sommighe gheestelicke van machte met haer gheschimpt hadden, maer voerdense up haer lancen.*" We know too that the Peters quarter prison in Ghent was called Vossensteert (Foxtail). Van Vaernewijck also mentions a captain, a German mercenary, who had two nicknames: Vossensteert of den vlieghenden Duvele (Foxtail or The Flying Devil).[96] The symbolic meaning of Bruegel's painting—and there is no doubt that it is symbolic— remains obscure. Obviously there is nothing comical about it. Seldom has evil been so forcefully depicted.

In their search for allusions in Bruegel's work many scholars have suggested that "The Massacre of the Innocents" (plates pp. 248–49) represents a violent protest against Spanish oppression. The leader of the mercenaries has even been taken for the Duke of Alba.[103] The analogy is certainly tempting and plausible. But this interpretation, persuasive as it is, is very questionable.[104] Since the painting is not dated, we have no proof that it was meant as an attack on the repressive regime. The Duke of Alba entered Brussels only in 1567, yet two other versions of this painting exist and both are dated 1564.[105] It is also worth recalling that Cardinal Granvelle, the orthodox adviser of Margaret of Parma, owned some of Bruegel's pictures. And we may well ask whether the Brussels city fathers would have honored with a commission a citizen who was in any way suspicious.

Unquestionably Bruegel wanted to bring home to his contemporaries man's brutality, but does that make him what would today be called a member of the resistance? We should not forget that Bruegel had never read Charles de Coster. His kinship with Till Eulenspiegel is of an entirely different nature. Many people imagine Bruegel roaming the back streets of Brussels and the Marolles quarter, his fists clenched in his pockets, muttering curses. Is this likely? Without doubt the painter realized that the common people were oppressed and exploited, that the teeming, amorphous, cowardly masses were held in check by professional soldiers and mercenaries, the scum of society. No doubt he realized that these mercenaries were themselves poor devils, illiterate boors faced with the necessity of earning a living, if only by the halberd and sword. Nevertheless the Bruegel scholar must finally confront the question of the artist's attitude toward the government and its official representatives. Being both sensitive and cautious, and possessing a remarkable talent for observation, an alert mind and a strong will, he no doubt kept his ideas about their fanaticism, intolerance and brutal cruelty to himself.

His age tolerated ironical remarks and even sarcastic farces as long as they were not aimed at any particular individual or group. It was all right to make fun of monks and monasticism, but dangerous to ridicule, say, the Franciscans. In his rebuttal of Martin van Dorp's criticisms of *Praise of Folly* Erasmus devoted several pages to pointing out that he never attacked any specific person or group: "To whom have I done the least harm? What country, order or individual have I specifically attacked? ... If there is any way of curing men of their vices without hurting anybody, the simplest one, if I am not mistaken, is never to make public mention of any name." He was always careful not to write "anything inflammatory or anything that might be taken as an insult to any order." And we know that Rabelais had to pay dearly for epithets such as *"sorbonagres," "sorbinotant"* and *"bornisortant,"* which he coined to apply to the Sorbonne. Apt as they were, they were considered too transparent.

The following typical quotation from the chapbook *Eulenspiegel* illustrates the kind of allusion Bruegel's age enjoyed:[106]

> The bishop answered: "Tell me point-blank how the matter stands, because we are in the habit of paying attention to what you people say."

> Eulenspiegel replied: "Your Grace, the spectacle makers' craft is dying out and may become completely extinct, because nowadays you and the other great men of the world: namely, the Pope and all the rest of them—cardinals, bishops, emperors, kings, dukes, judges, city fathers, governors—God save us!—look through your fingers [connive at wrongdoing] and refuse to distinguish right from wrong for the sake of the bribes this brings you. In earlier times those gentlemen diligently studied the law so that they would know to whom [fair and prompt] justice was to be dispensed, and in those days there was a great demand for eyeglasses, so we did good business. And the priests used to study much more than they do now, so we used to sell plenty of eyeglasses to them too, but today they often recite their hourly prayers by rote, and it can happen that they don't open a book in three weeks. So our trade is dying out. And this failing is so widespread throughout the land that our peasants are learning to look through their fingers too."

Apparently the bishop got the point. In 1570 *Eulenspiegel,* along with some other chapbooks, was placed on the Antwerp Index—one year after Bruegel's death. This supports the theory that Bruegel's work contains political allusions. By that time the situation was so tense that a man could be hanged for an insulting or sarcastic remark.[107]

Certain events which occurred in Brussels in 1559 suggest the restless atmosphere of the city where Bruegel was soon to marry and settle down. On April 6 of that year the Brussels city council ordered a celebration to commemorate the peace of Cateau-Cambrésis, which marked the end of the Italian wars between France and Spain. The rhetoricians were ordered to provide three evenings of "the finest, merriest, most enjoyable entertainments" with the reservation that the plays were to contain no taunts or gibes: *"behoudelyck zonder schimp oft vilonie."* As usual there was a play contest, with prizes. The Corenbloem (Cornflower) School of Rhetoric took first prize for its performance of a play entitled *De Bervoete Bruers* (literally, *The Barefoot Brothers*). Barefoot Brothers, however, was the usual Flemish nickname for the Franciscans or Minorites. The theme of the prize winning play was simple, not to say naïve. Hans and his wife complain that their "seven or eight" children have nothing to eat. Last night they had to go to bed "singing." So Hans takes his wheelbarrow and sets off for town, hoping to scrounge at least a crust of bread. He meets a nobleman who is getting ready for a banquet with the Franciscan prior. The nobleman entrusts his provisions to Hans, telling him to take them to "the barefoot brothers." What happens is not hard to imagine. After the inevitable thrashing and dousing with a bucket of water, Hans wins his case, for the magistrate himself has to admit that he carried out the nobleman's instructions. After all, seven or eight sons who have no shoes to wear can certainly be called barefoot brothers.

Harmless as the joke may seem to us, the Franciscans took it amiss. At a second performance of the play on Saint Matthew's Day, September 21, the rhetoricians preceded it with a prologue stating that nobody was being ridiculed: *"ten es op niemant schimp gedaen."* But this did not help matters, especially when two of the "entertainments" performed by other schools of rhetoric also aroused protests. Granvelle himself ordered an investigation. The testimony (some of which is preserved in the records) is revealing. The five witnesses for the prosecution: two Franciscans, a bed merchant, and the vicar and a canon of Saint Gudula's, alleged that the plays in question, particularly *The Barefoot Brothers*, were antireligious. The two monks protested against speeches they felt to be disparaging to their order on the grounds that they were detrimental to the order's pastoral work. In the canon's opinion the play was "a laughing matter, but nevertheless critical and obviously intended to ridicule the Minorite Brothers." Plays like this should not be tolerated because "you should never turn a louse loose in a fur." The parish priest of Saint Gudula asked for the texts of the plays under attack, but the rhetorician Gielken van Genuechte refused this request with the quick-witted retort that the authority probably only wanted to search the manuscript for more details to object to.

The three plays were banned. Apparently the magistrate simply shelved the case, but a few years later his negligence came under sharp attack: "Moreover, the said witness alleges that although the magistrate was ordered by the said cardinal to arrest and punish the performers of certain plays which are suspicious and therefore prohibited by express edict of the late emperor, after speaking with the actors he merely sent them to the said vicar to make their excuses, instructing them to tell him that he, the magistrate, demanded nothing of them and that he was satisfied so long as the vicar was."[108]

This case shows that certain subjects had become very sensitive. Anyone who made fun of a cleric could expect prompt action by the highest authorities. Doesn't this suggest that the potential censors of Bruegel's pictures never found them insulting or took them as direct personal attacks? Or is it rather a tribute to the artist's skill at camouflaging his satirical broadsides as orthodox Biblical scenes? Marcus van Vaernewijck says in his account of the Reformation: "A fisherman doesn't catch the fish with the bare hook. He covers it with a bait which tastes good to the fish. The devil doesn't simply set out his poison: he covers it with the handsome words of the Holy Writ."[109]

This gives food for thought. Modern man's critical mind is understandably quick to see in Bruegel an element of tongue in cheek slyness. Tempting as it is, this is a dubious assumption. Even if his work had really been loaded with political allusions, only a limited audience would have understood them. Would Bruegel have risked his neck for such a problematical effect? Painting pictures was certainly not the most effective way to influence public opinion in those days. Moreover, it would be absurd to assume that anyone with a quick mind was necessarily a Gueux or a freethinker. Probably Bruegel's criticism was not nearly as aggressive as many modern interpreters would like to think.

No observant viewer will doubt that his work abounds in allusions. Without question much of what he refrained from saying was immediately obvious to his contemporaries, especially to anyone acquainted with the subtleties of the Dutch language. The pun "*Alghe Mist*" is sufficient proof of this. What about the range of his criticism? After examining the problem carefully from various aspects, we must conclude that Bruegel was probably not nearly so sly as he has been made out to be. But this still does not explain why the authorities tolerated his obviously satirical attitude. Contemporary literature offers a very simple explanation quite in keeping with the Dutch national character: a fondness for moralizing. To be sure, this quality is not confined to the Dutch, but there is no denying that it was particularly highly developed and appreciated in the Netherlands. This can be explained in various ways: as a pragmatic knowledge of men as they are, or as a feeling of helplessness in confronting a "topsy-turvy world."

Sometimes moralizing crystallizes into simple pragmatic wisdom, but it is often no more than the long-winded maundering of a man who knows where the shoe pinches but cannot do anything about it. Didacticism at its worst is boring rather than provocative.

The sixteenth century in general was given to moralizing; in fact, for us this is one of the less attractive characteristics of Bruegel's contemporaries, which sometimes mars otherwise admirable passages of literature. Chronicles, lampoons,[110] plays, and farces—all literature in fact—are full of proverbs and precepts, relevant or irrelevant. Every would-be writer seems to have invented his own maxims. Of all sixteenth-century literary forms the song has probably retained the most spontaneity,[111] but even here the effect is often marred by a stanza of banalities. The didactic tone of a play is often evident in its list of characters, who frequently have allegorical names like Afjonstich Gheest, Ootmoedigh Herte, Sinnelijcken Appetijt (Envious Spirit, Submissive Heart, Sensual Desire). A seaman is called Jaep Seldenthuys (Jacob Seldom-at-Home), a peasant Jasper Goetbloet (Jasper Goodbloom). Obviously Bruegel's contemporaries enjoyed pointing a moral and never tired of puzzling out allusions and symbols.

Bruegel was a moralist through and through. Today this is no compliment, but it would be unfair to judge him by preconceived standards. We must see the artist in the context of his time, for he addressed himself to his contemporaries. And he was by no means the only moralist of his age. There was Erasmus and there was Thomas More, to mention only two. In his refutation of Martin van Dorp, Erasmus wrote: "I believed I had found the way to insinuate myself, as it were, into weak minds and to entertain and heal them at the same time."

Gotthard Jedlicka has pointed to a certain duality in Bruegel's art, saying that it produced two separate trends in painting, one leading to the Flemish art of Rubens and the other to the Dutch art of Rembrandt.[112] It is true that the separation of the northern and southern provinces of the Netherlands did not stem entirely from politics. To explain uprisings in the north entirely as a revolt against Spanish rule is to oversimplify. Critical historians have long emphasized the many differences between the Flemish mentality and that of the seven northern provinces (present-day Holland) thus to some extent justifying their separation.

Bruegel certainly never glorified the gluttony of intemperate people who stuff themselves *tot dbuycxken vol totter kinnen is* (until their belly is full to the chin). But neither does he blame a child for indulging in the simple pleasure of licking out his bowl, his face half hidden by his voluminous hood. The peasant in the foreground of the splendid drawing "Summer,"[160] (plate p. 71) with his leg stretched out and his scythe on his knee, has certainly earned the right to a refreshing drink. Anyone who knows the Dutch character will suspect that Bruegel sometimes approves of the very things he is criticizing. As a Brabanter, he is in some ways half Dutch and half Flemish.

Perhaps we should take this readiness to moralize as proof that Bruegel shared the sound common sense and popular wisdom which were to characterize the moral outlook of the Dutch bourgeoisie in the seventeenth century. We are reminded of the poet and politician Jacob Cats, popularly known as vader Cats (Father Cats), born in 1577, eight years after Bruegel's death, whose didactic works made him in a sense the mentor of the Dutch people. Vader Cats' works are imbued with a practical good sense which today seems commonplace and banal, not to say narrow-minded.[113] Bruegel, of course, is not to be equated with Cats. We merely wish to make the point that the literature of that age more often than not had a moralistic tone. We should not forget that Cats treated many of the same subjects as Bruegel.[86] Seventeenth-century Dutch painting's fondness for emblems and symbols proves that the didactic element in Bruegel's art which was so typical of his century persisted for a considerable time.[114]

Parallels have often been drawn between Bruegel's art and that of his contemporary, Rabelais.[115] They are more or less plausible, depending upon what characteristics the two artists are thought to have in common. It would be completely wrong to identify Bruegel with Gargantua, who, as we read in the eleventh chapter of Rabelais' account of his exploits, "wiped his nose on his sleeve, blew snot in his soup, piddled around everywhere, drank out of his slipper, chewed while he was laughing and laughed while he was chewing, pissed against the sun, often threw up" and so on. As we have seen, Bruegel's work often recalls Till Eulenspiegel's adventures, but it must be emphasized that Bruegel is never coarse; the revolting details he occasionally introduces into his pictures have nothing in common with the crude jokes that enliven the text of the chapbook.[106] And, after all, hygiene was an unknown subject to our sixteenth-century ancestors.

It would be fairer to Bruegel to link him with Erasmus.[76] These two men are among the few who achieved the difficult synthesis of passionate feeling and style. Charles de Tolnay rightly calls attention to the passage where Erasmus says: "In sum, if you might look down from the moon, as Menippus did of old, upon the numberless agitations among mortal men, you would think you were seeing a swarm of flies or gnats, quarreling among themselves, waging wars, setting snares for each other, robbing, sporting, wantoning, being born, growing old, and dying. And one can scarce believe what commotions and what tragedies this animalcule, little as he is and so soon to perish, sets a-going."[116]

Bruegel himself might well have been the author of some lines written by a French contemporary, Jacques Grévin (1538–70):

Je déplore mes ris, je me ris de mes pleurs
Je ris mon passe-temps, je pleure mes douleurs
Tout me tire à pleurer, tout à rire m'excite.

(I deplore my laughter and laugh away my weeping. I laugh at my fun; I weep at my griefs. Everything prompts me to cry; everything makes me laugh.)

An important leitmotif in Pieter Bruegel's work is "the topsy-turvy world" and its transience. Man's ignorance and foolishness prevent him from finding his soul's salvation. Only nature, the landscape in which all happenings occur, is immaculate, well ordered, pure, and beautiful.

We must guard against projecting our own view of the world onto Bruegel. If we try to transpose his work into our own time, we are amazed how up-to-date it seems. Day in and day out we all confront the terrifying yet laughable, meaningless yet tragic spectacle played out by society, just as Bruegel described it in his "Netherlandish Proverbs" (plates pp. 88–101).

An artist is interesting insofar as he reflects his age; he is great insofar as he transcends it. Bruegel belongs to all ages and places. What painter before him ever observed man with such insight? Peasant and rascal, merchant and clerk, cripple, dwarf and beggar woman, peddler and monk—Bruegel saw through them all. He knew their wiles and their simplicity. Poverty, hunger, incurable diseases, horrible mutilations, covetousness, cowardice, hate, death, religious fervor, idleness, sorrow, resignation, as well as indestructible vitality—all this he recognized, understood and portrayed. He knew how poor people enjoyed the spectacle of an execution; for them this was a show, a festive occasion. Without comment he shows us children continuing their games, heedless and undisturbed while the execution takes place. Like Rabelais, Bruegel builds with living stones: with men.

The longer we look at his work, the more insistently we ask ourselves what in his inmost heart he really thought of man. His love for the indestructible beauty of nature knew no bounds; he portrayed it with devout reverence—perhaps the only thing he openly revered. But he expresses his opinion of man very ambiguously. Was he really as tolerant as we like to think? With his Brabantine wiliness he manages to insinuate in our minds all kinds of notions about ourselves—some of them by no means flattering. Was Bruegel a joker? That would indeed be a joke.

Both versions of "The Tower of Babel" (plates pp. 190–95 and 196–97) are sublimely beautiful. Does another painting exist that so movingly expresses the absurdity of human existence within grandiose nature? Has there ever been a more perceptive rendering of the abysmal vanity of this two-handed creature known as man who, taking himself as master of the world, insists on trying to build the impossible?

None of Bruegel's works is grimmer or richer in meaning than "The Parable of the Blind" (plates pp. 304–13). Its matchless rhythm suggests a row of falling bowling pins photographed in slow motion. In this extraordinary composition Bruegel depicts the inescapability of ultimate catastrophe. Nature itself, reflected in the tranquil Brabantine landscape, seems to be implicated in it; beautiful and indifferent, it seems to condone the human tragedy. And what does the parish church signify in this context?

Bruegel painted "The Parable of the Blind" and "The Cripples" (plate p. 329) in the last year of his life. Looking at his paintings in chronological order is like watching a film. The camera pans across the dense crowd and finally moves in for a close-up of man, that wicked, halting, blind creature. Charles de Tolnay is right in saying that "The Parable of the Blind" seems to have been conceived "with an objectivity which has detached itself from everything human."

Although Bruegel is commonly taken for a joker, we search his work in vain for lightheartedness. In looking at his paintings, drawings and engravings, we are immediately struck by the seriousness of his human figures. Their faces bear the marks of age; their features are coarse; their expressions careworn, bad-tempered, pained, astonished, or worried. One feels that these people have never known happiness, laughter or a positive attitude toward life. The old-looking children are even more distressing. Absorbed in their games as they are, they do not seem to be having any fun but look more like adults forced to work hard all day long. The atmosphere of the famous "Children's Games" (plates pp. 106–9) does not suggest a playground; one wishes that the swarms of children would fill the air with a joyful hullabaloo. Bruegel went to great trouble to present a comprehensive catalog of children's games; he worked with the care and precision that mark the scientific methods of the modern folklorist. But this does not mean that his intention was to create an exhaustive documentary illustration for a lexicon or textbook on folklore. The moral that all human activity is ultimately no more than child's play was quite familiar to his contemporaries.

Until recent times Bruegel's style was not highly regarded. Critics who believed in the idealizing function of art found him disappointing. Scholars such as G. F. Waagen, Jacob Burckhardt and Henri Hymans spoke of him in uncomplimentary terms, calling him vulgar, unbearably coarse, occasionally grotesque, and so on. But if we take time to look at his works carefully and compare them with the copies his elder son, Pieter, made of them, Bruegel emerges as an incomparable stylist.

We must now examine Bruegel's esthetic values, which have rarely been properly appreciated. All too often he is identified with his plebeian models and themes. Beauty, as Bruegel conceived it, has nothing to do with the pleasing quality prescribed by classical antiquity or the Renaissance. His individual style achieved something unique: it portrayed clumsiness with elegance. Unlike his Romanist colleagues, he hardly ever painted nudes,[117] probably because his view of man was not the Italian one but something quite different which can only be grasped in the context of his cosmic landscapes. Bruegel tends to see the world from above—sometimes from a great height. Van Mander writes of "The Temptations of Christ" (now lost) that it is a picture "in which one looks down from above, as from the Alps, upon cities and country borne up by clouds." Bruegel apparently saw man as a helpless, insignificant creature lost in space. When he is placed in the foreground, he is swallowed up in the abyss of perspective.

We have come a long way from the evaluation of the critic who rediscovered Bruegel in 1890, Henri Hymans, who stated succinctly: "His scope is certainly not the broadest, and his ambition is kept within modest bounds. He confines himself to a knowledge of man and familiar things."[118]

The fact that parallels can be drawn between Bruegel and the rhetoricians or Father Cats is in no way disparaging to Bruegel. It is certainly unnecessary to prove that he was an incomparable master or to reiterate that the creations of contemporary versifiers become insignificant in the light of his genius. The parallels we have drawn are only relative; they merely try to show what was on the minds of the people of Brabant in the sixteenth century. Bruegel made himself a spokesman for his compatriots, giving expression to their cares and aspirations. The rhetoricians of the Pioen Bloeme (Peony) School tried their best to paint a cautionary picture of man's foolishness, but their verses leave us cold. Bruegel's pictures, however, still speak to us, despite the gap of four hundred years. His genius made an impact where his contemporaries' efforts failed. The human condition as seen by this sixteenth-century Brabantine artist became a universal one.

The artist creates his work; I look at it. Does it really contain a personal message for me? Does this message emanate from the drawing carefully preserved in a drawer in a print room or the painting hanging on a museum wall? The artist and I both have our sights set on a distant star. Is it the same one? For many years I believed so; today I am not so sure. Perhaps Pieter Bruegel has been trying to speak to me across the gulf of centuries but I have understood only part of his message. Is it not closer to the truth to say that I, the viewer, am seeking in his works confirmation of ideas which are important to me?

Unquestionably Bruegel was a perspicacious man of remarkable intelligence with a finely honed critical faculty unusual in his day, but this does not make him a freethinker or revolutionary. Every work he created testifies to his genius. Since the beginning of the twentieth century he has ranked high among the great geniuses of the West. Our attempts to comprehend his art are like the gropings of a man in some fascinating labyrinth whose extent and tortuous paths are unknown to him. We must avoid the pitfalls of book learning. Every Bruegel scholar will sooner or later have to admit that the seminal core of his work is difficult of access.

As we skim through Till Eulenspiegel's merry pranks, we are stopped by a profound observation. During his peregrinations Eulenspiegel played tricks on clerics, peasants, bakers, tailors, cobblers, clerks, barber-surgeons, and men of high degree. Now he is ill and weak and about to die. His poor mother is sitting at his bedside. "Give me some of your property," she says.

Eulenspiegel replies: "Mother, we must give to him who has nothing, just as we must take from him who has. So far as my property is concerned, it is so well hidden that nobody can find it. But if you chance upon it, don't wait to be asked. Just help yourself."

Bruegel too hid his treasure well.

"The Painter and the Connoisseur"
(Self-portrait of Pieter Bruegel
the Elder?)
Pen drawing. Vienna, Albertina.

36

Despite the existence of a vast Bruegel literature, many questions remain unresolved. The catalog of Bruegel's drawings and paintings[119], varies with every compiler. A picture which one scholar calls a masterpiece may be rejected as unauthentic by another. In our opinion it is essential to subject all Bruegel's work to laboratory analysis. Technical procedures such as macro-, infrared and fluorescent photography and microscopic examination of the drawings and signatures could settle many controversial attributions. The same applies to the paintings. Since Bruegel's technique is simple,[163] besides being consistent and of a high order, his work lends itself admirably to this kind of analysis.[164] A comparison of X-ray photographs would undoubtedly prove very useful too. Until an exhaustive analysis of this kind can be undertaken, we must rely on the data established by historical research.

The following notes do not seek to rectify other opinions; their purpose is rather to shed light on the range of Bruegel's ideas and particularly the content of his pictures. In the matter of authenticity, variant versions and copies, we refer the reader to the findings of the eminent scholars who have dealt with this subject from René van Bastelaer and Georges Hulin de Loo to Gotthard Jedlicka, Gustav Glück, Charles de Tolnay, Walter Vanbeselaere, and Fritz Grossmann.

1 "Landscape with Sailing Boats and a
  Burning Town"
  Wood panel, 7 by 10 inches. Private collection.

This work is first listed by Grossmann (*The Paintings*, plate 1 and p. 189). It should be noted that the dimensions cited in the plate caption (18 by 26 centimeters) differ from the size given in his catalog (24.4 by 34.8 centimeters). If the attribution is confirmed, this painting of about 1553 would be Bruegel's earliest extant work. (See Catalog No. 2.) The drawing of an "Alpine Landscape" published in 1959 (London, Collection of Counte Antoine Seilern) is signed "P. Brueghel 1547," but this date is not consistent with biographical data derived from various sources. There is no doubt that Bruegel did not go to Italy until after he had been admitted to Saint Luke's Guild in 1551. Lit.: F. Grossmann, "*New Light on Bruegel*"; L. Münz, *The Drawings*, p. 240, Appendix No. 2.

2 "Landscape with Christ Appearing to the
  Apostles at the Sea of Tiberias"
  Wood panel, 26 1/8 by 39 inches, 1553. Private collection.

Tolnay admits the possibility that the figures in the Biblical scene may be by another hand ("*An Unknown Early Panel*"). This is thought to be the oldest painting bearing Bruegel's signature. (See Catalog No. 1.)

3 "Landscape with the Fall of Icarus"
  Transferred from panel to canvas, 28 5/8 by 43 5/8 inches. Brussels, Musées royaux des Beaux-Arts. Plates pp. 74–81.

A slightly different version of this picture. Panel, 24 1/2 by 35 inches. Brussels, Van Buuren Collection. Plate p. 74.

While the authenticity of the composition is unchallenged, opinion is divided as to whether Bruegel actually painted either of these two versions. Jedlicka says: "... it is impossible to identify either version as the original. In my opinion Bruegel did paint a similar picture in his youth, but neither the Brussels version nor the one belonging to Mme. Herbrand in Paris [now in the Van Buuren Collection] is the original. At best they are copies (possibly from the same workshop), which were later painted over, and the Herbrand version of this narrative theme may well be the closer copy" (p. 545). See also Vanbeselaere, "*Bruegeliana*".

The picture is thought to have been painted between 1555 and 1562 or 1563, possibly as late as 1567 or 1568. The subject is probably taken from Ovid's *Metamorphoses*, Book VIII; Bruegel interpreted the details in his own way. The barely distinguishable figure of a dead man lying under the trees at the left (plate p. 80) has never been satisfactorily explained. One assumes that the picture's deeper meaning may be a moralistic one: the realist with both feet firmly planted on the ground fails to recognize the dreamer.

For a technical discussion of the ship and plow see Van Beylen, Smekens, Theuwissen, and Weyns.

Van Lennep believes that this picture is full of alchemistic symbolism ("*L'Alchimie et Pierre Bruegel*"). See also Stridbeck, *Bruegelstudien*, pp. 235–43.

4 "The Adoration of the Kings"
  Tempera on canvas, 45 by 63 1/2 inches. Brussels, Musées royaux des Beaux-Arts. Plates pp. 82–85.

Since this picture is neither signed nor dated, the attribution is controversial. Comparable paintings are very rare, so it is difficult to reach a decision. However, the work is quite consistent with Bruegel's style. Dating varies between 1555–57 and 1562–63. The picture has suffered badly from poor care and handling. Whether it is an original Bruegel or not, this composition is a valuable example of a once common genre.

5 "Landscape with the Parable of the Sower"

Wood panel, 28⁷/₈ by 39³/₄ inches, 1557. San Diego, Timken Art Gallery, Putnam Foundation. Plates pp. 86–87.

The inscription on a copy of this painting shows that it illustrates the parable of the sower from Matthew 13:3–8. Glück comments: "The details of how birds devour some of the seed scattered by the sower, how some of it falls among thorns and stones and only a little falls on good ground and sprouts and brings forth fruit are an admirable vehicle for the artist's ideas about the folly and vanity of human activity" (*The Large Brueghel Book*, No. 7).

6 "The Netherlandish Proverbs"

Wood panel, 45⁵/₈ by 63¹/₂ inches, 1559. Berlin, Staatliche Museen, Gemäldegalerie. Plates pp. 88–101.

In the fifteenth century conversation was well sprinkled with maxims and proverbs. (See J. Huizinga, *The Waning of the Middle Ages*, New York, 1954, pp. 229–31.) We recall Villon's "*Ballade des Proverbes*," his "*Ballade des Menus Propos*" and his "*Ballade des Contrevérités*." This liking for proverbial sayings persisted into the sixteenth century. Cervantes later made fun of it in *Don Quixote*. So Bruegel's proverb picture was no great novelty; such a painting was certain to appeal to his contemporaries. Louis Lebeer's "*De Blauwe Huyck*" is a comparative study of engravings dealing with the theme. The oldest print known to us is by Frans Hogenberg. The plate for this was probably engraved by Barthelemy de Momper in Antwerp about 1558, very close to the date of Bruegel's painting. The original title is mentioned on the engraving: "*Die Blau Huicke is dit meest ghenaemt | maer des weerelts abuisen hem beter betaempt.*" (This is usually called "The Blue Cloak," but a better name would be "The Folly of the World.") New versions of this print and its explanatory text appeared up until the eighteenth century. An engraving by L. Fruytiers, for instance, bears the legend: "*Deze witbeeldinghe wort die Blauwe Huyck ghenaemt | maer des Werelts ydel spreck-*

woorden beter betaemt—Par ce dessin il est monstré les abus du monde renversé." (This drawing shows the folly of the topsy-turvy world.)

The following key to the proverbs summarizes the explanations proposed by Jan Grauls and Louis Lebeer. Some details and allusions are still controversial or obscure; a few of the explanations seem unsatisfactory. As Grauls has shown (*Volkstaal*, p. 50), it is a mistake to try to interpret Bruegel's picture with Harrebomée's *Spreekwoordenboek* in hand, because this anthology of proverbs dates from the nineteenth century and later expressions cited by Harrebomée cannot be indiscriminately applied to a picture which illustrates sixteenth-century proverbs and idioms. We have to rely on literary sources of the fifteenth, sixteenth and seventeenth centuries. A comparative study of Flemish, French and German expressions is urgently needed. See also Wilhelm Fraenger, *Der Bauern-Bruegel*.

Expressions like the proverbs are to be found in Rabelais. Gargantua, for instance, "*se asseyoyt entre deux selles le cul à terre—pissoyt contre le soleil—se cachoyt en l'eau pour la pluye—faisoyt perdre les pieds aux mouches—baisloit souvent aux mouches—saultoyt du coq à l'asne..*" (sat between two stools with his arse on the ground, pissed against the sun, took shelter in the water from the rain, tore off flies' feet, often yawned at flies, jumped from the cock to the ass).

One of the chief claims to fame of Flemish art is its realism. This quality is by no means accidental: it reflects the character of the Flemish people and is another expression of their sound human understanding. Their sayings and proverbs reflect their positive, matter-of-fact wisdom. The Fleming is hardworking, cautious, jocose, and sardonic. He is quite aware that it is unwise to bite off more than one can chew or, as he puts it, "to try to open your mouth wider than an oven door."

It is worth noting that at least twenty of the idioms and proverbs that Bruegel illustrates deal with craftiness, hypocrisy or

deceit. The expression "to hang a blue cloak on someone" (No. 21) is depicted in the very center of the picture (plates pp. 89, 99), and the original title "The Blue Cloak" underlines the fact that deceit is its leitmotif. The theme of dishonesty and cheating constantly recurs throughout contemporary literature and plays. Idioms and proverbs are essentially moralistic. Bruegel was not merely presenting an anthology of proverbs; he was admonishing his audience: "Just look at the way you carry on!" Doesn't the despairing sigh "*En laet die werelt der werelt syn in haer verdoeltheyt*" (Let the world be the world in its aberrations—let the world go its own foolish way) reveal a longing for a better world? See O. van den Daele and F. van Veerdeghem, *De Roode Roos*, p. 220.

A list of the sayings and proverbs so far as they have been identified follows. The numbers begin at the lower left of the diagram. The proverb is quoted first in modern Dutch, then in as literal a translation as possible. The literal renderings are invaluable if we wish to acquire a sense of the psychological climate and mode of expression of Bruegel's age, when language was generally picturesque. Finally we give a corresponding English proverb or an explanation. See also F. A. Stoett and J. Sterck.

1. "*Zij zou de duivel op een kussen binden*" (she would [even] tie the devil to a pillow). She is spiteful and quarrelsome—a shrew, a real virago. See *Veelderhande geneuchlijcke dichten* (p. 7): "*Al waert een van die seven wijven | Die den duyvel opt kussen deden blijuen*" (as if she were one of the seven women who kept the devil lying on the pillow).

On the ground near the group is an object that looks like an enema syringe. It has not been explained.

2. "*Een pilaarbijter*" (a pillar biter). A hypocrite, sanctimonious person, bigot or dissembler. See Marcus van Vaernewijck, II, p. 122.

In a morality play performed in September, 1595, a character called Trauwe (Faithfulness) complains that she is reviled and rejected

while the hypocrites—the people with four cheeks to their face, the pillar biters—are received at court: "*Menschen met aensichten van vier wanghen / Die pilernen byten; / Dese sullen die Werelt noch verstranghen, / Want sy woerden al te hoeve ontfanghen / Metten ypocryten; / My siet men wt den lande bannen en smyten, / Grooten smaet achter rugge roepen en cryten.*" See Van den Daele and Van Veerdeghem, p. 156.

3. "*Zij draagt water in de ene hand en vuur in de andere*" (she carries water in one hand and fire in the other). She can blow hot or cold; she is two-faced or double-dealing. This phrase can probably also describe inconsistent behavior: to pursue virtue yet not keep out of the way of temptation. See, for instance, a morality play entitled *Tspel van*

den ontrouwen rentmeester (Play of the Unfaithful Steward) performed in Hasselt in 1588 and 1609 (Van den Daele and Van Veerdeghem, p. 107).

4. (a) "*De haring braden om de kuit*" (to broil the herring for the sake of the roe). To spend money for nothing. In an early-seventeenth-century play we find the expression "*Gy dunckt my een trawantgen Die om de kuijte den haring braet*" (You look to me like a vassal who would broil the herring for the sake of the roe).

(b) "*Zijn haring braadt er niet*" (his herring doesn't fry there). Things are not going according to plan. He gets the cold shoulder.

(c) "*Het deksel op de kop krijgen*" (to get the lid on the head). To have to face the music or pay for the damage.

(d) The herring hanging on the wall may

mean: "*De haring hangt aan zijn eigen kieuw*" (the herring hangs by its own gills). Everyone must bear the consequences of his own mistakes.

5. "*Hij valt tussen twee stoelen in de as*" (he falls between two stools into the ashes). He has missed his opportunity because he couldn't make up his mind.

6. "*De hond in de pot vinden*" (to find the dog in the pot or larder). To find the cupboard bare; to come the day after the fair; to find that someone has been there before you. To have all your trouble for nothing.

7. "*De zeug trekt de tap uit*" (the sow pulls out the bung). The innkeeper doesn't keep a strict eye on things, and everybody takes advantage of it. The funnel standing upside down on the cask probably also refers to a proverb. A funnel worn on the head—as, for instance, in Bosch's famous picture "The

Cure of Folly" in the Prado in Madrid—denotes a dupe. Is that what it means here? Have the pigs any particular significance?

8. "*Met het hoofd tegen de muur lopen*" (to run one's head against the wall). To pursue impetuously the impossible. To take a beating.

The man is in a rage, suggesting the Dutch expression "*terstont in't harnas zijn*" (to be quickly up in arms), to have a quick temper. (*Cf.* Catalog No.13, "*Dulle Griet.*")

Some details have still not been satisfactorily explained: the way the man is dressed; the bandage on his right leg; his left foot bare but his right one shod; and his big knife.

9. "*De ene scheert schapen, de andere varkens*" (one shears sheep, the other pigs). One man lives in luxury; another in poverty. This proverb was probably generally applied to greedy, unscrupulous people. In a play performed by the Brussels School of Rhetoric a character named Tswerelts Cruyen (Worldly Tricks) asks the other characters: "What [do you think] of all the people who scrounge and scrape the way I do, all those who let the pigs alone and shear the sheep, all those who are more interested in the skin than the hair? What do you think of them?" The other characters answer in chorus: "They know the tricks (*cruyen*) of the world." (*Alle die met mijne | rapen en schrapen | Al die tvercken laten | en scheyren de schapen | Al die voor thayr verkiesen de huyen | Wat segdy van die? ... Die kennen de cruyen [Spelen van Sinne]*).

10. "*De kat de bel aanbinden*" (to bell the cat). To attempt a difficult task. To pull the chestnuts out of the fire. To be courageous. "*La difficulté fut d'attacher le grelot*" (the difficulty was to attach the bell), says La Fontaine in "*The Fable of the Council of Mice.*" *Cf.* Van Vaernewijck, Vol. I, p.100.

11. "*Hij is tot de tanden gewapend*" (he is armed to the teeth).

12. "*Daar hangt de schaar uit*" (there the scissors hang out). The scissors hanging at the window like an inn sign denote a place where the customer is cheated or fleeced—a clip joint.

13. "*Aan een been knagen*" (to gnaw at a

bone). To keep harping on the same subject; to fret and fume.

14. "*De hennetaster*" (the hen feeler, one who feels a hen to see if it is going to lay). This expression seems to have two meanings: (1) a busybody; a rough, good-natured fellow; possibly a man who helps around the house, and (2) a skirt-chaser. It still survives in this sense in the region of Arendonk near Turnhout in the province of Antwerp. See Sterck.

15. "*Hij spreekt uit twee monden*" (he speaks with two mouths). He is double-tongued, two-faced, deceitful.

16. "*Hij draagt de dag met manden uit*" (he carries the day out in baskets). He kills time, loafs, fritters away his hours.

17. "*De duivel een kaars ontsteken*" (to light a candle to the devil). To flatter people (even the untrustworthy) in order to gain their help or support.

18. "*Bij de duivel te biecht gaan*" (to make one's confession to the devil). To disclose confidential information to an enemy or rival.

19. "*De oorblazer*" or "*iemand iets in het oor blazen*" (the ear blower or to blow in somebody's ear). The tattletale. To whisper something in someone's ear. To put ideas (usually bad ones) in other people's heads.

20. (a) "*De ene rokkent wat de andere spint*" (one winds on the distaff what the other spins). Here the phrase is applied to two gossips, but it can also mean to finish off something that someone else has begun. For example: "*Ick gaent dan haspelen dat ghy gheroct hebt* (then I have to unwind all that you've wound on the distaff [*Spelen van Sinne*, Zoutleeuw School of Rhetoric]).

Van Vaernewijck (Vol. I, p.190), speaking of fights instigated by women, says: "*Die vrauwen haddent gheroct maer die mans zoudent af spinnen*" (the women had wound the distaff, but the men had to unwind it).

(b) "*Zie dat daar geen zwarte hond tussen komt*" (watch out that a black dog doesn't intervene). Be careful: something could go wrong. A black dog was a bad omen.

21. "*Zij hangt haar man de blauwe huik om*" (she hangs the blue cloak on her husband).

She deceives or cuckolds her husband; makes him wear horns.

22. "*Als 't kalf verdronken is, dempt men de put*" (after the calf has drowned, they fill in the ditch). They lock the stable door after the horse is stolen. *Cf.* Van Oesbroeck, p. 50, line 121.

23. "*Men moet zich krommen wil men door de wereld komen*" (one has to squirm if he wants to get through the world). The following details have not been satisfactorily explained: the man's left foot is bare, but he wears a shoe on his right foot. His left leg is bare; on his right he wears a legging or some kind of orthopedic brace.

24. "*Rozen voor de varkens strooien*" (to strew roses before the pigs). To cast pearls before swine; to give somebody a gift he cannot appreciate. *Cf.*, for example, Van Oesbroeck, p. 45, line 108.

25. "*Hij steekt het varken door de buik*" (he sticks the pig through the belly). (1) He settles a disputed question. He plunges boldly into something. He gets down to brass tacks. (2) It's a put-up job, a foregone conclusion.

26. "*Twee honden [knagen] aan één been*" (two dogs [gnaw] on one bone). They both lay claim to the same object or have their minds set on the same thing. They are fighting—or soon will be.

27. "*De vos en de kraan hebben elkander te gast*" (the fox and the crane entertain one another). They have both been bamboozled. They have fallen into their own trap; they are hoist with their own petard. "*Honteux comme un renard qu'une poule aurait pris*" (as ashamed as a fox trapped by a chicken), says La Fontaine in "*The Fable of the Fox and the Stork.*"

28. The saying or proverb illustrated by the scene at the spit has not been positively identified. The following suggestions have been made:

(a) "*Het is gezond in het vuur te pissen*" (it is healthy to piss in the fire).

(b) "*Zijn vuur is uitgepist*" (his fire is pissed out). He is completely discouraged. He has given up. He has had it.

(c) "*Het vlees aan het spit moet begoten*

worden" (the meat on the spit must be basted). Anything that is to succeed must be done with care.

29. "*Hij doet de wereld op zijn duimpje draaien*" (he spins the world on his little thumb). He only needs to crook his finger and everybody comes running. Everyone dances to his tune. The phrase is not restricted to the rich man who gets everything he wants in this world. In *Bruer Willeken*, a play performed in Hasselt in 1565, the world is said to spin "on the little thumb" of all those who lead a frivolous life: "*Ruyst, tuyst, drinct, sprinct daer en hier, | Verkeert al omme int cranck bestier; | Sweert, vloeckt, liecht, bedriecht, weest loos en boes, | Rammelt, dammelt, weest luye en lecker altoes | Hoort vrye nae my en dwoert verstaet; | Ghy sult vinden dat die werelt op u duymken drayt.*" (Van den Daele and Van Veerdeghem, pp. 201–2.)

30. "*Een stok in het wiel steken*" (to put a stick in the wheel). To put an obstacle in someone's path.

31. "*Hij die zijn pap gestort heeft, kan niet alles weder oprapen*" (he who has spilled his porridge cannot scrape it all up again). A blunder can never be completely retrieved.

32. "*Hij zoekt het bijltje*" (he is looking for the hatchet). He is looking for an excuse or a pretext.

33. "*Hij weet kwalijk van 't ene brood tot 't andere te geraken*" (he can barely reach from one loaf to another). He can barely make ends meet. He is a bad manager.

The implement on the table, a dough scraper, may also be an allusion to some saying. See Weyns.

34. (a) "*Zij trekken om het langste (eind)*" (they pull to get the longest [end]). They are engaged in a power struggle, fighting over a pretzel. Everyone seeks his own advantage. The scene recalls the drawing "*Elck*" (plate p. 60).

(b) "*De liefde is aan die kant waar de beurs hangt*" (love is on the side where the money bag hangs). Everyone knows on which side his bread is buttered.

35. "*Hij gaapt tegen de oven*" (he gapes against the oven). He tries to open his mouth wider than an oven door. He overestimates himself, bites off more than he can chew.

36. "*Ons Heer een vlassen baard aandoen*" (to tie a flaxen beard on Our Lord). To try to trick someone by sanctimonious behavior. To be hypocritical.

37. "*Men zoekt de andere niet in de oven tenzij men er (vroeger) zelf in geweest is*" (you don't look for someone in the oven unless you've been there yourself). If you suspect someone else of wrongdoing, you've probably already been guilty of it yourself. It takes one to know one.

38. "*Ze neemt het hoenderei en laat het ganzeëi lopen*" (she takes the hen's egg and lets the goose egg go). She makes a bad bargain. See, for instance, *De legende vanden Geusen Troubele over Zeelant inden jare 1572 ende 1573*, G.D.T. Schotel ed., Leiden, 1872.

39. "*Door de mand vallen*" (to fall through the basket). To fail or come to grief. To be turned down. The figure's left leg looks clean, while the right is dirty. In a copy of this painting by Pieter Bruegel the Younger in a private collection in Brussels the figure wears a white stocking on his left leg. The expression "*witte voeten hebben*" (to have white feet) meant "to be *persona grata*," "to be in favor." Cf. Stoett, No. 1487.

40. "*Op hete kolen zitten*" (to sit on hot coals). To be on tenterhooks, on pins and needles.

41. "*De verkeerde wereld*" (the topsy-turvy world). The opposite of the way things ought to be.

42. "*Hij schijt op de wereld*" (he shits on the world). He has nothing but contempt for the world.

43. "*De gekken krijgen de (beste) kaart(en)*" (fools get the [best] cards). Fortune favors fools. The meaning of the game bag slung over the man's shoulder is not clear.

44. "*Ze nemen elkander bij de neus*" (they take each other by the nose). They lead each other by the nose; trick each other.[137]

45. "*Door het oog van de schaar halen*" (to pull through the eye [the handle] of the scissors). To engage in sharp practice; to make a dishonest profit.

46. "*Een ei in het nest laten*" (to leave an egg in the nest). To refrain from spending one's last penny; to keep a nest egg.

47. "*Hij ziet door de vingers*" (he looks through his fingers). He winks or connives at something (usually fraud, injustice or wrongdoing). He doesn't need to see what he's doing because he stands to gain in any case. The expression was most commonly used when a poor man was not being treated fairly. Literature is full of complaints like this: "*Heeft hy gelt, men sal duer den vinger kycken; | Men siet den armen dus in der noot syn; | Justitie slaept of sy moet doot syn; | Den rechter wordt duer faveur en gelt verblint nu.*" ([Adultery, usury, murder]—what do they matter so long as you have money! But if you're a poor, needy man, they don't look through their fingers. Justice is either asleep or dead. The judge is blind from taking bribes. [Van den Daele and Van Veerdeghem, pp. 218–19].)

What is the significance of the hanging dagger? The wooden sabots *(platijnen)* on the window sill are also unexplained.

48. "*Vrijen onder één dak, is het schande, 't is gemak*" (courting under a roof may be shameful, but it's comfortable). Clandestine liaisons were common, though not sanctioned.

49. "*De bezem uitsteken*" (to stick out the broom). To celebrate. The symbolic meaning certainly dates back to the thirteenth century. See *Le vieil rentier d'Audenarde (ca. 1275)* in the Cabinet des Manuscrits of the Brussels Bibliothèque royale. In Limburg girls used to stand a broom outside the front door to let the boys know when their parents were out.

50. "*Daar zijn de daken met vladen gedekt*" (there the roofs are tiled with pies). That is a land of plenty, the Land of Cockaigne. There you can live in clover, live the life of Riley.

51. (a) "*Tegen de maan pissen*" (to piss against the moon). To attempt the impossible.

(b) "*Hij heeft tegen de maan gepist*" (he has pissed against the moon). Things have turned out badly. See D.T. Enklaar, *Varende Luyden,* pp.117–18. The figure wears a bandage around his cheeks and ears as if he had a toothache. Perhaps this means that he must grin and bear it.

52. (a) "*Het zijn twee zotten onder één kaproen*" (they are two fools under one hood). Two souls with but a single thought, two like-minded or inseparable people, two peas in a pod.

(b) "*Twee zotten in huis is te veel*" (two fools in the house are too many). What is the meaning of the branch protruding from the window?

53. "*De gek scheren (met iemand)*" or "*Hier wordt de gek geschoren*" (to shave the fool—here the fool is shorn). To take advantage of someone or make a fool of him.

54. "*Achter het net vissen*" (to fish behind the net). To miss an opportunity; to come away emptyhanded.

55. (a) "*Zijn achterste aan de poort vegen*" (to rub one's backside on the door). To clean off one's backside on the door: to take a devil-may-care attitude; not give a damn.

(b) "*Hij loopt met een pakje*" (he goes around with a burden). He has something on his conscience. It is uncertain whether the expression was used in this sense in Bruegel's day. If it was, Bruegel was using one figure to illustrate two contradictory sayings—though there would be nothing particularly surprising about that.

56. "*De ring van de deur kussen*" (to kiss the door ring [knocker]). (1) To be out of one's mind with love. (2) The lover who has been shown the door now finds himself on the wrong side of it. The following passage in *Le voyage et navigation que fist Panurge*[91] sheds some light on this: "After [the green goats'] ears are cut off, they turn into women and are known as curly-haired goats. Plenty of fools fall in love with them, [and behave] like lovers, often kissing the door handle behind what they take to be their sweetheart." (chapter 22.)

57. "*Van de os op de ezel springen*" or "*Van de os op de ezel vallen*" (to jump or fall from the ox onto the donkey). (1) To go from riches to rags; to fall on bad times. (2) To skip from one subject to another. To talk nonsense. To chop and change. To be moody or changeable. Another common phrase expressed the same idea: "*Van der kerre op den waghen vallen*" (to fall from the cart onto the wagon). See "*Van drie Sotten*" in W. van Eeghem's *Drie schandaleuse spelen*, p. 61.

58. "*Hij speelt op de kaak*" (he plays on the pillory—or on the jawbone). He appropriates other people's belongings. Corruption is everywhere.

Bruegel's illustration involves a pun. The word "*kaak*" has several meanings, including both "jawbone" and "pillory." This saying is illustrated in the engravings of "Twelve Flemish Proverbs" made between 1568 and 1569. Van Bastelaer's interpretation of it in *Les Estampes* (No.173) seems to be based on a misunderstanding of the Flemish text. His explanation, "The rich man's music is always agreeable, even when played on an animal's jawbone," is not compatible with the meaning of the phrase.

The legend on the engraving reads: "*Tis goet Ontfangher sijn, inden Crijch principael. Hij vult den Aessack, en men laudeert sijn sake. Al is sijn gagie groot noch weet hy sij[n] v[er]hael. Hy hout hem heerlijck en speelt op die kake.—Qui de recevoir a moijen, Sur la machoire il ioue bien.*" (The man who is on the receiving end plays well on the jawbone.)

59. (a) "*Al zijn pijlen verschieten*" (to shoot all one's arrows). To exhaust all one's weapons and be left defenseless. To run out of arguments. To try everything to no avail.

(b) "*De ene pijl na de andere zenden*" (to send one arrow after another). To persevere.

60. "*Waar het hek open is, lopen de varkens in het koren*" (where the hedge is open, the pigs run into the corn). A warning against careless supervision. When the cat's away, the mice will play.

61. "*Hij loopt of hij het vuur in zijn achterste had*" (he runs as if he had fire in his backside).

62. "*De huik naar de wind hangen*" (to hang one's coat according to the wind). To be a turncoat. To make up one's mind according to how the wind blows or how the cat jumps.

63. "*Zij kijt naar de ooievaar*" (she stares after the stork). She stands staring into space. She is wool-gathering, loafing.

64. "*Hij want pluimen in de wind*" or "*Hij want koren in de wind*" (he winnows feathers or corn into the wind). He puts the cart before the horse. To go at a job impetuously and unsystematically.

65. "*Grote vissen eten de kleine*" (big fish eat little ones).

66. "*Een spiering werpen om een kabeljauw te vangen*" or, as we say today, "*een bliekske smijten on een snoek te vangen*" (to throw out a smelt to catch a cod or a sprat to catch a pike).

67. "*Hij kan niet velen dat de zon in het water schijnt*" (he cannot bear the sun to shine on water). He is envious of other people's prosperity or success. What is the significance of the hat floating on the water?

68. "*Tegen de stroom opzwemmen*" (to swim against the stream). Has the swimmer's cap any significance?

69. "*Een paling bij de staart hebben*" (to hold an eel by the tail). To take a tiger by the tail. To be engaged in a risky undertaking.

70. "*Het is goed riemen snijden uit andermans leder*" (it's easy to cut straps out of other people's leather). It's easy to spend other people's money.

71. "*De kruik gaat zo lang te water tot ze breekt*" (the pitcher goes to the water until it breaks). You may do that once too often!

72. "*De kap op de tuin hangen*" (to hang one's cape on the fence). To quit. To throw in one's cards. To give up one's job.

73. "*Zijn geld in het water smijten*" (to throw one's money in the water). To throw money down the drain or down a rathole.

74. "*Zij schijten alle twee door één gat*" (they both shit through one hole). They are inseparable.

75. "*Hij vangt twee vliegen in één klap*" (he kills two flies with one stroke). He kills two birds with one stone. He achieves a double purpose.

76. (a) "*Als het huis brandt warmt men zich aan de kolen*" (when the house burns, one warms himself at the coals). Every cloud has a silver lining. In our opinion this proverb is

too optimistic to fit the sixteenth-century context.

Another proverb reflects the attitude of Bruegel's contemporaries much more faithfully:

(b) "*Hij geeft er niet om wiens huis in lichtelaaie staat, als hij zich maar aan de gloed kan warmen*" (he doesn't care whose house burns to the ground so long as he can warm himself at the glow). He is a confirmed egoist. In a play entitled *Suzanna* performed in 1607 in Hasselt this line occurs: "*Ons en raect wiens huys dat bernt achermen, Te minsten dat wy ons aen die coelen wermen*" (We don't care whose house burns down so long as we can warm ourselves at the coals [Van den Daele and Van Veerdeghem, p. 48]).

(c) "*Hij steekt zijn huis in brand om zich aan de kolen te warmen*" (he sets his house on fire in order to warm himself at the coals). He risks everything for a problematical gain.

77. "*Het blok slepen*" (to drag the stocks). To court an unattainable woman. To assume a burden for the sake of the woman one loves. See *Een schoon liedekens Boeck*, p. 328.

78. "*Paardekeutels zijn geen vijgen*" (horse droppings are not figs). Don't let anybody pull the wool over your eyes. All is not gold that glitters.

79. This scene at the upper right of the picture has not been satisfactorily explained. Some scholars associate the bears (?) with idling or being burdened with debts. Others think they represent an exemplary male-female relationship in the animal kingdom which is being held up as a model for married couples in everyday life. No one has yet established any meaningful connection between the bears and the shepherd (?) on the other side of the hedge.

80. (a) "*Hierom en daarom gaan de ganzen barrevoets*" (for this reason or that reason geese walk barefoot). There must be some good explanation for it.

(b) "*Ben ik niet geroepen om ganzen te hoeden, laat het ganzekens wezen*" (if I'm not smart enough to watch the geese, [at least] let me watch the goslings). Each according to his means. Everyone must do the best he can, cut his coat according to his cloth.

81. "*Een oogje in het zeil houden*" (to keep one's eye on the sail). To be on the alert, not miss anything.

82. "*Hij beschijt de galg*" (he shits on the gallows). He is not deterred by any penalty. He is a gallows bird; he will come to a bad end.

83. "*Angst en vrees doen (zelfs) de ouden rennen*" (fear and fright set [even] old people running). See Van Vaernewijck, Vol. II, p. 251.

84. "*Als de ene blinde de andere leidt, vallen ze beiden in de gracht*" (when one blind man leads another, they both fall into the ditch). See Catalog No. 42.

85. "*Niemand ooit zo klein iets spon, of het kwam wel aan de zon*" (everything, however finely spun it may be, [finally] comes to the sun). Nothing remains hidden or unrequited forever.

7 "The Fight Between Carnival and Lent"
Wood panel, 46 by 64¹/₈ inches, 1559. Vienna, Kunsthistorisches Museum. Plates pp. 102–5.

Bruegel did not invent the subject, which certainly dates back to the thirteenth century. (See Huizinga, *The Waning of the Middle Ages*, p. 212.) He later treated separately three motifs from this painting: "*De vuile Bruid*" ("The Dirty Bride"[155] also known as "The Marriage of Mopsus and Nissa"), "Ourson and Valentine,"[156] and "The Cripples" (Catalog No. 41 and Grossmann, *The Paintings*, p. 190).

The picture is a rich source of information about popular life in the Netherlands. The scenes it depicts can best be appreciated when they are compared with contemporary literary sources. The following excerpt from an early seventeenth-century play will supplement the references already given and incidentally explain why the figure in the lower left corner is wearing waffles in his cap. It describes some popular carnival traditions of Bruegel's day: wearing a disguise, making a racket (with a "rattle pot"), getting drunk, staring at sights like the man with a monkey, dancing in the streets, and decorating one's clothes with delicacies such as waffles, chicken drumsticks, and sausages: "*Aensiet eens dese kalesbent. De vuyle druyt stofferen, | Sy loopen mommen onbekendt Im omgekeerde kleren; | Sy spelen op een roeste tangh, En drillen op 't gebrom van 't schot | Of rommelpot Met berrevoetsche sangh. | Som rollen 't slootgen om de stadt, Men siet het turfgen rapen, | En drincken haer dan vol en sadt, Som commender met apen, | Die brenghen vreemde grillen voort, Se comen danssen op de straet | Als 't veêltgen gaet, En buytlen om een koordt. | U hoeden rondom dight bekleedt, Met lecker hoenderbouten | De varckensbillen niet vergeet, Al sijn se wat ghesouten, | En an u halsen kransen maeckt Van worsten en sausijsen veel | Ghepepert êêl, Daer wel een dronck op smaeckt*" (Van Vloten, Vol. II, p. 59).

Weyns is helpful in identifying some of the articles depicted, as well as Lenten food such as pretzels, mussels, figs, and fish. Lent has a rush basket of figs at her feet. The expression "*vijgen na Pasen*" (figs after Easter) probably comes from the tradition of eating figs during Lent.

8 "Children's Games"
Wood panel, 46 by 62³/₄ inches, 1560. Vienna, Kunsthistorisches Museum. Plates pp. 106–9.

In *L'espinette amoureuse* the chronicler Jean Froissart (*ca.* 1337–1404) mentions some sixty games he played as a child in Valenciennes. Even better known is the catalog in chapter 23 of Rabelais' *Gargantua*. The theory that "Children's Games" is a didactic picture is supported by Jacob Cats' treatment of the same theme in *Kinder-Spel* (1625): "*Dit spel, al schijnt' et zonder sin, | Dat heeft een kleyne werelt in, | De werelt en haer gants gestel | En is maer enckel kinder-spel.*" (This game, which seems meaningless, contains a whole world in microcosm. The world and all its activity is only a children's game.)

Lit.: Grossmann, *The Paintings*, p. 191; Glück, *The Large Bruegel Book;* De Meyere, *De Kinderspelen;* De Cock and Teirlinck, *Kinderspel;* Tietze-Conrat; Würtenberger, pp. 95–100; Van Lennep, *L'Alchimie.*

9 "View of Naples" sometimes called "The Sea Battle"

Wood panel, 15½ by 27⅛ inches, 1562? Rome, Galleria Doria. Plates pp. 182–89.

We believe this to be an early painting, but Winkler (*Die Altniederländische Malerei*, p. 345) and Grossmann (*The Paintings*, p. 194) think it is stylistically closer to Bruegel's mature work. Smekens (pp. 27–29) thinks it represents a naval battle outside the harbor of Naples, possibly an event in the war between the Turks and the imperial fleet. *Cf.* the engraving "Naval Battle in the Straits of Messina."[37]

10 "The Suicide of Saul" or "The Battle on Mount Gilboa"

Wood panel, 13 by 21½ inches, 1562? Vienna, Kunsthistorisches Museum. Plates pp. 180–81.

The composition, especially the sweep of the lances, recalls Altdorfer's famous "Battle of Alexander" (1529) in the Munich Pinakothek. Grossmann interprets the moral theme as pride punished: "The subject is exceptional in painting, though not infrequent in illustrated bibles. The explanation for the surprising choice of subject may lie in the fact that Saul's suicide was interpreted as punished pride. In Dante's *La Divina Commedia* (*Purgatorio*, XII, 25 ff.), Lucifer, Nimrod who built the Tower of Babel, and Saul are among the examples of punished pride" (*The Paintings*, pp. 193–94). This would suggest that "The Fall of the Rebel Angels" and "The Tower of Babel" are also warnings against pride.

11 "The Resurrection of Christ"

Pen and wash on paper, mounted on a wood panel, 16¾ by 12 inches, 1562? Rotterdam, Boymans-van Beuningen Museum. Plates pp. 136–37.

The signature has been inscribed over an earlier one. The work is undated.

Grossmann (*The Paintings*, p. 192) relates this work to Bruegel's two other extant grisailles (which, however, are oil paintings) and finds that they "have something of a personal or private character within Bruegel's oeuvre." This suggests that "The Resurrection" may have been painted for a friend.

Discussing the engraving after this picture, Bastelaer says: "No engraver's signature. The engraver seems to have taken a painting as his model, conscientiously copying every detail—even the frame. It seems to be by the same hand as 'The Death of the Virgin,' that is, by Philippe Galle" (*Les Estampes*, No. 114, p. 43). See Catalog No. 21.

Van Lennep notes that "the subject of this engraving is a fairly common one in alchemy: Christ, wearing a halo, is actually ascending from the tomb and pointing to a sun rising from the sea. Beside the soldiers is the hermetic hollow tree, with a bundle of dry twigs leaning against its trunk. De Tolnay is puzzled by this engraving and says: 'The exact meaning of this mysterious work is obscure.' We must, I think, assume a connection between this engraving and the 'Resurrections' in the *Rosarium philosophorum* (published in 1550) or the *Liber Trinitatis* (written between 1410 and 1419), which symbolize the triumphant materialization of the philosophers' stone. Christ, like the stone, emerges from the darkness of base matter to enter the realm of light. The transformation has taken place in the darkness of the Athanos, symbolized by the hollow tree [A.J. Pernety, *Dictionnaire mytho-hermétique*, Paris, 1787, p. 77]. There decomposing matter suffers a temporary death like Christ's only to rise again, sublimated. The bundle of dry twigs and the grave are symbols of the decay which matter must undergo before the red color appears, the color of the philosophers' stone. Christ's sojourn inside the earth is the spiritual equivalent of the wanderings of the alchemist, who *must seek the hidden stone inside the earth*.

"In his '*Dulle Griet*' Bruegel had depicted the final stages of this descent into Hell. His 'Resurrection' presents the fulfillment, unmistakably heralded by the sunrise. The alchemists used this as a symbol of the materialization of the philosophers' stone" (*L'Alchimie*, p. 116).

Attractive as this interpretation is, we must ask whether the hollow trees in "The Triumph of Death," "The Numbering of the People at Bethlehem," "The Netherlandish Proverbs," and in several engravings also have this symbolic or hermetic significance. In "The Numbering of the People at Bethlehem" a hollow tree is being used as a tavern—the White Swan. The swan was in those days an evangelical symbol. Obviously Bruegel's work lends itself to many interpretations.

In our opinion it cannot be convincingly maintained that "The Resurrection of Christ" represents anything more than the Resurrection in the traditional Biblical sense. If we accept Grossmann's assertion that the work, along with the two other grisailles, has "a personal or private character," this might indicate that Bruegel was a devout man.

On the beer jug and the torch, see Weyns.

12 "The Fall of the Rebel Angels"

Wood panel, 45½ by 63⅛ inches, 1562. Brussels, Musées royaux des Beaux-Arts. Plates pp. 138–51.

According to Bastelaer and Hulin de Loo, this painting "is like a breath of fresh air among the serious works Bruegel created" (p. 118). Grossmann, on the other hand, comments that "in the years around 1563 Bruegel's mind was filled with thoughts of Last Things" (*The Paintings*, p. 192). So we see that a traditional Biblical theme of Western art can suggest conflicting interpretations when treated by Bruegel. See also J.B. Knipping.

13 "*Dulle Griet*" sometimes called "Mad Meg"

Wood panel, 44⅞ by 62¾ inches. Antwerp, Musée Mayer van den Bergh. Plates 152–77.

The date is almost illegible. Photographic enlargements made in 1953 (A.C.L. No. L. 628 B and L. 629 B) suggest MDLXII (1562), confirming the generally accepted date.

This is one of Bruegel's most discussed works. Van Mander's comments have given rise to some misunderstandings[9,10], and in

44

any case a picture like this must inevitably seem foreign to us. Several scholars think it represents armed force and alludes to religious strife and brutal repression. A few concur in Friedländer's perceptive opinion that "the subject of this dramatic and exciting scene, which we would have difficulty in interpreting if Van Mander had not recorded the title for us, is ridiculously commonplace. It is nothing more nor less than the traditional figure of the wicked woman who is stronger than the devil himself. This figure, popularized in various symbolic versions, must have fired Bruegel's imagination. Contemporary expressions referred to 'making a raid on the gates of hell' and 'going to hell with a dagger in your fist'" (*Pieter Bruegel*, p. 92).

Grauls' penetrating study in *Volkstaal* (pp. 42–76) analyzes the various explanations and urges a critical examination of old texts which might help in interpreting this picture. He agrees with Jedlicka's explanation of the significance of the armor and the gauntlets. These refer to idioms: (1) "*terstont in 't harnas zijn*" (to be quickly up in arms; to be quick-tempered); (2) "*iets met ijzeren handschoenen aangrijpen*" (to tackle something with iron gloves; to use the mailed fist; to be violent).

Grauls may be right in suggesting that the curious figure with a boat on his back is an allusion to the expression "*opscheppen met de grote lepel*" (to ladle with the big spoon; to be wasteful or extravagant). While he cannot identify the figure, he thinks Bruegel is making fun of extravagance and carousers, noting that the *blauwe schuit*, the blue boat, was a symbol of profligacy. The boat, however, is not blue now. This detail could be resolved by laboratory tests.

A detail of the entrance to hell is worth noting. The entrance is represented by the mouth of a monster: a traditional medieval image for the jaws of Hell (plate p. 156). The eyebrows of the grotesque face are formed of rows of round, narrow-necked jars. To quote Van Puyvelde: "Birds perch on the eyebrows which are formed by a row of flagons. Similar flagons are scattered like ex-votos throughout the picture and perhaps

serve as a reminder that drink provides one of the well-trodden paths to hell" (pp. 4–5). According to this interpretation, these jars or flagons would be a reminder that drunkenness leads to hell. But it also seems plausible that they are nesting jars for starlings—another allusion to "roof," thievery and robbery. Jars like these used to be hung up outdoors as nesting boxes for starlings, but the nests were removed or plundered before the young birds were fledged. The Bokrijk museum owns a rare example. See Weyns.

14 "The Triumph of Death"

Wood panel, 45⅝ by 63⅛ inches. Madrid, Prado. Plates pp. 110–35.

The picture is neither signed nor dated. The consensus is that it was painted about 1562. Tolnay says that Bruegel here combined two themes: the Triumph of Death, a subject in the Italian tradition, and the Nordic theme of the Dance of Death (*Pieter Bruegel*, p. 31.)

Once again the moralistic tone is indisputable: everyone, no matter who he is, is doomed to death. Neither age nor social position nor wealth can protect him from this inescapable end. As Grossmann says: "In accordance with Christian doctrine death is for Bruegel the wages of sin and thus the men and women are not only representatives of various human occupations and stations of life, as in the Dance of Death, but of certain sins, among which covetousness, greed, the placing of worldly possessions above salvation, above faith in God seems to be the dominant one" (*The Paintings*, p. 192). This interpretation of death as a punishment for sin is supported by literature.

In the lower right corner Death interrupts the merrymaking of carefree young men and women. Cards, dice and backgammon board fall to the floor. The wine spills. The fool tries to hide under the table. The lovers' song is about to be silenced forever. The elegant nobleman drawing his sword recalls the young man in the song "*Vanden Leeraer opter tinnen*" (*Een schoon liedekens Boeck*, pp. 247–50). In answer to the moralist's admonitions, he says that he is young and wants to enjoy life,

dance, and be merry. He finally admits that he has strayed from the right path and promises to reform.

15 "Two Monkeys"

Wood panel, 7¾ by 9 inches, 1562. Berlin, Staatliche Museen, Gemäldegalerie. Plate p. 179.

Terlinden rejects the theory that this work is symbolic: "Given the opportunity of closely observing a monkey—not an ordinary Barbary ape but a monkey of a rare species from equatorial Africa—he makes use of it to produce a very careful study. He places the model in a window embrasure so that the light will come from behind and shows it full face and in profile. Not wanting the window to look like a hole opening on an empty sky, he puts in the familiar panorama of Antwerp—like the good landscapist he is. In art history, as everywhere else, the simplest solution is always the best" (pp. 248–50).

Grossmann, however, challenges the view that the work is a purely realistic study by a first-class animal painter. Citing H. W. Janson's *Apes and Ape Lore in the Middle Ages and the Renaissance* (London, 1952), he concludes that since the ape could be interpreted as a symbol for many different and even conflicting notions, it is "all the more difficult to arrive at a correct solution" (*The Paintings*, p. 193).

16 "The Tower of Babel"

Wood panel, 44½ by 60½ inches, 1563. Vienna, Kunsthistorisches Museum. Plates pp. 196–97.

Bruegel painted three versions of this subject, which must have particularly interested him. See Catalog No. 17. The Colosseum in Rome is supposed to have been his model and inspiration. The painting has rightly been compared to a builder's manual. Its meaning is generally assumed to be the punishment of human pride and the ultimate vanity of even the boldest human endeavors.

Van Vaernewijck draws a parallel between the internal quarrels of the Protestants and the Tower of Babel: "*Maer meerct hier, mijn leser, hoe een ghedeelt rijcke bestandich blijven mach: daer waren up desen tijt drij diveersche leeringhen upgheworpen, als Calvinische, Martinische ende Anabaptistsche. Elc maker een ghoet veers af: eijst niet de temmeringhe vanden turre van Babel, daer Godt haer sprake verwerrende ende alzoo haer boos weerc verstoorde? Want babel heet confuzie. Aldus waren zij confuus ghemaect onder malcanderen, ghelijc zonder twijffel dees sectarissen van onsen tijde zijn. Elc brijnct een bijsonder leeringhe voort, als een monster met veel hoofden, daer de keercke eenstemmich es"* (Vol. I, p. 255).

This passage, which compares the feuding Calvinists, Lutherans and Anabaptists with the builders of the Babylonian tower, whose pride God punished by confounding their language, could of course be easily misinterpreted to support the theory that Bruegel's picture is actually ridiculing the Reformation.

17 "The Tower of Babel" sometimes called "The Small Tower of Babel"
Wood panel, 23³/₈ by 29 inches. Rotterdam, Boymans-van Beuningen Museum. Plates pp. 190–95.

This picture is neither signed nor dated. It may have been trimmed, because the unpainted margins covered by the original frame are missing. The attribution is based on Van Mander's chronicle. (See p. 7.) Glück believes it was painted in 1554 or 1555 (*The Large Bruegel Book*, No. 9). Grossmann, however, dates it about 1563 (*The Paintings*, p. 194). *Cf.* Catalog No. 16.

18 "The Flight into Egypt"
Wood panel, 14¹/₂ by 21⁵/₈ inches, 1563. London, Collection of Count Antoine Seilern. Plate p. 199.

This painting poses no particular problems. The landscape in which Bruegel has placed the Holy Family obviously owes something to memories of his own journey through the Alps. Here he has chosen a theme which since Patenier had often inspired Flemish painters. Unlike most versions, this one does not show the Holy Family in a moment of rest during its flight. Nevertheless the religious theme is by no means secondary; it is in fact effectively emphasized by the use of contrasting colors.

19 "The Adoration of the Kings"
Wood panel, 43¹/₄ by 32¹/₂ inches. London, National Gallery, Plates pp. 212–17.

Discussing the date of this painting, usually given as 1564, Grossmann says: "There is a vertical crack in the panel between the *L* and the *X* of the date, and this *X* and the following four figures lack the beautiful calligraphic character of Bruegel's script; the *L* seems to be drawn over the original figure" (*The Paintings*, p. 196). The dating should be clarified by laboratory analysis.

The problems here are primarily stylistic: the question of Bruegel's relationship to the works of Hugo van der Goes on the one hand (see Vanbeselaere) and Italian Mannerism on the other. His closeness to Mannerism actually underlines the originality of his own style. Bruegel takes the Biblical subject as an occasion for observing ordinary people.

20 "The Procession to Calvary"
Wood panel, 48³/₈ by 66³/₈ inches, 1564. Vienna, Kunsthistorisches Museum. Plates pp. 200–211.

Many critics have stressed the closeness of this painting to works by Bruegel's predecessors, Herri met de Bles and the artist known as the Brunswick Monogrammist (probably Jan van Amstel, also known as Jan de Hollander). The composition itself, however, is original: for instance, in its swinging movement from left to right. The detail of the thieves in the cart with their confessors recalls a motif by Hieronymus Bosch on the back of the right-hand panel of the altarpiece of Saint Anthony in Lisbon. One of the drawings in the *naer het leven* (from life) series in the Boymans-van Beuningen Museum in Rotterdam seems to have a certain relationship with this picture. See Münz, *The Drawings*, Catalog No. 95 and Grossmann, *The Drawings*. Although the dramatic incident of Christ falling under the weight of the cross is at the very center of the composition, it is almost obscured by the crowd, and this heightens the dramatic effect. Here Bruegel shows mankind as foolish, gaping, hypocritical creatures.

Critics have rightly called attention to the stylistic contrast between the picture as a whole and the group of figures around the Virgin Mary, painted entirely in the Flemish primitive tradition. We do not know why Bruegel introduced this contrast, but his motive was probably religious.

The windmill on the hilltop is so conspicuous that we feel it must have some symbolic significance, but no convincing explanation has yet been offered. The skull—probably of a horse—in the right foreground may also have a special meaning. Weyns points out that skulls had a magical function; in Black Forest folklore an ox skull was a token of good luck. The engraving of "The Kermess of Saint George"[138] shows a horse's skull on the thatched roof of the barn at left.

The theory that this picture proves Bruegel's sympathy for the Anabaptists seems far fetched. *Cf.* Auner, pp. 103–9.

21 "The Death of the Virgin"
Grisaille. Oil on wood panel, 14 by 21¹/₂ inches, 1564? Banbury, England, Upton House, National Trust.

Bruegel probably painted this picture for his friend, Abraham Ortelius.[50] In any case, in 1574 Ortelius commissioned Philippe Galle to make an engraving from it (Bastelaer, *Les Estampes*, No. 116). The print has two insets containing three four-line stanzas of Latin verse and the following inscriptions: "*Sic Petri Brugelij archetypu Philipp. Galleus imitabatur*" and "*Abrah. Ortelius, sibi & amicis fieri curabat.*" D. V. Coornhert and B. A. Montanus acknowledge receipt of the print from Ortelius. See Popham.

Probably at some later date Rubens acquired this painting. No. 193 in the inventory of his pictures is listed as "*Le trépas de nostre Dame, blanc et noir, du vieux Breugel*" (death of the Virgin, black and white, by Bruegel the Elder).

In our opinion there is no reason to think

that "The Death of the Virgin" has any meaning beyond the Christian iconographical one. Grossmann thinks Bruegel's inspiration was Jacobus de Voragine's *Golden Legend* (*The Paintings*, p.196).

Stylistically this is an important work. While the influence of Van der Goes is still recognizable, Bruegel here uses light in a truly avant-garde manner. We must not forget that Caravaggio was not even born when this picture was painted.

22–26 "The Series of the Months"

22 "Haymaking"
Wood panel, $44^1/2$ by $61^5/8$ inches, 1565. Prague, Museum of Fine Arts. Plates pp. 224–37.

23 "The Corn Harvest"
Wood panel, $45^5/8$ by $62^3/8$ inches, 1565. New York, Metropolitan Museum. Plates pp. 244–47.

24 "The Return of the Herd"
Wood panel, $45^5/8$ by 62 inches, 1565. Vienna, Kunsthistorisches Museum, Plates pp. 242–43.

25 "The Hunters in the Snow"
Wood panel, $45^5/8$ by $63^1/8$ inches, 1565. Vienna, Kunsthistorisches Museum. Plates pp. 238–39.

26 "The Gloomy Day"
Wood panel, $45^5/8$ by $63^1/8$ inches, 1565. Vienna, Kunsthistorisches Museum. Plates pp. 240–41. See Notes 47 and 48.

Only five paintings from this set survive, and it is uncertain whether there were originally six or twelve. If six, we have to assume that of the sixteen Bruegels given to the city of Antwerp by Nicolas Jongelinck eight were of unidentified subjects. If there were originally twelve, then only two paintings are not mentioned by name. Grossmann, as quoted by Novotny (p. 29), thinks it more likely that two out of sixteen paintings by a famous master should be omitted from the list of

titles than that eight should be entirely passed over, as would be the case if the "Series of the Months" originally comprised only six. This does not seem entirely convincing. Frans Floris (whose paintings are identified) may well have been more famous than Bruegel in Antwerp at that time. Novotny makes a valid point when he says: "On the other hand the hypothesis that seven in a series of important works by Bruegel have vanished arouses some skepticism."

Tolnay was the first to defend the thesis that the set originally consisted of six pictures, each representing two months (*"Studien zu den Gemälden"*). Many critics share his opinion. Jedlicka thinks there were twelve: "The division of the year into twelve parts was enriched by certain associations. The way sixteenth-century artists related man's life to the months of the year was quite in keeping with the psychological outlook of the age. Here they were harking back to a fourteenth-century poem, which they altered and weakened in some respects" (p.187). Grossmann believes that "further extensive examinations of comparative material are needed" (*The Paintings*, p.198).

In our opinion the accounts kept by Blaise Hütter, secretary to Archduke Ernst, provide a decisive argument in favor of Tolnay's position. On July 5, 1594, the Antwerp city fathers presented the archduke with six paintings representing the twelve months: "On the fifth," says Hütter, "when the gentlemen of Antwerp presented to His Highness six paintings representing the twelve months and eight tapestries, I gave the usher eight taler" (*Bulletin de la Commission royale d'Histoire*, XIII, 1847, pp. 85–147; Glück, *The Large Bruegel Book*, pp. 70–71). In *Albrecht en Isabella* (pp. 53 and 455–56) De Mayer cites an early seventeenth-century inventory which mentions the pictures: "*elck schilderije twee maenden met hunne figueren*" (each picture representing two months, with their figures). That seems to settle the question.

The identification of the months depicted in "Haymaking" and "The Corn Harvest" obviously presents no problem, and it would

seem simple enough to identify deductively the others in the series. But the matter is still controversial. "The Hunters in the Snow" is assumed to represent the period from November to February and "The Gloomy Day" (probably an erroneous title) the period from January to April. Attempts to relate some of the activities depicted in the paintings to any one season and to reconcile the cycle with the calendar year as we know it lead to confusion.

Sterck has made the valuable suggestion that the series be studied in relation to the traditional popular names for the months: January: *Lauwmaand, Hardmaand, Lechmaand;* February: *Sprokkelmaand, Blijdemaand, Dollemaand, Schrikkelmaand;* March: *Lentemaand, Mertemaand;* April: *Grasmaand, O(o)stermaand;* May: *Bloeimaand, Braekmaand, Wonnemaand;* June: *Zomermaand;* July: *Hooimaand, Dondermaand;* August: *Oogstmaand, Koornemaand, Bouwmaand;* September: *Herfstmaand, Oest-Speltmaand;* October: *Zaaimaand, Roschmaand, Arselmaand, Bedemaand;* November: *Slachtmaand, Martinsmaand, Dodemaand;* December: *Wintermaand, Hoeremaand, Wijnmaand.*

Folklorists might well investigate the names commonly used in Brabant in Bruegel's day. The whole question still needs clarification. On the basis of these traditional names, "The Hunters in the Snow" would cover the months of November (Slachtmaand) and December (Wintermaand). Then "Haymaking" would have to represent May and June, which does not fit with the use of the name "hay month" for July. "The Corn Harvest" (July–August), however, fits nicely into this scheme. The so-called "Gloomy Day" would then represent the months of January and February.

In the right foreground of "The Gloomy Day" (plate p. 241) is a group of three figures: a woman, a man and a child. The man is eating waffles. The child is dressed up in a paper hat, with two pillows tied around him like a chasuble and a bell jangling on his belt; he holds a lantern in his right hand. The paper hat and waffles recall Carnival traditions. It seems more likely, however, that the group represents an allusion to *dertienavond*, Twelfth Night, Epiphany, or the Feast of the Three Kings, commemorated on January 6. Van Vaernewijck speaks of the Spanish soldiers' traditional celebration of this day (Vol. III, p. 196–97). They would run about the streets disguised, pulling faces and distributing oranges and sweets. "*Men wilt ooc zegghen, datter daer was die ghijnghen met een belle ende met eenen lamteerne met een keersse, ende hadden een manniere van casule anne, als oft zij ghespot hadden met tdraghen vanden H. Sacramente*" (they also said that many [Spanish soldiers] went about with a bell and a candle in a lantern, wearing a kind of chasuble as if they were aping the carrying of the Holy Sacrament). While the triple coincidence of chasuble, bell and lantern is striking, it does not elucidate the problem.

We would tentatively reconstruct the series as follows (bearing in mind that in Bruegel's day the year began at Easter [47]): (1) The missing picture, which probably represented the months of March and April; (2) "Haymaking": May–June; (3) "The Corn Harvest": July–August; (4) "The Return of the Herd": September–October; (5) "The Hunters in the Snow": November–December; (6) the so-called "Gloomy Day": January–February. At the same time we emphasize most strongly that the whole question is still open.

The "Series of the Months" is a landmark in the development of European landscape painting. It also offers valuable insight into Bruegel's view of the relationship between man and his world, which sees him as dominated and conditioned by nature.

27 "The Massacre of the Innocents"
   Wood panel, 42⅝ by 60⅜ inches. Hampton Court, Collections of Her Majesty the Queen. Plates pp. 248–49.

There are several versions of this composition. The one in the Vienna Kunsthistorisches Museum (45¼ by 62⅜ inches), signed "BRVEG" but undated, is now thought to be a copy. Many scholars believe the Hamp-

ton Court picture to be the original, although it is neither signed nor dated. See Grossmann, *The Paintings*, p. 199. Grossmann dates it between 1565 and 1567. In this case the date is significant because the picture has been interpreted as a protest against Spanish tyranny.

It is worth noting the existence (in the Antwerp Musée des Beaux-Arts and the collection of Dr. Delporte in Brussels) of two versions of this subject by Pieter Brueghel the Younger apparently copied from a painting by his father, though quite different in composition. They are signed "P. BREVGHEL" and are both dated (presumably after the original) 1564—the year of Pieter Brueghel the Younger's birth. See Marlier's catalog in *Le Siècle de Bruegel*. If we assume these to be copies of an original by Pieter Bruegel the Elder dated 1564, then Bruegel could not have painted "The Massacre of the Innocents" as a protest against Spanish oppression because the Duke of Alba's troops did not enter Brussels until 1567.

On Bruegel's winter landscapes see Catalog No. 30.

28 "Winter Landscape with Skaters and a Bird Trap"
   Wood panel, 14⅞ by 21⅞ inches, 1565. Brussels, Collection of Dr. Delporte. Plates pp. 218–23.

Since this painting was first published in 1927, its authenticity has been challenged. It is now regarded as a prototype of a common seventeenth-century genre: winter landscapes. Many copies and variants survive.

In our opinion this is not really a genre painting but a didactic one. Possibly Bruegel meant it as a warning against light-mindedness; the happy skaters are as carefree as the birds pecking at the ground underneath the fatal trap. The village is said to be Sint-Anna-Pede near Brussels.

On Bruegel's winter landscapes see Catalog No. 30.

29 "Christ and the Woman Taken in Adultery"

Grisaille oil painting on panel, 9⅜ by 13¼ inches, 1565. London, Collection of Count Antoine Seilern. Plate p. 198.

This work belonged to Jan Brueghel. In 1609 he wrote to his patron Federigo Borromeo, Cardinal of Milan, that he had not been able to find a single painting by his father on the art market because Emperor Rudolph II had bought up all the available ones at considerable expense. This was the only work by his father that Jan Brueghel owned, and he bequeathed it to the cardinal in his will of January 12, 1625.

Lit.: Grossmann, *Burlington Magazine*, XCIV, 1952, p. 218, and *The Paintings*, pp. 26, 197. See also Catalog No. 11.

30 "The Numbering of the People at Bethlehem"
   Wood panel, 45⅝ by 64⅛ inches, 1566. Brussels, Musées royaux des Beaux-Arts. Plates pp. 250–67.

The picture is signed and dated, but the signature is almost illegible. (Macrophotographs A.C.L., L. 12896 B, L. 12912 B and L. 12548 B.)

Bruegel is *the* painter of winter scenes. His famous winter landscapes may well have been inspired by the unusually hard winter of 1564–65, when the ground was frozen for ten weeks. In a rhymed chronicle entitled *Cleyn Memoriael* (edited by M. Sacré) the rhetorician Daniel van Oesbroeck tells us that the population suffered terribly from the cold and many poor people died of cold and starvation.

"The Numbering of the People at Bethlehem" is extremely important for the light it sheds on the popular culture of Brabant. See Weyns. Some of the details are very interesting. The green wreath is an inn sign, like the jug hanging on the wall to denote that beer is served. The beehive under the eaves appears in several engravings and in the "Peasant Wedding" (Catalog No. 35) and is probably a nesting box. Outside the window above the doorway is a woven wire-blind known as a *hor*. On the façade of the brick house in the center of the picture are three starling jars.

(See Catalog No. 13.) Other details show Bruegel's gift for meticulous observation: the skates, the child's bowllike sled propelled by pronged sticks (see Catalog No. 33), the top for spinning on ice, the carts, the pig being stuck, the boy with straw sandals. A particularly good example of this talent is the little scene of a boy and girl playing on the ice with a three-legged stool while another child stands on the bank shivering with cold. (Plate p. 266.)

31 "The Sermon of Saint John the Baptist"
Wood panel, 37 by 62⅝ inches, 1566. Budapest, Museum of Fine Arts. Plates pp. 268–70.

Several scholars believe this painting was inspired by the *hagepreken*, the clandestine outdoor services of the reformed groups, and there is no denying that every detail of the scene fits Van Vaernewijck's description of them. Common people took part in them just for amusement, he tells us, but they were also attended by God-fearing, blameless men whom one would not have expected to see there. There are indications that Bruegel himself attended some of these meetings, but to conclude on this evidence that he was an Anabaptist seems premature. See Auner.

In the thick of the crowd a nobleman is talking to a fortune-teller who is reading his palm. This is obviously a portrait, though we do not know of whom. Auner thinks this painting may well be the "Triumph of Truth" which Bruegel, according to Van Mander, considered his best work, but this is purely conjectural.

32 "The Wedding Dance in the Open Air"
Wood panel, 46⅜ by 61¼ inches, 1566. Detroit, Institute of Arts. Plates pp. 271–73.

On the moralistic element in subjects of this type see Note 133.

Many versions of this picture exist. Most critics consider the one reproduced here the best; some identify it as the original. Tolnay suggests that a miniature on parchment in the Uffizi Gallery in Florence signed "B.I.L.F."

is the long-sought original ("*Das aufgefundene Original des 'Hochzeitstanzes im Freien' von Pieter Bruegel d.Ä.*" in the *Neue Zürcher Zeitung*, July 13, 1969, p. 49). He interprets the initials as standing for "*Bruegel invenit laboravit fecit*"—which seems somewhat presumptuous, since so far as we know Bruegel never used such a signature. We have seen only the reproduction published in Tolnay's article and cannot of course reach a final judgment without seeing the original, but as of now the stylistic characteristics do not seem to us to substantiate his case.

33 "The Adoration of the Kings in the Snow"
Wood panel, 13⅝ by 21½ inches, 1567. Winterthur, Switzerland, Collection of Dr. O. Reinhart. Plates pp. 278–89.

Grossmann stresses that Bruegel "made the Biblical event, which in the Christian year is connected with January 6, as 'real' and lifelike as possible" (*The Paintings*, p. 200). Although the picture has something of the religious atmosphere of Flemish primitive art, it is much more secular in spirit.

In the foreground is a child in a bowllike sled (plate p. 285). These sleds were made of the jawbones of large animals—horses or oxen. See Weyns.

34 "The Conversion of Saint Paul"
Wood panel, 42⅛ by 60⅞ inches, 1567. Vienna, Kunsthistorisches Museum. Plates pp. 290–93.

True to one of his principles of composition, Bruegel again places the thematic motif in the center of a busy crowd scene. The composition is sophisticated. The figures seen from behind as they look into the center of the picture combine with the movement of the landscape to lead the eye toward the place where Saint Paul has fallen from his horse and is being converted. The landscape is an echo of Bruegel's journey through the Alps fifteen years earlier. Grossmann is certainly right in rejecting any association with the Duke of Alba (*The Paintings*, p. 201).

35 "The Peasant Wedding" sometimes called

"The Wedding Banquet"
Wood panel, 44½ by 63½ inches. Vienna, Kunsthistorisches Museum. Plates pp. 294–97.

The signature and date were probably lost when the frame was sawed off along the lower edge. Assuming that the restorer had the original dimensions in mind when he attached a 2¼-inch strip, this picture must have been the same size as "The Peasant Dance" (Catalog No. 36). This seems to confirm the theory that they were painted as a pair. They may have been part of an unfinished series on peasant life. The picture is generally dated 1565–67.

Various answers have been given to the question of which man is the bridegroom; perhaps it is the young man filling the pitcher. The serious-faced figure sitting listening to the monk at the extreme right has not been positively identified. Van Mander's statement that Bruegel and his friend Franckert often mixed with the peasants at country weddings or fairs is not a substantial argument for assuming this to be a self-portrait.

On the content Grossmann has this to say: "If one accepts the interpretation here suggested for the Detroit "Wedding Dance" [Catalog No. 32. *Cf.* Note 133], then one must agree that this peasant banquet is meant as a picture of gluttony. The strong accent of the man pouring out wine in the foreground, the still life of wine jugs, the greedy child, these motifs sound the leitmotif which can be followed through the whole composition" (*The Paintings*, p. 201). Grossmann is certainly right in noting the moralistic tone, but in our opinion this work is neither bitter nor ambiguous (except perhaps for the striking detail of the peacock feather in the cap of the child in the foreground, who is unconcernedly licking off his plate). The harvest is in, and the table has been set up in the barn. Over the bride's head hangs the bridal crown, and in the background we see a beehive used as a nesting box. According to Weyns, the two sheaves of corn hanging from the rake are the *zantekoren* or *santekoren*—the gleanings reserved for the poor. ("*Sante*" in Middle

Dutch means "sheaf.") Weyns gives further information on objects in this picture.

36 "The Peasant Dance" sometimes called "The Kermess"

Wood panel, 44¹/₂ by 64 inches, Vienna, Kunsthistorisches Museum. Plates pp. 298–301.

Vanbeselaere dates this painting 1569, the year of Bruegel's death. Grossmann says: "We find here a further development of the tendencies observed in the Detroit 'Wedding Dance' [Catalog No. 32. *Cf.* Note 133]. But now it is not only the sin of lust which Bruegel portrays: anger and gluttony appear combined with it.... The man next to the bagpipe player wears on his hat the peacock feather of vain pride.... The occasion for all this sinful behavior is a kermess, to celebrate some saint's day! The church appears in the background, but all figures are shown with their backs to it. Moreover they do not pay the slightest attention to the picture of the Madonna which looks down on the sinner from the tree on the right" (*The Paintings*, p. 202).

The tankard on the table is a *drinkuit* (drink-up) or *stortebeker* (turnover mug); it had to be turned upside down when empty. The farmhouses are of great documentary interest to folklorists because they show that the mud and straw walls were not whitewashed. However, Bruegel seems to have embellished these houses a little, because most farmhouses of that period had no chimney but just a smoke hole in the gable. See Weyns. See also Catalog No. 35.

37 "The Land of Cockaigne"

Wood panel, 20¹/₄ by 30⁵/₈ inches, 1567. Munich, Pinakothek. Plates pp. 274–77. See Friedländer, "*Bruegels Schlaraffenland.*" On the literary sources see Notes 91 and 92.

According to Grossmann, "the picture is obviously intended as a condemnation of the sins of gluttony and sloth" (*The Paintings*, p. 200). The legends on the engraving after the painting (Bastelaer, *Les Estampes*, No. 147) confirm this interpretation. They read: "*Insvla fortvnata—Abscondit piger manus sub*

ascella sua, et laborat si ad os suum eas converterit. Prov. 26:15—*Le pais guleux et paresseux.—Le paresseux cache ses mains soubs son eschasse, et luij est peine de les tourner vers sa bouche.—Het luy leckerlandt. Den luijaert berght sijn handen onder sijne ockselen, ende 't valt hem suer, dat hijse ten mondewaerts heffe.*" (This is the Land of Cockaigne. The lazy man has his hands in his arm-pits, and it is an effort to him to move them as far as his mouth.)

See Lebeer, "*Le Pays de Cocagne,*" an engraving signed "P.B." (probably Peeter Balten).

38 "Head of an Old Peasant Woman"

Wood panel, 8⁵/₈ by 6⁵/₈ inches. Munich, Pinakothek. Plate p. 328.

Because of the close-up technique, several critics believe that Bruegel painted this study in the last year of his life (1569). He probably painted several more like it.

39 "The Peasant and the Bird Nester"

Wood panel, 23 by 26¹/₂ inches, 1568. Vienna, Kunsthistorisches Museum. Plates pp. 330–31.

Bastelaer and Hulin de Loo interpret this picture as an illustration of the Flemish proverb inscribed on the drawing "The Beekeepers": "*Dye den nest weet dyen weeten, dyen ro[o]ft dy[en] heeten*" (he who knows where the nest is has the knowledge; he who robs it has the nest).[161] While the point of the proverb is clear—the good-natured man opposed to the go-getter—it does not seem quite applicable to this picture. The moral apparently hinges upon the fact that the stupid-looking peasant boy is about to fall into the stream, and in that case the proverb quoted above was probably not the one Bruegel had in mind. Bastelaer and Hulin de Loo (p. 299) mention a picture in the estate of the Archduke Leopold Wilhelm inventoried in 1659: "*Ein Landschaft von Öhlfarb auf Holcz, warin ein Baur mit einem Prügel in der linckher Handt einen Jungen trohet, welcher auf einem Baum Vögel ausnimbt*" (a landscape in oil on wood, in which a peasant with a cudgel in his left hand is threatening a boy robbing bird

nests up in a tree). Are we to conclude that by 1659 the point Bruegel was trying to make was no longer clear? The main figure, who faces the viewer as though explaining the situation, is quite obviously not threatening the bird nester.

According to Boström, the plants have a symbolic significance ("*Das Sprickwort vom Vogelnest*"). See also Grauls, *Volkstaal*, pp. 160–74.

40 "The Misanthrope" or "The Perfidy of the World"

Tempera on canvas, 33¹/₂ by 33¹/₈ inches, 1568? Naples, Museo Nazionale. Plates pp. 302–3.

Hulin de Loo says of this work: "Although Bruegel himself inscribed on the picture the proverb he was illustrating, the subject is almost incomprehensible" (Bastelaer and Hulin de Loo, p. 288). We are skeptical about the first part of this statement. Even in reproductions the difference between the ground color of the picture itself and that of the background of the inscription is obvious, which suggests that the caption could be on an overpainted ground. This is confirmed by a careful examination of the writing. Vervliet dates the inscription "not earlier than 1680" (p. 81, note 5. Could "1680" be a typographical error for "1580"?) Only laboratory analysis can resolve this problem. Despite the apocryphal character of the inscription, the lines do seem to fit the theme of the picture. They read: "*Om dat de werelt is soe ongetru / Daer om gha ic in den ru*" (because the world is so faithless, I wear mourning).

While Bruegel's symbol of the world can hardly be misunderstood, the character and tribulations of the central figure have been variously interpreted. The picture is unquestionably moralistic. Roggen (p. 125) thinks the caption comes from some unknown *cluyte* or farcical playler.

The engraving of this subject (Bastelaer, *Les Estampes*, No. 171) has the following legend: "*Je porte deuil voijant le monde / Qui en tant de fraudes abonde*" (I wear mourning, seeing the world, which abounds in so much fraud). The Flemish text is somewhat more explicit, deploring not only faithlessness but also injustice, hypocrisy, thievery, and covetousness: "*De sulck draecht rou | om dat de weerelt is onghetrou | Die meeste ghebruijcken minst recht en reden | Weynich leefter nou als hy leuen sou. | Men rooft men treckt elck steeckt vol gheueijsde seden.*"

41 "The Cripples" sometimes called "The Beggars"

Wood panel, 7 by 8³/₈ inches, 1568. Paris, Louvre. Plate p. 329.

Marlier says in the catalog of *Le Siècle de Bruegel*:

"On the back of the picture we can decipher several Flemish and Latin inscriptions apparently from the sixteenth century. They begin with some half-effaced lines: '*[K]ruepelen, hooch, dat u nering beteren moeg*' (Good luck and good business to you, cripples!—a phrase commonly used when giving alms). Then come two Latin couplets deciphered and translated by R. Genaille and published with his permission by Édouard Michel: '*NATURAE DEERAT NOSTRAE QUOD DEFUIT ARTI | HAEC DATA PICTORI GRATIA TANTA [FUIT] | ALIUD | HIC NATURA STUPET PICTIS EXPRESSA FIGURIS | VISA SUIS CLAUDIS HUNC BRUEGEL ESSE PAREM*' (Nature has nothing that is not to be found in our art; so great is the grace bestowed upon the painter. Here Nature, expressed in painted images and seen in her cripples, must recognize with amazement that Bruegel is her equal)."

The Latin text recalls the words of Abraham Ortelius. [See note 50.]

Van Puyvelde discusses the interpretation of this painting in his posthumous article '*De poëtische waarheid,*' citing the legend of an engraving after Hieronymus Bosch in the Vienna Albertina: '*Al dat op den blauwen trughelsack gheerne leeft | Gaet meest al cruepel op beyde syden. | Daerom den Cruepel Bisschop veel dienaers heeft | Die om een prove den reghten ghanc myden*' (All those who like to live from the blue juggler's bag usually limp on both sides. Therefore the cripple-bishop has many servants who, for the sake of a dole, avoid walking properly).

According to Van Puyvelde, the figure wearing a miter represents the cripples' Prince of Carnival. Bastelaer and Hulin de Loo had already called attention to this text (pp. 135–38). Remarkable as it is, it does not solve the problem.

In interpreting this picture it is important to remember that in Bruegel's day there was little humanitarian sympathy for cripples.

42 "The Parable of the Blind"

Tempera on canvas, 33¹/₂ by 60³/₄ inches, 1568. Naples, Museo Nazionale. Plates pp. 304–13.

The church is said to be Sint-Anna-Pede near Brussels. See Bastelaer, "*Le paysage ...*". The subject is probably taken from Matthew 15: 14.

Grossmann says of this picture: "The inner blindness, which is meant by the parable, is a greater defect than the blindness of the eyes. Those who are blind to true religion, who do not perceive its message which is symbolized in the background by the church, a strong and firm structure with its spire pointing to heaven and contrasted with the unsteady broken row of the wretched men—such people must lose their way and fall into the abyss" (*The Paintings*, p. 204).

Several literary sources suggest that the saying "If the blind leads the blind, both shall fall into the ditch" did not necessarily have a religious connotation in Bruegel's time. A character named Catyvighe (Poor Wretch) exclaims: "I see the blind man leading the way. He leads the other blind men into the ditch." Deugd (Virtue) points the moral: "That is certainly a bad example. Those who should show us the way go astray. Everyone is frail, alas." (The original text reads: "*Ey, jaet, jaet, ick sien[t] die blinde gaet voeren | En leyt den anderen blinden in den gracht, ... Dat exempel is quaet dier wel op acht; | Die ons dlicht souwen draeghen te deghe, | Dolen selve wel uuten weghe; | Een iegelyck, lacen, is gebreckelyck*" (Van den Daele and Van Veerdeghem, p. 217).

Van Vaernewijck quotes this common saying in connection with the degeneration of a religious tradition. Every year, he tells us, a statue of Saint Anthony used to be carried from Belle in western Flanders to Ghent. In recent years the procession has degenerated into a brawl because young men from the various quarters of Ghent began to fight over the statue. Van Vaernewijck takes this as evidence of moral laxity but also blames the clergy for not taking steps to correct the deplorable state of affairs—and so one blind man leads the others into the ditch: "*Men hoorde ooc niet datter eenighe sermoenen jeghen ghedaen waren: den eenen blenden leedde den anderen in de gracht*" (Vol. I, p. 65).

In Dedekind's *Grobianus*, the saying is applied to a drunkard: "And so one blind man leads the other."

43 "The Magpie on the Gallows"

Wood panel, 17⁷/₈ by 19⁷/₈ inches, 1568. Darmstadt, Hessisches Landesmuseum. Plates pp. 314–27.

Grossmann finds Van Mander's commentary on this picture "not quite satisfactory" (*The Paintings*, p. 204). Other interpretations by modern critics are equally unconvincing. Does "The Magpie on the Gallows" represent the final word of Bruegel's sermons against frivolity and stupidity? It shows people making merry in the shadow of the gallows, and his contemporaries would have probably recognized the implied warning without difficulty. Grossmann speaks of "the rapturous rhythm of the dance in which even the gallows seems to join" and thinks the painting has a general air of optimism. "Is this a new departure, a new development cut short by Bruegel's premature death?" he asks. This, of course, is pure conjecture.

44 "The Storm at Sea"

Wood panel, 27¹/₂ by 37⁷/₈ inches, 1569? Vienna, Kunsthistorisches Museum. Plates pp. 332–35.

Formerly ascribed to Joos de Momper, this picture is now thought to be by Bruegel. Some scholars believe it to be his last—unfinished—work. Whether it is actually unfinished is difficult to say. We should not forget that Bruegel often applied semitransparent layers of paint directly to the ground[163] almost like a glaze. These thin layers become increasingly transparent with age. Nor should we forget that Rubens was a master of this technique, especially in his oil sketches. Rubens' admiration for Bruegel may have been based on appreciation of his technique.

A drawing in the collection of Count Antoine Seilern (Münz, No. 50) has been linked with "The Storm at Sea." This drawing is neither signed nor dated; moreover, it depicts not a seascape but a view of the Scheldt near Antwerp.

The picture may be read in a moralistic sense. The whale which allows itself to be distracted by the empty barrel thrown overboard by the crew of the menaced ship may stand for man unmindful of the one essential: his eternal salvation. The church on the horizon would then be a symbol of refuge. Many scholars, including G. W. Menzel, think the picture contains a political allusion.

The sailors' trick of throwing a barrel overboard is traditional in sixteenth-century chronicles such as *Tvoyage van Mher Joos van Ghistele* (Ghent, 1557) and *De wonderlycke Historie vande Noordersche landen* (Antwerp, 1572).

NOTES

1 For a transcription see Marijnissen, *Pieter Bruegels kleurnotities.* See also notes 25 and 122.

2 On Bruegel's drawings which served as models for engravings we sometimes find Flemish or Latin inscriptions which may or may not be in his hand. The question is controversial. To quote Münz: "The composition drawings are ... preliminary drawings designed to be reproduced.... This is apparent technically because on some of them clear traces are to be seen of the burin with which the outlines were impressed on the copper plate. Another clue lies in the fact that the inscriptions are in a distinctive handwriting, which is certainly not that of Pieter Bruegel himself, but probably that of a calligrapher, who neatly described the purpose of the sheet, often in a lighter ink than that used for the drawing itself" (*The Drawings*, p. 28).

3 Carel van Mander, *Het Schilder-Boeck waer in voor eerst de leerlustighe Jeught den grondt der edel vry Schilderconst in verscheyden deelen wort voorghedraghen. Daer nae in dry deelen t'leuen der vermaerde doorluchtighe Schilders des ouden, en nieuwen tyds. Eyntlyck d'wtlegghinghe op den Metamorphoseon...*, *voor Paschier van Wesbvsch Boeckvercooper tot Haerlem 1604. Met Priuilegie.*

The section containing the biographies of painters is entitled: "*Het Leven der Doorluchtighe Nederlandtsche* / *en Hooghduytsche Schilders. By een vergadert en beschreven door Carel van Mander Schilder. Alles tot lust* / *vermaeck* / *en nut der Schilders* / *en Schilder-const beminders. Tot Alckmaer, Ghedruckt by Jacob de Meester* / *voor Passchier van Westbusch* / *Boeckvercooper* / *woonende in den beslaghen Bybel* / *tot Haerlem. Anno 1604."*

A second edition of this *Book of Painting* appeared in Amsterdam in 1618. A translation into modern Dutch was published by A.F. Mirande and G.S. Overdiep (Amsterdam, 1936; 4th ed., 1950). English translation: C. van de Wall, *Dutch and Flemish Painters* (New York, 1936); German annotated translation: H. Floerke, *Das Leben der niederländischen und deutschen Maler* (two vols., Munich, Leipzig, 1906); French translations: H. Hymans [M. Koloff], *Le livre des peintres*, with notes and commentary (two vols., Paris, 1884, 1885), R. Genaille, *Le livre de peinture*, annotated (Paris, 1965).

4 The original text reads as follows (1604 ed., pp. 233–34): "*Het leven van Pieter Brueghel, uytnemende Schilder van Brueghel.*

De Natuer heeft wonderwel haren Man ghevonden en ghetroffen / *om weder van hem heerlijck ghetroffen te worden* / *doe sy in Brabant in een onbekent Dorp onder de Boeren* / *om Boeren met den Pinceel nae te bootsen* / *heeft uyt gaen picken* / *en tot de Schilderconst verwecken* / *onsen gheduerighen Nederlandtschen roem* / *den seer gheestighen en bootsighen Pieter Brueghel, den welcken is gheboren niet wijt van Breda* / *op een Dorp* / *gheheeten Brueghel* / *welcks naem hy met hem ghedraghen heeft* / *en zijn naecomelinghen ghelaten. Hy heeft de Const gheleert by Pieter Koeck van Aelst* / *wiens dochter hy naemaels trouwde* / *en hadse doe sy noch cleen was dickwils op den arem ghedraghen* / *doe hy by Pieter woonde. Hy is van hier gaen wercken by Ieroon Kock, en is voorts ghereyst in Vranckrijck* / *en van daer in Italien. Hy hadde veel ghepractiseert* / *nae de handelinghe van Ieroon van den Bosch: en maeckte oock veel soodane spoockerijen* / *en drollen* / *waerom by van velen werdt gheheeten Pier den Drol. Oock sietmen weynich stucken van hem* / *die een aenschouwer wijslijck sonder lacchen can aensien* / *ja hoe stuer wijnbrouwigh en statigh hy oock is* / *hy moet ten minsten meese-muylen oft grinnicken. In zijn reysen heeft hy veel ghesichten nae t'leven gheconterfeyt* / *soo datter gheseyt wort* / *dat hy in d'Alpes wesende* / *al die berghen en rotsen had in gheswolghen* / *en t'huys ghecomen op doecken en Penneelen uytghespoghen hadde* / *soo eyghentlijck con hy te desen en ander deelen de Natuere nae volghen. Hy vercoos en nam zijn wooninghe t'Antwerpen* / *en quam aldaer in het Gildt oft Schilderscamer* / *in 't Jaer ons Heeren 1551. En wrocht veel voor een Coopman* / *gheheeten Hans Franckert, dat een edel goet borst was van een Man* / *die geern by Brueghel, en met hem daeghlijcks seer gemeensaem was. Met desen Franckert gingh Brueghel dickwils buyten by den Boeren* / *ter Kermis* / *en ter Bruyloft* / *vercleedt in Boeren cleeren* / *en gaven giften als ander* / *versierende van Bruydts oft Bruydgoms bestandt oft volck te wesen. Hier hadde Brueghel zijn vermaeck* / *dat wesen der Boeren* / *in eten* / *drincken* / *dansen* / *springen* / *vryagien* / *en ander kodden te sien* / *welck dingen hy dan seer cluchtigh en aerdigh wist met den verwen nae te bootsen* / *soo wel in Water als Oly-verwe* / *want hy van beyden seer uytnemende was van handelinghe. Dese Boeren en Boerinnen op zijn kempsche en anders wist hy oock seer eyghentlijck te cleeden* / *en dat Boerigh dom wesen seer natuerlijck aen te wijsen* / *in dansen*

gaen / *en staen* / *oft ander actien. Hy was wonder vast in zyn stellingen* / *en handelde seer suyver en aerdigh met de Pen* / *makende veel ghesichtkens nae t'leven. Terwijlen hy noch t'Antwerp woonde* / *hiel met een Meyt oft Dochter huys* / *welcke hy oock soude hebben ghetrouwt* / *dan hem mishaeghde* / *dat sy altyt (soo seer de waerheyt sparende) ghewent was te liegen. Hy maeckte met haer een verbondt en bespreck* / *hy soude al haer loghenen kerven op eenen kerfstock* / *waer toe hy eenen maeckte redelyck langh* / *en so den kerfstock met der tydt quam vol te worden* / *soude t'Houwlyck gantsch uyt en te nieten zijn* / *ghelyck het eer langhen tyt geschiede. Eyndlinghe* / *also de Weduwe van Pieter Koeck ten lesten woonde te Brussel* / *werdt hy te vrijen haer dochter die als verhaelt is* / *hy dickwils op den arem had gedraghen* / *en is met haer ghetrouwt: doch besprack de Moeder* / *dat Brueghel Antwerpen verlatende most comen woonen te Brussel* / *op dat hy mocht verlaten en vergheten dat vooeighe Meysken* / *het welck also gheschiede. Hy was een seer stille en gheschickt Man* / *niet veel van woorden* / *dan wel bootsigh in't gheselschap* / *doende den luyden* / *oft oock zijn eyghen knechten* / *t' somtijt verschricken met eenigh ghespoock* / *oft gherammel* / *dat hy te weghe bracht. Eenighe zijner besonderste wercken zijn althans by den Keyser* / *te weten een groot stuck* / *wesende eenen thoren van Babel* / *daer veel fraey werck in comt* / *ock van boven in te sien. Noch een der selver Historie* / *cleen oft minder wesende: oock twee stucken Cruys-dragingen* / *seer natuerlijck om sien* / *met altyt eenige drollen daer onder. Voort een Kinder-doodinghe* / *daer veel wercklycke dinghen zijn te sien* / *waer van ick elder hebbe verhaelt* / *hoe dat daer een gantsch gheslacht soecken te verbidden een Boerigh kindt* / *dat een der moordighe kryghs-luyden ghevat heeft om te dooden* / *den rouwe en t'versterven der Moeders* / *en ander werckingen wel naghenomen wesende. Voorts een Bekeeringhe Pauli, met seer aerdige Clippen. T'waer qualyck te verhalen wat hy al ghemaeckt heeft* / *van tooverijen* / *Hellen* / *boerige geschiedenissen* / *en anders. Hy heeft gemaeckt een temptatie Christi, daer men van boven* / *als in de Alpes, neder siet Steden en Landen* / *overspreyt met wolcken* / *daer men te som plaetsen door siet: oock een dulle Griet, die een roof voor de Helle doet* / *die seer verbystert siet* / *en vreent op zijn schots toeghemaeckt is: ick acht dees en ander stucken oock in s'Keysers' Hof zijn. Daer is oock t'Amsterdam tot den Const-liefdigen Sr Herman Pilgrims, een Boeren Bruyloft van Oly-verwe* / *die seer aerdigh is* / *alwaer men siet der Boeren tronien en naeckten* / *gheel en bruyn | als van de Son verbrandt | en leelyck van huydt wesende | den Steeluyden niet ghelijckende. Hy heeft oock ghemaeckt een stuck | daer den Vasten teghen den Vasten-avondt strijdt: een ander | daer alle de remedien worden ghebruyct teghen de doot: een ander van allerley spelen der kinderen | en meer ontallijcke sinnekens. Daer zijn oock te sien twee doecken van Water-verwe | by den Const-liefdighen Heer Willem Jacobsz. by de nieuw Kerck t'Amsterdam | wesende een Boeren Kermis | en Bruyloft | daer veel drollighe bootsen in zijn te sien en t'rechte wesen der Boeren: onder ander | daer sy de Bruydt begiften | is een ouden Boer | hebbende t'buydelcken aen den hals | en is doende met in zijn handt t'gheldt te passen | en zijn seer uytnemende stucken. De Heeren van Brussel hadden hem een weynigh voor zyn doot aenbesteedt te maken eenighe stucken van het delven van de Brusselsche vaert nae Antwerpen | dan is door zijn sterven achterweghe bleven. Veel vreemde versieringhen van sinnekens sietmen van zijn drollen in Print: maer hadder noch seer veel net en suyver geteyckent met eenighe schriften by | welcke ten deele al te seer bijtich oft schimpich wesende | hy in zijn doot-sieckte door zijn Huysvrouwe liet verbranden | door leetwesen oft vreesende sy daer door in lijden quaem | oft yet te verantwoorden mocht hebben. Hy liet zijn Vrouwe in Testament een stuck met een Exter op de galgh | meenende met d'Exter de clappighe tongen | die hy de galgh toe eygende: hadde verder gemaeckt | daer de waerheyt doorbreeckt: dit soude (nae zijn seggen) t'beste zijn | dat van hem ghedaen was. Hij liet nae twee sonen | die mede goede Schilders zijn | den eenen Pieter gheeten | leerde by Gillis van Conincxloo, en is een Conterfeyter nae t'leven. Ian by zyn Groot-moeder | de Weduwe van Pieter van Aelst | hier van Water-verwe hebbende gheleert | quam en leerde van Oly-verwe by eenen Pieter Goe-kindt, daer veel fraey dinghen waren in huys. Hy reysde voort nae Colen | en soo in Italien | en is seer groot achten ghecomen | met te maken Landtschapkens | en seer cleen, beeldekens | daer hy een uytnemende fraey handelingh van heeft. Lampsonius spreeckt op desen sin tot Brueghel, vraghende: Wie is doch desen Bos....*"

For the end of this text see Note 49.

5 We know almost nothing about this good friend of Bruegel's except that he came from Nuremberg and was a member of the Violiere (Gillyflower) School of Rhetoric in Antwerp.

6 We do not know whether Bruegel did actually train pupils. Van Mander's statement that he did has not yet been corroborated by other sources. The word *"knecht"* can mean a "house servant" as well as an apprentice.

7 In the "Leerdicht" which is part of the introduction to the *Schilderboeck*. (See Note 3.)

8 This painting is lost. It is last mentioned in the "Inventory of paintings in the house inhabited by the late Sieur Peter Paul Rubens at his death" (1640). No. 210 in this inventory is listed as "The Temptation of Our Lord and Saviour by Bruegel the Elder." See J. Denucé, *De Konstkamers*, p.65.

9 Van Mander's phrase *"een roof voor de helle doen"* has been interpreted in various ways. Hymans translates it: *"en train de recruter pour l'enfer"* (engaged in recruiting for hell); Genaille has *"qui fait une razzia pour l'enfer"* (who is making a raid for [or on] hell). The interpretation of Bastelaer and Hulin de Loo (*Peter Bruegel l'Ancien*, p. 287) seems more plausible: *"Dulle Griet est le sobriquet populaire de la mégère, de la femme méchante et querelleuse (d'où par métaphore ce nom fut étendu aux pièces d'artillerie, tel le Grand Canon de Gand, tels aussi ceux de Londonderry, d'Edimbourg, etc., appelés Mad Meg). Faire une rafle devant la porte de l'enfer, c'est évidemment le braver."* (Dulle Griet is the popular nickname for a virago, a shrewish, quarrelsome woman. Hence the name was metaphorically extended to pieces of artillery, such as the great cannon of Ghent or the ones in Londonderry, Edinburgh, etc., called Mad Meg. To make a raid on the gate of hell obviously means to defy it.) J. Grauls sheds important light on this in *Volkstaal* (p. 43 ff.). He takes Van Mander's words to mean *"een stout stuk verrichten op hoop van winst, bang zijn voor duivel noch hel en alle gevaar trotseren"* or *"met de uiterste stoutheid, onaangezien alle gevaar, om winst iets durven ondernemen"* (p. 69): that is, to perform a daring action in the hope of reward, to fear neither hell nor the devil, to defy danger, or to embark boldly on an enterprise which promises to be profitable, heedless of danger.

In a farce performed by the Lischbloeme (Iris) School of Rhetoric of Malines at the Landjuweel of 1561 (Note 143) *"Griete die den roof haelt voorde helle"* (Griete who fetches the loot from hell [or before the gate of hell]) is mentioned as one of the women whom a fool would send to market.

10 Van Mander's phrase *"vree(m)t op zijn schots toeghemaeckt"* has been misunderstood. It is often translated—by Hymans, for example, and by Bastelaer and Hulin de Loo (p. 286)—as *"accoutrée à l'écossaise"* (dressed in the Scottish fashion) or as *"she ... wears a strange Scottish costume"* (L. Van Puyvelde, *Pieter Bruegel's "Dulle Griet,"* p. 3). In this context, however, the word *"schots"* has nothing to do with Scotland. In Middle Dutch it was used in the sense of "strange," "foolish" or "perverse." See J. Verdam, *Middelnederlandsch Handwoordenboek* and D.T. Enklaar, *Uit Uilenspiegel's kring*. Grauls says in *Volkstaal*: "'*Schots*' must be read as a synonym for '*vreemt*' [strange]."

Modern Dutch still uses the expression *"schots en scheef"* meaning "topsy-turvy," "cockeyed," "all mixed up." Today the adjective *"schotsbont"* means "gaudily variegated." This meaning may indeed derive from Scottish tartans.

11 Perhaps "The Triumph of Death." Cat. No. 14.

12 Perhaps "The Peasant Dance." Cat. No. 36.

13 We do not know what became of this painting.

14 It is not known whether Bruegel began work on this commission before he died.

15 The document has never been found.

16 Bruegel's contemporaries often complain of *clappaerts* (gossip) and *quade tonghen* (evil tongues). See, for example, *Spelen van Sinne* and *Een schoon liedekens Boeck*. The same complaints also occur in early seventeenth-century literature, in G. A. Bredero's *Spaansche Brabander* (1617), for instance. Perhaps Van Mander is just using a cliché.

17 Apparently this picture is lost. An analogy with "The Fall of Icarus" or "The Sermon of Saint John the Baptist" does not seem very plausible. See J. B. F. van Gils, *Een andere kijk*. Also M. Auner. Could Van Mander be referring to the drawing "The Calumny of Apelles" (Note 151) discovered in London in 1959? See Glück, *The Large Bruegel Book*, No. 53.

18 Pieter the Younger (1564–1638), sometimes called Helsche (Hell) Breughel, became a free master in Antwerp in 1585. See F.-J. van den Branden, *Geschiedenis der Antwerpsche schilderschool*, Vol. I (1883), pp. 440–44; L. van Puyvelde, *La peinture flamande au siècle de Bosch et Bruegel* (1962), pp.138–40; H. Demoriane, *"Bruegel et son fils," Connaissance des Arts*, February, 1968; G. Marlier, *Pierre Brueghel le Jeune* (Brussels, 1969).

19 Van Mander corrects himself in an appendix to his book, saying that he was misinformed and that Pieter Brueghel the Younger (Brueghel II) does not paint portraits but is highly skilled in the art of copying his father's works.

20 Jan the Elder (1568–1625), also called Samtbrueg(h)el (Velvet Breughel) became a free master in Antwerp on his return from Italy in 1596. From 1601 to 1602 he was president of St. Luke's Guild. See Van den Branden, *Geschiedenis*, pp.

444–55; E. Michel, *Les Breughel*; M. Eemans, *Breughel de Velours* (Brussels, 1964); Denucé, *Bronnen*, III.

21 On the relations between the Goetkindt and Bruegel families see Denucé, *Bronnen*, III.

22 Today the name of the Dutch village is spelled "Bruegel." The *Nomina Geographica Neerlandica* lists the following earlier spellings: "Breughel" (1560); "Brogel" (1500); "Broeghel" (1288). See Bastelaer and Hulin de Loo, p. 45.

23 L. Guicciardini, *Descrittione di tutti i Paesi Bassi* (Antwerp, 1567, 1581, 1588); *Description de tout le Pays-Bas* (Antwerp, 1568, 1609, 1625); *Niderlands Beschreibung* (Basel, 1580); *The Description of the Low Countreys* (London, 1593).

24 Bastelaer and Hulin de Loo, p. 145; R.-L. Delevoy, *Bruegel. Étude historique*, pp. 10–11.

25 "It is hardly necessary to recall that in those days family names were almost unknown among common people, especially peasants. In his own village a man was known by his patronymic; non-natives often added the name of their birthplace" (Bastelaer and Hulin de Loo, p. 42).
    We have already referred to handwritten notes on many of Bruegel's sketches in the *naer het leven* (from life) series (Notes 1 and 122). According to the recent investigations of F. Van Leeuwen "*Jets over het handschrift*" and J. Spicer "*The 'Naer he t Leven' Drawings*" the series in question should be attributed to Roelandt Savery.

26 C. Bossus, "*Sur la date de naissance.*"

27 G. Marlier, *La Renaissance flamande: Pierre Coecke d'Alost.*

28 *Ibid.*, p. 74.

29 A. Vermeylen, "*Bruegel et l'art italien*"; Charles de Tolnay, "*Bruegel et l'Italie*"; Ludwig Münz, *The Drawings*; W. Vanbeselaere, *Pieter Bruegel*; F. Lugt; H. Vlieghe. Many scholars have investigated Bruegel's debt to the Italian masters, including Domenico Campagnola, Boldrini, Baldovinetti, Pollaiuolo, Rosso Fiorentino, Raphael, Titian, Tintoretto, and Michelangelo. Obviously the style of any master, however great, always owes something to his predecessors. While this applies to Bruegel too, his mature style is a very personal and independent one.

30 E. Michel, "*Pierre Bruegel le Vieux et Pieter Coecke d'Alost.*"

31 Malines City Archives, DD S, No. 32, Fol.64: "*...Aen den welcken geleert heeft Claude Dorisi, hebbende naerderhant alle de vier exercitien gehouden met seer grooten winckel, waer by de principaelste meesters hebben gewerckt als den ouden vermaerden Breugel, die de deuren van de Hantschoenmaekers tsynen huyse heeft gemaekt, ende Pieter Baltens op den selven winckel het binnenste....*" This document has been published in A. Monballieu's "*P.Bruegel en het altaar*" (pp.109–10). Claude Dorisi, born about 1517, was enrolled in the Malines painters' guild in 1536 and died on June 16,1565 (*ibid.*, p. 97).

32 Malines City Archives, D³, *Handschoenmakers, Lijst der Meesters en Cnapen*, Fol.166 x verso—167: "*Int jaer ons heeren Jesu cristi doemen screef duijsent vijf hondert ende vijftich int jaer van Jubileen soo sijn de ghesworene metten deken vanden ambachte vanden hanscoemakers verghert omme haer tafele te besteen... Ende sijn als doen minnelijcken met malcanderen verghert gheweest int leeuken over de grootebrugghe metten scilders te wetene meester ghelaeudi [*CLAUDE DORISI*] ende hebben als doen ons tafele besteet te scilderen en daer in te stellen de legende van onsen patroon sinte gummaer ende dat met seker condicien hier naer volghende, te wetene; (dat hij) inden iersten dat hij sal legghen goede scoone vaste verven ende soo binnen inde tafele sal maken de voorseijde legende van onsen patroon ende dat hij die lijsten binnen sal vergulden met goeden fijnen goude ende noch moet hij van buijten stellen op de dore twee groote personasijen te weten: sinte gommaer ende sinte rombout ende daer int middene eenen boom ende boven de hoofden vanden voorseijden personasijen moet hij noch maken hoeijen metten wapenen vanden ambachte daer inne hanghende ende ditte alte samen, te wetene datter buijten op de doren staene moet en derf hij maer maken van witten ende van swerten verwen ende de lijsten di^e buijten aen de doren staen, die moet hij marmoren oft swert maken met een cleyn boordeken van goude daer rontomme loopende ende noch soo moet hij het sambrant datter boven omme loopt ende den voet daer die tafele op staet mede stofferen alsoo dat het behoort ende noch soo moet hij ons maken een stuck doeck scilderije metter Verrijsenisse daer inne ende ditte altesamen hebben wij hem besteet te maken voor de somme van xij pont vlems ende dits noch op voorweerde als dat hijse moet voldaen hebben teghen sinte gummaers dach [11. Oktober] anno. lj*"; V. Hermans, *Inventaire des Archives de la Ville de Malines* VIII, 1894, p. 243. Monballieu, "*P. Bruegel en het altaar,*" pp.108–9.

33 See Marlier, "*Peeter Balten, copiste ou créateur?*" *Bulletin des Musées royaux des Beaux-Arts de Belgique*, 1965, pp. 127–42.

34 "*A° 1551. In 't jaer Ons Heeren doen men screef XVe ende een en vijftich doen waeren Dekens ende Rhegeerders van S. Lucasgulde, Gommaer van Eerenbroeck [ende] Kerstiaen van den Queeckborne, ende hier na volghen haer vrijmeesters die zy ontfangen hebben in 't jaer voorscreven: ...*" There follow the names of twenty-two free masters, twelve of them painters, including "Peeter Brueghels, *schilder.*" This list also includes "Joorge Mantewaen, *coperen plaetsnyder,*" i.e. George of Mantua (Giorgio Ghisi), engraver. See P. Rombouts and T. van Lerius, *De Liggeren*, p. 175. F. Crucy asserts that "Brueghels" is a Flemish adjectival form meaning literally "Pieter from the village of Brueghel" (*Les Bruegel*, p. 5). Delevoy also says that the final *s* denotes an adjectival form indicating that Peeter comes from the village of Brueghel (*Brueghel*, p. 9). Actually, however, the final *s* denotes a genitive, so that "Brueghels" signifies "Brueghels *zoon*" (Brueghel's son). The name of the Amsterdam art lover mentioned by Van Mander is Willem Jacobsz., i.e., Willem Jacobszoon, or William, Jacob's son.

35 Münz, *The Drawings.*

36 D. Bertolotti, *Giulio Clovio*; Jedlicka, *Pieter Bruegel*, pp. 28–32 and 485, Notes 28, 5. All the works mentioned in this document are lost. On the lower margin of a miniature of the *Last Judgment* attributed to Clovio, now in the New York Public Library, is an inset of storm-tossed ships. Could it be from Bruegel's hand?

37 The engraving is entitled "*Freti Sicvli sive Mamertini vulgo el faro di Messina optica delineatio*" ("Picture of the Sicilian or Mamertine Straits commonly called the Straits of Messina"). It is signed "*Hieronymus Cock pictor excudebat. M.D. lxi Cum Gratia et priuilegio. Bruegel Inuen.*" See Bastelaer, No. 96; Lebeer, No. 40.

38 Michel, "*Bruegel le Vieux a-t-il passé à Genève?*"; Lebeer, *Les Estampes.*

39 No.192 in the "Rubens Inventory" (Note 8) is a picture entitled "Le Mont S.Godard du vieux Breugel".

40 Bastelaer, *Les Estampes*; Münz, *The Drawings.*

41 Is it really necessary to seek a deeper reason for this change of signature? As we know, spelling in those days was largely a matter of taste. G.W. Menzel believes that Bruegel changed his signature as a precautionary measure: "Bruegel too may have been impelled by the threatening events of 1559 to restrain his social criticism and dissociate himself from his earlier works by a

change of signature" (*Pieter Bruegel*, pp. 52–53). This seems very questionable. It is most unlikely that the Inquisition would have been taken in by a minor change in the spelling of a name.

42 Münz, Nos. 47, 48, 49. See Note 144.

43 Brussels City Archives, Church of Notre Dame de la Chapelle, marriage register, Folio 5. Menzel gives a facsimile (p. 66).

The building at No. 132 Rue Haute in Brussels is supposed to be Bruegel's house. This is substantiated by the entry recording the death of his great-grandson David Teniers III (d. 1685) which reads: "*den ii e Sr. Daùid Teniers in de kercke van Caudenbergh opde hooghstraete naest de roode poorte*" (on 11 [February, 1685] Sieur David Teniers [was buried] in the church of Caudenbergh. [He lived in the] Rue Haute next to the red door). Since this quarter has partly been rebuilt, the location of Teniers' house cannot be established. Moreover, it has never been proved that Teniers III inherited the house from his mother. See V. G. Martiny, "*A propos de la maison dite de Breughel rue Haute à Bruxelles*" in *Bulletin de la Commission royale des Monuments et des Sites*, Vol. XV, 1964, pp. 7–45.

44 Second definitive edition: *Le vite de' piu eccelenti pittori, scultori ed architetti, scritte da maestro Giorgio Vasari, pittore ed architetto aretino di nuovo ampliate, con i ritratti loro, e con l'aggiunta delle vite de' vivi e de' morti, dell anno 1550 insino al 1567.*

45 In a letter dated Bologna, 16 June, 1561, a certain Scipio Fabius asks Abraham Ortelius for news of "Martinus Vulpes [Maarten de Vos] and his dear friend, the excellent painter Petrus Bruochl." In another letter of April 14, 1565, the same correspondent again sends greetings to "Petrus Brouchel." See Popham.

46 The epitaph in memory of "Petro Breugelio," renewed in 1676 by David Teniers III, bears the inscription "*Obiit ille anno MDLXIX.*" It is still to be seen in the third chapel of the right aisle of Notre Dame de la Chapelle in Brussels.

The historian A. Wauters asserted in "*La Famille Breughel*" that Bruegel died on September 5, 1569, but the author did not state his source.

47 Antwerp City Archives, City Protocols 1563–70, VIII, No. 1551: "*Nicolas Jongelinck verclaerde dat alsoo hy hem op den VIIen dach van September anno 1563 borge geconstitueert heeft aen dese stadt voor Daniel de Bruyne voor het voldoen van den Collectatien dije hy gehadt heeft van den Wynaccynse*

deser stadt totter sommen toe van Sesthien duysent Carolus gulden ende hy eghene speciale panden tot versekerheyt van der selver stadt alsdoen gestelt en heeft. Soo eest dat hy om de stadt te beter te bewaeren anderwerff borge geconstitueert heeft, ende beloeft dat ingevalle den voors. Daniel der stadt nijet en voldoet oft contenteert van alle tghene dat by slote van reckeninghe bevonden is oft noch sal worden der stadt schuldich ende ten achter te zijn van den Collectatien van den voors accysen, imposten ende pondtgelt, tselfde te voldoen ende der Stadt opteleggen ende te betalen totter voors.sommen toe van Sesthien duysent Carolus gulden eens. Daer voer verbindende alle alsulcken schilderyen als hij heeft nu ter tyt staende in zynen huijse geleghen ter Beken. Te weten thien stucken van de historie van Hercules, acht stucken van de slapende Conste, het Oordeel van Paris, een zee Triumphe, een Bancket van de Goeden, een stuck van Spes, Fides et Caritas, al gemaect by Franchoïjs Floris; een stuck van Albordura; Sesthien stucken van Bruegel onder de welcke is den Thoren van Babilonyen, eenen Cruysdrager, de Tweelf maenden, ende voorts alle dander hoedanich dye zyn, ende voerdane hem selven ende alle zijne goeden quaecumque et ubicumque. Mede compareerde Daniel de Bruyne ende heeft beloeft opt vonnisse etc. binnen de sesse weken naestcommende der stadt gereet op te leggen ende te betalen de somme van ses duysent Carolus guldenen eens, tot twintich stuvers den gulden... An° 1565, XXI Februarij."

The year is to be read as 1566, not 1565, because the date is not based on the Gregorian calendar. The calendar in use when this document was written was the so-called Easter Calendar (*stylus Gallicanus, Camerancensis* or *Brabantiae*) according to which the year began with Easter, on Good Friday or Saturday. Since February 21 comes before Easter, the year would be 1566 by our reckoning. The document was published by Denucé in *Bronnen* (Vol. II, p. 5).

The text reads in translation: "Nicolas Jongelinck has declared that on the 7th day of September in the year 1563 he pledged himself as surety to this city for Daniel de Bruyne and [promised] to pay the excise duties on wine owed by him in the amount of 16,000 guilders. Having given no specific guarantees to our city at that time and in order to offer the city better security, he has put up a pledge and promised to pay off in one lump sum the outstanding debt of 16,000 guilders in case the said Daniel should fail to meet his obligations to the city of all he owes after the closing of accounts, or all arrears, whether in the aforementioned excise duties or in other taxes or tolls. To this end [Jongelinck] gave to the city as security all the pictures at present in his own house, Ter Beken, to wit: ten pieces [paintings] of the 'Story of Hercules,' eight pieces of 'Art Sleeping,' one 'Judgment of Paris,' one 'Triumphant Sea' [?],

one 'Banquet of the Gods,' one 'Faith, Hope and Charity,' all executed by Frans Floris; one piece by Albordura [Albrecht Dürer]; sixteen pieces by Bruegel, including a 'Tower of Babel,' a 'Calvary,' the 'Twelve Months,' and furthermore all other [paintings], whatever they may be, and finally himself and all his possessions, whatever and wherever they may be. At the same time Daniel de Bruyne appeared and promised in accordance with the judgment etc. to pay the city the lump sum of 16,000 guilders cash within the next six weeks [at the rate of] twenty pennies to the guilder. Anno 1565, February 21."

48 It is interesting to note that all Frans Floris' works are identified in the document, while only three of the sixteen Bruegels are mentioned by name. This point is significant in tracing the famous series of "The Months," Cat. Nos. 22–26.

Nicolas Jongelinck had a brother named Jacques, a sculptor who worked for Cardinal Granvelle. This connection may explain how Granvelle came to own some Paintings by Bruegel.

49 "*Petro Brvegel, Pictori. – Quis nouus hic Hieronymus Orbi | Boschius? ingeniosa magistri | Somnia peniculoque, styloque | Tanta imitarier arte peritus, | Vt superet tamen interim & illum? | Macte animo, Petre, mactus vt arte. | Namque tuo, veterisque magistri | Ridiculo, salibusque referto | In graphices genere inclyta laudum | Praemia vbique, & ab omnibus vllo | Artifice haud leuiora mereris.*"
Dominicus Lampsonius, Pictorum aliquot celebrium Germaniae inferioris effigies. Antwerpen 1572.

In the translation of Van de Wall: "Who may be this other Jeroon Bos, / Who came in this world again, / Who pictures to us the fantastic conceptions of his own master again, / Who is most able with the brush, / Who is even surpassing his master? / Ye, Pieter, ye work in the artistic style of your old master. / But you rise still higher: / For reason that you select / Pleasant topics to laugh about. / Through these you deserve great merit / And with your master you must be praised for being a great artist."

Van Mander (Note 4) gives the following Dutch translation: "*Wie is doch desen Bos? Jeroon van nieuws ghecoomen | Ter Weerelt, die ons boost zijns Meesters cloecke droomen, | Ervaren met t' Penceel, en stijl soo abel daet, | Dat hy hem ondertusch[en] nochtans te bóven gaet? | Neemt Petre toe in moet, soo ghy in Const doet vruchtigh, | In dijn oudt Meesters wijs, van schild'ren bootsen cluchtigh, | Wel lacchens weerdt, ghy doch verdient te zijn eenpaar | Heerlijck ghelooft, niet min als eenigh Constenaer.*"

There is a reproduction of the Lampsonius engraving Grossmann's *The Paintings*.

50 Pembroke College, Cambridge, *Album amicorum,* ca. 1573:

"*Dijs Manibus sacrum*

Petrum Brugelium Pictorem fuisse sui seculi absolutissimum, nemo nisi invidus, emulus, aut eius artis ignarus, umquam negabit. Sed quod nobis medio etatis flore abreptus sit, an hoc Morti, quod fortasse eum ob insignem artis peritiam, quam in eo viro observaverat, etate provectiorem duxerat; an Nature potius, quod eius artificiosa ingeniosaq[ue] imitatione, sui contemptum verebatur, impectavero, non facile dixerim

AMICI MEMORIAE
ABRAHAMUS ORTE-
LIUS LVGENS CON-
SECRAB.

Eupompus pictor interrogatus quem sequeretur antecedentium, demonstrata hominum multitudine, dixisse fertur, naturam ipsam imitandum esse, non artificem. Congruit nostro Brugelio hoc, cuius picturas ego minime artificiosas, at naturales appellare soleam. Neque eum optimum pictorum, at naturam pictorum vero dixerim. Dignum itaque indico, quem omnes imitentur.

Multa pinxit, hic Brugelius, quae pingi non possunt, quod Plinius de Apelle. In omnibus eius operibus intelligitur plus semper quam pingitur. Idem de Timanthe Eunapius in Iamblicho. Pictores qui formosulos in etatis flore constitutos (p)ingunt voluntque picture lenocinium quoddam et gratiam de suo adjicere, totam depravant representatam effigiem et ab exemplari proposito pariter et a vera forma aberrant. Ab hac labe purus noster Brugelius."

The text is published in A.E. Popham's "*Pieter Bruegel and Abraham Ortelius*" and in Tolnay's *Pierre Bruegel l'Ancien* (p. 61). In English it reads: "Sacred to the gods of the underworld. No one except through envy, jealousy or ignorance of that art will ever deny that Peter Bruegel was the most perfect painter of his century. But whether his being snatched away from us in the flower of his age was due to Death's mistake in thinking him older than he was on account of his extraordinary skill in art or rather to Nature's fear that his genius for imitation would bring her into contempt, I cannot easily say.

Abraham Ortelius dedicated this
with grief to the memory of his friend.

The painter Eupompus, asked which of his predecessors he should take for a model, is said to have mentioned numerous names and finally replied that it is Nature herself that should be imitated, not the artist. This applies to our Bruegel, whose pictures, as I always say, bear the stamp of Nature rather than art. Indeed I would call him not the best of painters but the essence of painters. I therefore name him as the painter who deserves to be imitated by everyone.

This Bruegel painted many things that cannot be painted, as Pliny said of Apelles. In all his works more is always communicated than is actually painted. According to Iamblichus, Eunapius says the same of Timanthes. Painters who paint handsome models in the flower of their age and who seek to introduce the picture a charm and grace of their own distort the total portrait and are equally untrue to the model and to the true form. Our Bruegel is free from this fault."
(First paragraph translated by Popham.)

The sentence "painted many things that cannot be painted" has been interpreted as evidence that Bruegel's contemporaries recognized the esoteric nature of his work (Tolnay, *Bruegel l'Ancien,* p. 62). The sentence "*in omnibus eius operibus intelligitur plus semper quam pingitur*" seems to us an excellent characterization of the didactic tone of Bruegel's art.

51 See bibliography, esp.: Denucé, *Bronnen* I and II; C. Piot, *Correspondance,* p. 524; Popham; S. Speth-Holterhoff, *Les peintres flamands;* L. von Baldass, "*Die niederländische Landschaftsmalerei*"; H. Zimmermann, "*Quellen*"; Bastelaer and Hulin de Loo; G. Glück, *The Large Bruegel Book.*

52 G.P. Lomazzo, *Trattato della Pittura, Scultura* (Milan, 1585); Cornelis de Bie, *Het Gulden Cabinet* (Antwerp, 1661, p. 89); Joachim Sandrart, *Teutsche Academie* (Nuremberg, 1675–78, Vol. I, part 2, p. 259); Florent Le Comte, *Cabinet des singularités* (Paris, 1699–1700, Vol. II, pp. 255–57); P.-J. Mariette, Catalogue collection Crozat (Paris, 1741); J.B. Descamps, *Vie des peintres flamands, allemands et hollandais* (Paris, Vol. I, 1753); J. Reynolds, *Journey to Flanders and Holland in the year MDCCLXXXI (The Works of Sir Joshua Reynolds,* London, 1797, Vol. II, p.112).

53 For a bibliography on the sixteenth century, see H. Sée, A. Rebillon and E. Préclin, *Le XVIe siècle.*

54 H. Hauser, *La modernité du XVIe siècle.*

55 L. Febvre, *Le Problème de l'incroyance au XVIe siècle. La religion de Rabelais* (Paris, 1947, p. 500).

56 M. van Vaernewijck, Vol. I, p. 23.

57 *Ibid.,* Vol. I.

58 *Ibid.,* Vol. I, p. 8: "*Tvolc welfde daerwaert niet met honderden maer met duysenden, maer almeest ghemeen puepel die lettel te verbueren hadde; waer af dat sommighe van hemlieden spraken menigheranden ongheschaefden caut achter straten.*"

59 *Ibid.,* Vol. I, p. 170: "*die niet dan tabbijt gheestelic en hadden.*"

60 *Ibid.,* Vol. I, p. 227: "*men quam hem snachts van zijnen bedde upcloppen om te ghaen helpen breken, ende en wiste niet dat hij daer in mesdoen zoude, ende beclaechde zeere dat hij onschuldich starf.*"

61 Equally brutal events are recorded in Van Vaernewijck's chronicle.

62 Philip II is damned by some, praised by others. The documents portray him as a ruler mindful of his duty. He was deeply religious, not to say sanctimonious, a conscientious, compulsive worker, a cruel man yet a good father, despite what has been written of him. His mistake probably lay in believing that his function as a ruler consisted in scribbling notes in the margin of the numerous state documents presented to him. See L.E. Halkin, "*Le caractère de Philippe II*" in *Initiation à la critique historique* (2nd ed., Paris, 1953, pp. 99–119).

63 Especially in "The Fight Between Carnival and Lent" (Cat. No. 7), the drawing "*Caritas*" in the Boymans-van Beuningen Museum, Rotterdam, and the painting of "The Cripples" (Cat. No. 41).

64 F. Braudel, *Civilisation matérielle et capitalisme (XVe–XVIIIe siècle),* (Paris, 1967, pp. 55–56).

65 The colophon of this book reads: "*Marie Ver-/ hulst vefue dudict Pier-/ re d'Alost trespassé en l'An M.D.L. / a faict imprimer / lesdictes figures. / soubz Grace & / Privilege de / l'Imperi / alle Ma-/ ieste / En l'An / .M. / .CCCCC. / L.III.*"

66 *Spelen van Sinne.*

67 D. van Oesbroeck, *Cleyn Memoriael,* M. Sacré, ed., line 257. Van Vaernewijck devotes a whole chapter to high grain prices: "*Hoe tvolck beghonde te murmureren, te Gendt, anghaende de dierte vanden coorne*" (Chapter XVIII, Vol. I, p. 91).

On the list of suggested themes for the Landjuweel of 1561 (Note 143) the following question has been inserted under Item XII: "*Hoe compt dat dagelix alle dingen verdieren?*" (How is it that everything gets more expensive every day?) See E. van Even.

68 *Bruer Willeken.* See O. van den Daele and F. van Veerdeghem, p. 219.

69 J. van Vloten, Vol. I, p. 209.

59

"*Elck*" or "Everyman." Pen drawing. London, British Museum. See Note 79.

"The Battle Between the Money Banks and the Strongboxes." Engraving. See Note 83.

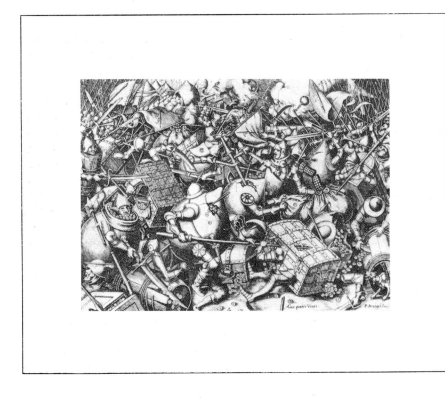

70 See Enklaar, *Varende Luyden*. Aernouts-broeders (Arnold's Brothers) were vagabonds and drifters. The name was sometimes also applied to wandering students, who often practiced quack medicine. A play entitled "*Vanden jonghen Aernout | ende hoe hij eerst inde werelt comt*" (*Veelderhande geneuchlijcke dichten*, p.104) gives us an idea of what their life was like. Young Aernout's life falls into four-year periods. As a foundling, he is dependent on public charity for four years, then he becomes a beggar and finally a leader of blind men. At the age of twelve he finds himself a *mosse*, a girl on whose earnings he can live. His vagabond career ends, like all dissolute lives, in the poorhouse.

Aernout gives a lively description of how he treats his girl: "Aernout, what are your household goods? / A needle and thread / So that I can patch my tattered clothes. / And a stick with four slashes. / With this yardstick I measure / All my girl's limbs / So every morning she struts around like a peacock / dressed in green and blue" (p.72).

71 The Ghesellen van Sint Reynuyt (Companions of Saint Reynuyt) was a nickname four carousers and young men who lived by their wits and who in case of necessity would "sell their shirt with the fleas and lice thrown in." "*Het wonderlijcke leven van sinte Reynuyt de welcke een Patroon is van alle Deur-brengers*" (The wonderful life of Saint Reynuyt, patron of all wastrels) can be found in *Veelderhande* (p.110). See Enklaar, *Varende Luyden*.

72 *Ghildekens* (tipplers) are also referred to as *banckgeselle* and *cadille*. See Van Vaernewijck, for instance.

73 "*Der Fielen, Rabauwen oft der Schalcken Vocabulaer, ooc de beueysde manieren der bedeleeren oft bedelerssen, daer menich mensche deur bedrogen wort, wort hier geleert, op dat hem elck daer voor wachten mach, ende is seer nut ende profijtelijck om lesen voor alle menschen. Ghedruct Thantwerpen by Jan de Laet in die Rape. Anno M.D.LXIII.*" The Antwerp museum of folklore has a copy of this little work. The text, like that of *Till Eulenspiegel*, is based on an older German one. The Dutch version published in Antwerp in 1563 shows that the kind of begging it describes was just as prevalent in the Netherlands. Excerpts were published in 1600 in *Veelderhande geneuchlijcke dichten*. See the edition of V. de Meyere and L. Baekelmans.

74 On population figures, see J. Cuvelier. He cites figures from the census of 1526, when Antwerp had not yet reached its peak of development. At that time there were within the city walls of

Antwerp 8, 994 houses, of which 1,262 were un-occupied. Comparative figures for Brussels were 5,844 and 407; for Bois-le-Duc 3,864 and 61; for Louvain 3,204 and 137. Brabant had a total of 97,013 occupied houses. In the 1560's, when the port of Antwerp was at the height of its activity, there were some 13,500 houses in the city, and the population numbered between 100,000 and 105,000. See *Antwerpens Gouden Eeuw*, p.14.

75   R. Ehrenberg; J.A. Goris.

76   A. Deblaere, "*Erasmus, Bruegel.*"

77   D. Roggen, "*J. Bosch: literatuur en folklore*" in *Gentsche Bijdragen tot de Kunstgeschiedenis* VI, 1939–40, pp.107–26; D. Bax, *Ontcijfering van Jeroen Bosch* (The Hague, 1949), *Beschrijving en poging tot verklaring van het Tuin der Onkuisheid-drieluik van Jeroen Bosch* (Amsterdam, 1956), "*Jeroen Bosch en de Nederlandse taal*" in *Jheronimus Bosch, Bijdragen* (Bois-le-Duc, 1967), pp. 61–71; Grauls, *Volkstaal.*

78   R.H. Marijnissen, *Bruegel, 16de eeuwse Brabander.*

79   London, British Museum. Münz, No. 138; Bastelaer, No.152; Bastelaer and Hulin de Loo, pp. 90–91; Grauls, "*Ter verklaring*" and *Volkstaal*; C.G. Stridbeck, *Bruegelstudien*, pp. 43–61. Lebeer, No. 26.

The legends read: "*Nemo non quaerit passim sua commoda, Nemo | Non querit sese cvnctis in rebus agendis, || Nemo non inhiat priuatis undique lucris, | Hic trahit, ille trahit, cunctis amor vnus habendi est || – Sur le monde vn chacun par tout recherche, | Et en toutes choses Soymesme veut tronner. | Veu qu'vn chacun donques tousiours se cherche, | Pourroit quelqu'vn bien perdu demeurer? || Vn chacun pour le plus long tire aussy, | L'vn par haut & l'autre par bas s'efforce. | Nul se cognoist Soymesme presque en ce monde icy: | Ce bien noté s'esmerueiller est forcé. || Elck soect hem seluen in alderley saken | Ouer al de werelt, al wort hy ghevloect, | Hoc can dan iemant verdoelt gheraken | Als elck hem seluen nu altijt soect. | Elck trect oock om dlancste soomen hier siet | Deen van bouen, dander van ondere. | Niemant en kent schier hem seluen niet | Diet wel aenmerct die siet groot wondere.*" (Everywhere in the world everyone seeks himself and in all things wants to find himself. How could anyone get lost, when everyone seeks himself? Everyone pulls to get the longer end [seeks his own advantage], one from above, the other from below. Hardly anyone knows himself. Whoever recognizes this will have to marvel at it.)

80   *Spelen van Sinne;* Van Even.

"The Alchemist." Pen drawing. Berlin, Kupferstichkabinett. See Note 86.

81   Van Even, p. 44, Nos. VI, XIII, XIV, and XV.

82   Brussels, Bibliothèque royale, Print Collection. See *Quinze ans d'acquisitions* (1954–68), Brussels, 1969, No. 242.

83   Bastelaer, No.146; Lebeer, 54. The legends read: "*Quid modo diuitie' quid fului vasta metalli | Congeries, nummis arca referta nouis, || Illecebres inter tantas atq[ue] agmina furum, | Inditium cunctis efferus vncus erit, || Preda facit furem, feruens mala cuncta ministrat | Impetus, et spolijs apta rapina feris. Wel aen ghij Spaerpotten, Tonnen, en Kisten | Tis al om gelt en goet, dit striden en twisten. || Al seetmen v ooc anders, willet niet ghelouen. | Daerom vuere[n] wij den haec die ons noijt en miste[n], || Men soeckt wel actie om ons te uerdoouen, | Maer men souwer niet krijgen, waerder niet te roouen.*" (The Money Banks and the Strongboxes in the guise of *landsknechts* fight over money and possessions so that they may continue to get their share of the loot on which they live.)

The second version has the following inscriptions: "*Divitiae faciunt fures | Multos perdidit aurum et argentum | Ecc^{le}, 8.3. || Les Richesses font les larrons | L'or et l'argent en a destruit plusieurs || Ryckdom maeckt dieven | Goudt en silver heeft vele bedorve[n].*" (Riches make thieves. Gold and silver have ruined many a man.)

84   In our opinion modern antithetical interpretations of all these legends are exaggeratedly critical. Why should their meaning always be the opposite of what they actually say?

85   B. Claessens, *Aimer Brueghel*, p. 52.

86   Berlin, Kupferstichkabinett. Münz: No.139. Münz mistranslates the pun "*ALGHE MIST*" as "all is dirt" (p. 33), and the translation "all is in vain" on p. 227 is equally incorrect.

Bastelaer and Hulin de Loo do not mention the original drawing. They say (p.110): "*Un éditeur postérieur de l'estampe de l'Alchimiste, jouant sur les mots, ajouta dans la planche les mots flamands 'Al-Ghemist' (tout est perdu).*" (A later publisher of the engraving of "The Alchemist" added to the plate the Flemish pun "*Al-Ghemist*"—"all is lost".) In fact this pun is part of the original drawing; there is no question of its having been added at a later date. Bastelaer's translation is no more correct than Münz's.

Bastelaer says (No.197): "*Le dessin de cette composition, daté de 1558, se trouvait dans la collection Crozat*" (the drawing for this composition, dated 1558, was in the Crozat collection). See Mariette, "*Abecedario,*" p.189. We should note that the drawing has no legend. This means that the commentary from Bruegel's own hand consists only

61

of the pun itself. The text on the sheet of paper pinned above the alchemist's head is practically illegible. We can just make out the word "*misero*" and an alchemistic symbol.

The first and second state engravings from this drawing each have two legends—warnings to stay away from alchemy, which leads its followers to the poorhouse. The first reads: "*Debent ignari res ferre et post operari | ivs lapidis cari vilis sed deniq[ue] rari | vnica res certa vilis sed vbiq[ue] reperta || Qvatvor inserta natvris in nvbe referta | Nvlla mineralis res est vbi principalis | Sed talis qvalis reperitvr vbiq[ue] localis*"

"*L'art Alchemiste ha son nom bien à plain | Le bien d'autruy & le nostre s'y pert, | De fain mourons, n'ayant pitance ou pain | Tous dessirez allons comme il appert, | Malheureux est qui a tel art s'assert || Voyez en hault comme bien sont receuz | Par Madame la bonne hospitalliere | Tous ceulx qui sont par cest art cy deceuz | Comme la chose en est bien coustumiere, | Heureulx sont ceulx qui s'en tirent arriere || Cette fois cy encoir' veulx je esprouuer | De cercher l'art, c'est tout mon pensement | Si à ce coup je ne le puis trouuer | Ie brusleray mes liures, puis vrayement | A l'hospital men yray briefuement | I'enraige au vif voyant que nostre bien | Par ce sot cy en la cendre demeure | Credit perdons, en bourse n'auons rien | En la fumee est tout fondu pour l'heure | A l'hospital irons, c'est chose seure.*"

The second state print has the following four-line stanza in addition to the Latin text: "*Voy comme ce folastre en ses fioles distille | Le sang de ses enfans, ses tresors et ses sens | Voy comme il cherche après la recherche inutile | Du Mercure son pain auecque ses enfans.*"

"*Den Alcomist, seer veel verquist, aen goet en tyt | Ghelt, goet en schat, heeft hij gehat, maer ist nu quyt | Hy vint int vier, gans niet een sier, dan syn bederuen | In d'eynde dan moet hy erm man int gasthuys steruen.*" While the French and Flemish Alexandrines are unambiguous, the Latin is an example of the abracadabra used by adepts of the Great Art. On the basis of Van Lennep's French translation in "*L'Alchimie*" (p.112) it may be rendered as follows: "The ignorant must acquire knowledge and then go to work. The identifying characteristic of the plentifully available yet ultimately rare and precious stone is that it is a manifestly common, unique thing, which is found everywhere. It is incorporated in nature in four forms and is common in that which is worthless, where no mineral is predominant, but as such it is encountered everywhere."

Van Lennep believes that this Latin inscription "ridicules those who do not know that the material of the stone is common and at the same time rare because it can be found everywhere and because it brings salvation to him who finds it."

Hence he argues that Bruegel was a great inititate "who defends the spiritual nature of alchemy" and that the drawing of "The Alchemist" proves that he "despised the numerous charlatans who brought hermetic philosophy into disrepute with their trickery." By "charlatans" Van Lennep means the "bellows boys"—the master alchemists' apprentices who sometimes tried to repeat their masters' experiments without sufficient knowledge or experience. In his discussion of this drawing Van Lennep says: "The kinship between the fool and the bellows boy ... is plainly stated. The wife of the bellows boy is showing her empty purse, indicating that her husband's obsession has reduced her to such poverty that only one course remains: to accept the charity of the poorhouse. This scene is depicted outside the big window of the workshop" (p.112).

We disagree. In our opinion the print is to be interpreted as an indictment of *folastres*—madmen carried away by the figments of their own brains. Of course many of Bruegel's paintings and drawings, like the works of other old masters, lend themselves to various interpretations, especially when one is trying to bring out the symbolic or hermetic aspect of his subjects. Without doubt Bruegel had seen alchemists at work. But are not his paintings and engravings pervaded through and through by sound common sense?

Tolnay and Würtenberger (p. 70) call attention to a similar criticism in the writings of the German philosopher Agrippa von Nettesheim (1486–1535): "The making of gold is indeed a very fine discovery and a pretty, unpunishable fraud, whose vanity and futility are apparent in its promise to do what nature can neither suffer nor attain. All other arts and sciences imitate nature but never surpass it, for the force of nature is much stronger than the power of art." (*Über die Eitelkeit und Unsicherheit der Wissenschaften*, 1527). S. Brant in his *Narrenschyff* (1494) and J. Cats in his *Sinn'-en Minne-Beelden* (1618) make also fun of alchemists. See Lebeer, No. 27.

On alchemy see M. Berthelot, *Les origines de l'alchimie* (1885) and *La chimie au Moyen Age* (3 vols, 1893); C.G. Jung, *Psychology and Alchemy* (1953); E.J. Holmyard, *Alchemy* (1957); M. Caron and S. Hutin, *Les alchimistes* (1959); F.S. Taylor, *The Alchemists* (1962).

87 *Spelen van Sinne*. The passage occurs in a play performed by the Cauwoerde (Pumpkin) School of Rhetoric of Herenthals: "*Ick heb alree mijn handen gheslegen | Aen menich begrijp | en veel handels verwect | Maer noyt connen comen tot consten perfect | Daer ick volchde vroech en late nochtans | Appetijt van eeren | en der baten dans | Dies ick nu D'alchimisterie bekeure | Gheen conste ter werelt en*

prijsicker veure... | Ick hebs veel deurloopen | en wel beproeft | Maer tgheen dat den vlieghenden gheest behoeft | En hebbic niewers connen ghevinden | Soo dat ick beghonst hebben tondervinden | Der Alchimisteryen practijcke | Onder vele consten gheen haers ghelijcke."

88 *Ibid.*, in a play given by the Berchem School of Rhetoric known as De Bloeyende Wijngaert (The Flowering Vineyard): "*Soo waert dan oirboirlijcker t[e] sijn een Alchemist | Die van luttel veel maken blijckelijck | Oft eenen conterfeytmunter | die rijckelijck | Van slechten aloye | groot ghelt maken can? | Dats al oneerlijck | tsal naemaels suer smaken | man | Tis menschen inuentie | niet dan bedroch.*"

89 J. van Vloten (pp. 206–15): "*Weest vrolyck, weest vrolyck, hout Vastenavondfeesten, | Ghy reine geesten, lichtvaerdich van sinnen! | Ick groet u, de minste en de meeste; | Weest vrolick, hout vastenavondfeesten... | Toont nu uwen aert, die my beminnen, | Backt pannekoecken, wafelen in't openbaar, | Worpt die worst op die kolen, slaet hoop werck binnen; | Want die Vastenavont comt maer eens in't jaer!...*
Haest u, haest u, 't is meer dan tijt! | Eet met naers, met mont, drinckt bier en wijn | Het moet op, dus smest met vlijt, | Want de cost sou Asselewoonsdachs bedorven sijn...
Sy sijn lanck van kinne en magher van kaecken... | Haer gebeent dat rammelt, haer rebben die craekken... | Want die vis ende olie is haer cost, | Sy en drincken geen stercken dranck, wijn noch most, | Sy sijn beveynst, al waren sy vol vreesen, | Van buyten sijn sy seer simpel gedost, | Maer daer onder is een quaet hert geresen...
In één cop bloemen sijn twaliff eyeren geraemt, | Sy sijn seer cort met suycker/overgestroeyt, | Omdat die Vasten sou sijn beschaemt, | Leckerder pannekoecken en at ghy noeyt, | Sy druypen van de butter, datter al vermoeyt | Daer en is voorwaer geen cost aengespaert; | Al souden wy morgen syn beroeyt, | Soo moet die Vastenavonts eer sijn bewaert. | Dan breng ick oock wafelen, die se begaert, | Die wel gecruyt sijn, lecker en êel, | Die schenck ick dit geselschap vermaert, | Ghy en aet u leven geen leckerder morseel; | Daer is nagelpoër in en caneel, | Peper ende alderhande cruyt, | Sofferaen van Noerden, daerom sijn sy soo geel | ..."

90 P. de Keyser, "*Rhetoricale toelichting.*"

91 *Le voyage et navigation que fist Panvrge disciple de pantagruel aux isles incongnues & estranges de plusieurs choses merveilleuses & diffciles à croire, qu'il dict auoir veues, dont il faict narration en ce present volume & plusieurs aultres ioyeusetez, pour inciter les lecteurs & auditeurs a rire* appeared under various titles. The first known edition, dated 1538, is attributed to Denis Johannot. The text is quoted

62

for comparative purposes in *Oeuvres complètes de Maître François Rabelais. Texte établi et annoté par Marcel Guilbaud* (Paris, 1957), Book V, pp. 240–82.

The Land of Cockaigne is described in detail in chapters 18 to 28. We quote some of the chapter headings: Chapter 18: "*Comme Panurge navigua tant qu'il trouva une montaigne de beurre fraiz & auprès d'icelle ung fleuve de laict portant bateau*" (how Panurge sailed until he found a mountain of fresh butter and beside it a river of milk on which the boat floated). Chapter 19: "*Comme Panurge arriva en ung pays plat, qui n'est point labouré, mais fort fertil, là où croissent les pastez chauldz, & d'une nuée dont tombent les alouettes toutes rosties, & comme l'on y couvre les maisons de tartelettes toutes chauldes*" (how Panurge arrived at a flat country which is not cultivated but is very fertile, where hot pies grow. And about a cloud from which roast larks fall, and how the houses are roofed with warm tartlets). Chapter 21: "*De l'isle des Papillons, & la manière dont les gens du pays font les maisons & habitations & les églises, & comme les grues volent en l'aer toutes rosties par belles bandes*" (about the Isle of Butterflies and how its inhabitants build their houses and habitations and churches, and how roast cranes fly through the air in great flocks).

92 The humorous title of this work is: "*Van't Luyeleckerlandt / twelcke is een seer wonderlijck / over schoon ende costelijck Landt vol van alder gheneuchten / ende wellustighheeden. Ende is nu eerst ghevonden int Jaer doemen schreef duysendt Suycker koecken / vijfhondert Eyer-vladen / ende ses en veertich gebraeden Hoenderen / in de Wijn maent / doe de Pastyen wel smaeckten. Ende is seer ghenoecklijck om te lesen*" (Of the Land of Cockaigne, a most wonderful, extremely beautiful and delightful land full of all kinds of pleasures and amusements, which has just been discovered in the year written as follows: one thousand sugar cakes, five hundred pancakes, and forty-six roast chickens, in the wine month, when the pies were good and tasty. And it is very amusing to read). The text was included in *Veelderhande Geneuchlycke Dichten* (Antwerp, 1600). See Grauls, *Volkstaal*, p. 206, and Lebeer, "*Le Pays de Cocagne*."

93 The engraving known as "The Fool Who Hatched a Big Empty Egg" (Bastelaer, No. 182) is clearly ridiculing drunkenness, as the Flemish inscription proves beyond doubt. Van Lennep's reading of it as a gibe at "the bellows boys [see note 86] who play around with the vessel of divine quicksilver without any knowledge of the rules of Hermes or the subtleties of the art" ("*L'Alchimie*," pp. 110–11*)* is unconvincing. The eggshell does not contain "another fool" but a fool's bauble.

94 Amsterdam, Rijksmuseum. Münz: No. 142. See note 141.

95 Brussels, Bibliothèque royale, Print Collection. Münz: No. 143. See note 141.

96 Van Vaernewijck, Vol. II, pp. 119–20; Vol. IV, pp. 167, 240.

97 Bastelaer, "*Sur l'origine de la dénomination des Gueux du XVIᵉ siècle*," *Mélanges Godefroid Kurth* (Liège, 1908); Bastelaer and Hulin de Loo, p. 137.

98 *Papiers d'État de Granvelle*, Vol. VIII, p. 138.

99 Bastelaer and Hulin de Loo, p. 138.

100 Bastelaer, *L'origine*.

101 Tolnai, "*Studien*," pp. 130–31; E. Sudeck, *Bettlerdarstellungen*.

102 *Kunsthistorische Mededelingen van het Rijksbureau voor Kunsthistorische Documentatie* (The Hague, 1947), pp. 32 ff.
On lepers see F. de Potter, *De leproos in de Middeleeuwen* (Belfort, 1891).

103 Menzel, p. 77.

104 C. Terlinden, "*Pierre Brueghel*."

105 Antwerp, Musée des Beaux-Arts; Brussels, Collection of Dr. Delporte. See Cat. No. 27.

106 The oldest extant edition of the chapbook recounting Till Eulenspiegel's deeds and experiences appeared in Strasbourg in 1515 under the title *Ein kurtzweilig lesen von Dyl Vlenspiegel gebore usz dem land zu Brunszwick. Wie er sein leben volbracht hatt. xcvi. seiner geschichten.* Probably the original version (also in German) dated back to about 1500, possibly to the last decade of the fifteen century. The Flemish version published in Antwerp by Michel van Hoogstraten is undated but is assumed to have appeared about 1519. The book became very popular all over Europe, went through many editions, and was translated again and again well into the nineteenth century. See L. Debaene and P. Heyns, *Het volksboek van Ulenspiegel* (Antwerp, 1948).
Charles de Coster's famous masterwork appeared in 1867 under the title *La Légende des aventures héroïques, joyeuses et glorieuses d'Ulenspiegel et de Lamme Goedzak au pays de Flandre et ailleurs*. This is a work of literature completely distinct from the historic chapbook discussed above. Although the setting is the sixteenth cen-

tury, De Coster's Till Eulenspiegel is a nineteenth-century man, as shown, for instance, by his typical nineteenth-century anticlericalism.

107 A royal decree of January 26, 1560, prohibited the *Rederijkers* from singing songs or performing plays which had not previously been approved by the authorities. This was in effect censorship. The text of the edict is quoted in F. de Potter and P. Borre, *Geschiedenis der Rederijkerskamer van Veurne* (Ghent, 1870), pp. 33–36.

108 The plays in question and the protocols of the testimony are published in W. van Eeghem's *Drie schandaleuse spelen* and the Brussels City Archives, *Geel Correctie Boeck*, Fol. 491 ff. (mss. div. 182).

109 Van Vaernewijck, Vol. I, pp. 83–84: "*Een visscher en vancht gheen visschen met een bloote hynghene, maer hij bedectse met een haes dat de visschen gheerne eten. Den duvel en stroijt zijn fenijn niet bloot uut, maer decket met die schoone letteren der scriftueren.*"

110 *Cf.* Van Vaernewijck. Also the famous pamphlet *Bienkorf* attributed to Marnix van Sint Aldegonde.

111 See, for instance, the *Schoon liedekens Boeck*.

112 *Pieter Bruegel*, pp. 432, 433, 441, 448, 449, and 467.

113 His very popular works were entitled: *Sinnen-Minne-Beelden* (1619); *Spiegel van den Ouden en Nieuwen Tijdt* (1632); *Trouringh* (1637).

114 E. de Jongh, *Zinne- en Minnebeelden*.

115 Rabelais' first book, entitled *Pantagruel. Les horribles et espoventables faictz & prouesses du tres renomme Pantagruel Roy des Dipsodes, filz du grand geant Gargantua, composez nouvellement par maistre Alcofrybas Nasier*, appeared in Lyons at the time of the November fair of 1532. The second book, *La vie inestimable du grand Gargantua père de Pantagruel*, followed in 1534. These two volumes were combined in a revised edition published in 1542. The *Tiers livre des faictz & dictz Héroïques du noble Pantagruel composez par M. Franç Rabelais docteur en Médecine & Calloier des Isles Hieres* appeared in Paris. The definitive version, *Reveu et corrigé par l'Autheur*, was published in 1552, also in Paris. The first version of the *Quart livre*, containing only eleven chapters, appeared in Lyons in 1548. The complete edition of the *Quart Livre des faicts & Dicts Héroïques du bon Pantagruel*.

Composé par M. François Rabelais docteur en Méde-cine, containing sixty-seven chapters, was published in Paris in 1552. The fragmentary fifth volume of sixteen unnumbered chapters, *L'Isle Sonnante*, is dated 1562. *Le Cinquième & dernier livre des faicts & dicts héroïques du bon Pantagruel, composé par M. François Rabelais, Docteur en Méde-cine* was published in 1564.

116 *Praise of Folly*, translated by H. H. Hudson (Princeton, 1941), p. 70.

Was Bruegel familiar with the original Latin text of *Praise of Folly*? It is entirely possible that he was, since the famous satire was well known during its author's lifetime. Bruegel seems to have had some connections with humanistic circles (Note 50), but can we take this to mean that he knew Latin? In our opinion the data currently available is not sufficient to establish any direct relation between *Praise of Folly* and Bruegel's drawings or paintings. Let us simply say that the work of Erasmus offers certain parallels: for instance, his reference to "this tremendous, powerful beast, the people," or the paragraph where he speaks of the Brabanters: "And rightly do they bruit it about concerning the people of Brabant, that although time brings prudence to others, the older Brabanters grow, the more foolish they are. Yet no other race is more genial than theirs in the ordinary converse of life, and no other race feels so little the misery of old age. Neighbors to the Brabanters, by affinity of temperament as much as by geography, are my Hollanders—for why should I not call mine those who are such eager amateurs of folly that they have won a proverbial name for it, a name they are not ashamed of, but bandy back and forth among themselves" *(Praise of Folly*, p.19*)*.

Huizinga noted this parallel: "As Holbein illustrated the *Moria*, we should wish to possess the *Colloquia* with illustrations by Bruegel, so closely allied is Erasmus' witty, clear vision to that of this great master" *(Erasmus and the Age of Reformation*, New York, 1957, p.114*)*.

117 While nudes appear fairly frequently in Bruegel's engravings, the only instance in the paintings is the one in "The Triumph of Death" (plate p. 115). Certainly the nude was never a major subject for Bruegel.

118 *"Pierre Breughel le Vieux,"* p. 20.

119 See Münz. *The Drawings.*

120 See catalogs of Bastelaer, Lebeer and La-valleye.

121 "The Ripa Grande." Chatsworth, Devon-shire Collection. This drawing, formerly thought to be by Pieter Bruegel the Elder, is now attributed to his son, Jan. Its date must therefore be later. Münz comments: "Egger was the first to introduce this drawing into the literature as the work of Pieter Bruegel, though it is significant that he mentions other drawings of 1559 and 1560 as stylistically related to it. Even today it is still considered to be an authentic work by Pieter Bruegel, but I am convinced that the original attribution to Jan Brueghel the Elder is the correct one. Certain interrelated flourishes in the drawing, and also the schematic division between fore-ground, middle distance and background, support this assumption. The drawing can certainly not be accepted as documentary evidence of Pieter Bruegel's having worked in Rome in 1553" *(The Drawings*, p. 234).

122 Münz's catalog of the drawings lists 154 items: 50 landscapes, 28 compositions and 76 sketches of people, animals, etc., *naer het leuen* (from life). Thus the *naer het leuen* sketches account for half of Bruegel's surviving graphic work. Unlike his regular drawings, they are neither dated nor signed, but they usually bear the notation *"nart het leuen"* in various orthographical variations. Their chronological order is still con-jectural, since the only available criterion is the stylistic one. The study of these sketches, which has much to contribute to a deeper understanding of Bruegel, is hindered by the fact that they are dispersed and reproductions are inconsistent in quality. The draftsmanship in several of them is too weak to be Bruegel's, and the attribution of the entire series has recently been challenged. This whole complex of problems calls for radical reexamination.

See Notes 1 and 25.

123 Lebeer, Nos. 81, 82.

124 "Alpine Landscape Series." The series is undated. All the engravings except the first bear Bruegel's signature as *"inventor"*:

"*Prospectvs Tybvrtinvs*" (Bast. 3)
"*S. Hieronymvs in deserto*" (Bast. 7)
"*Magdalena poenitens*" (Bast. 8)
"Alpine Landscape" (Bast. 9)
"*Insidiosvs avceps*" (Bast. 10)
"*Plavstrvm Belgicvm*" (Bast. 11)
"*Solicitvdo rvstica*" (Bast. 12)
"*Nvndinae rvsticorvm*" (Bast. 13)
"*Evntes in Emavs*" (Bast. 14)
"*Fvga deiparae in Aegyptvm*" (Bast. 15)
"*Pagus nemorosvs*" (Bast. 16)
"*Milites reqviescentes*" (Bast. 17)

The last print in the set, an "Alpine Landscape" (Bast. 18), is slightly larger than the rest. It is undated.

Certain elements seem to have been borrowed from earlier drawings. Lebeer summarizes expert opinion and concludes that the drawing on which the "Alpine Landscape" (Bast. 9) was based can only be the Louvre "Mountain Ravine" (Louvre No. 20720, Münz, No. 13), which is signed "[br]ueghel [15]55." Bastelaer suggests that many of the human figures in the print may have been added by the engraver.

125 "The Ass at School." Berlin, Kupferstich-kabinett. The drawing has the following legend: "*Al reyst den esele ter scholen om leeren—Ist eenen esele, hy en sal gheen peert weder keeren.*" ([It is useless] for the ass to go to school to learn. Since he is an ass, he will not come back a horse.) On the engraving this is preceded by a Latin inscrip-tion: "*Parisios stolidvm si qvis transmittat asellvm—Si hic est asinvs non erit illic eqvvs.*" See Lebeer, No. 17. Münz (No. 129) quotes Tolnay's incorrect translation: "Although the ass goes to school to learn—this one here is [nevertheless] an ass and will never become a horse." He also comments: "Since Brandt's *Narrenschiff*, to which Tolnay draws attention, the ass as a teacher had been a favorite subject for humanistic illustrators." But the drawing shows the ass as pupil, not teacher. It seems more likely that Bruegel is making fun of stupid and inattentive pupils.

The skin of the blood sausage hanging from the saltbox is tied off with a thorn. This was common in Campine until about 1900. See Weyns.

126 "Big Fish Eat Little Fish." Vienna, Alber-tina. The engraving is signed "Hieronijmus Bos inuentor," but according to Lebeer (No. 16), the signature was a later addition. Above the group in the foreground is the word "*Ecce.*" The legend reads: "*Grandibvs exigvi svnt pisces piscibvs esca—Siet sone dit hebbe ick zeer langhe gheweten dat die groote vissen de cleyne eten*" (See, son, I have long known that big fish eat little ones). Both engrav-ing and legend have a sort of Till Eulenspiegel sauciness, and it has been suggested that the use of Bosch's signature may have been dictated by caution. Yet Bruegel signed the original drawing with his own name, and so long as its authenticity remains unchallenged there are no grounds for believing that he was trying to hide behind Bosch's signature.

The earthenware pitcher in the boat was known as a *Jacobakannetje*. See Weyns.

127 "The Temptation of Saint Anthony." Oxford, Ashmolean Museum. The lower edge

of this drawing may have been trimmed. The engraving bears the following legend: "*Mvltae tribvlationes ivstorvm de omnibvs iis liberabit eos Dominvs—Psal. 33.*" According to Tolnay, the head represents the corrupt Church. Münz disagrees (No. 127). Any explanation of scenes like this must depend to some extent on the interpretation of Bosch's work.

Lebeer (No. 14) rightly warns against explanations based on Dutch, German, English or French proverbs but does not exclude the possibility of a satirical meaning: in this case satirization of a one-eyed political state and the plight of a church (in the shape of a fish—I. CH. TH. U.S.) supported by it.

128 "The Sleeping Peddler Robbed by Monkeys." Brussels, Bibliothèque royale. Bastelaer, No. 148. The date 1557 is perhaps a misreading; see Lebeer, No. 53. The legend: "*Qvand le mercier son dovlx repos vevlt prendre, en vente les signes ses marchandises vont tendre*" (When the peddler wants to take a nice rest, the monkeys get ready to sell his wares).

This is an old folktale which, according to the *Mémoires de Messire Olivier de la Marche (ca. 1426–1501)*, first published in 1562, was the didactic subject of a play performed at the wedding of Charles the Bold and Margaret of York in 1468. In his chapter on Herri met de Bles, Van Mander (Note 3) refers to a painting in Amsterdam illustrating this story. This may be the picture now in the Dresden Staatlichen Gemäldegalerie. Van Mander notes that this painting has been taken for a caricature of the Pope. The monkeys robbing the peddler could be "the Martirs or Martinists," followers of Luther, who are squandering the Pope's "goods." Van Mander is skeptical but does not go into his reasons, merely remarking that art should not be satirical.

Some items in the peddler's stock, especially the flute and the spectacles, were symbols of deception in the sixteenth century. Given a certain amount of dialectical skill, one may interpret this print to support the theory that Bruegel sympathized with the Gueux.

The farmhouse in the background has no chimney (*cf.* Cat. No. 36). Other details are also of interest to folklorists: the hobbyhorse, the game bag, the money pouch, and the boxes made of thin wood shavings. See Weyns.

129 "The Seven Deadly Sins." All the drawings have a Dutch legend. These legends are repeated on the engravings (with slight variations of spelling) after a Latin inscription.

"*auaritia.*" London, British Museum. "*Eere beleeftheyt schaemte noch godlyck vermaen | En siet die scrapende giericheyt niet aen*"—"*Qvis metvs avt pvdor est vnqvam properantis avari?*"

"*ira.*" Florence, Uffizi. "*Gramschap doet den mont swillen, en verbittert den moet | sy beroert den geest, en maeckt swert dat bloet*"—"*Ora tvment ira nigrescvnt sangvine venae.*"

"*desidia.*" Vienna, Albertina. The legend has been cut off and pasted on the back. It reads: "*Traechheyt maeckt machteloos en verdroocht | Die senuwen dat de mensch niewers toe en doocht*"—"*Segnities robvr frangit, longa ocia nervos.*"

The print reproduced by Lavalleye (No. 42) is signed "Hieronymus Bos inventor" and does not belong to this series. It does, however, contain some informative illustrations of proverbs.

"*superbia.*" Paris, Lugt Collection. "*Hoouaerdye wert van Godt bouen al ghehaet | Sghelycx wert godt weder an hoouerdye versmaet*"—"*Nemo svperbvs amat svperos, nec amatvr ab illis.*"

"*gula.*" Paris, Lugt Collection. "*Schout dronckenschap ende gulselyck eten | Want ouerdaet doet godt en hem seluen vergeten*"—"*Ebrietas est vitanda inglvviesque ciborvm.*"

"*inuidia.*" Basel, Collection of Baron R. von Hirsch. "*Een onsterffelycke doot es nyt | en wreede peste | Een beest die haer seluen eet met valschen moleste*"—"*Invidia horrendvm monstrvm, saevissima pestis.*"

"*luxuria.*" Brussels, Bibliothèque royale, Print Collection. "*Luxurije stinckt sij is vol onsuijuerheden | Sij breeckt die crachten en sij swackt die leden*"—"*Lvxvria enervat vires, effoeminat artvs.*"

The engraving of "The Last Judgment" may possibly belong to this set (Note 132). For an analysis of the whole series see Stridbeck, pp. 63–126; H. A. Klein; Lebeer, Nos. 18–24; J. G. van Gelder and J. Borms.

130 "The Excision of the Stone of Madness" or "The Dean of Renaix." Brussels, Bibliothèque royale. Print Collection. Like "The Witch of Mallegem" (Note 136), this print recalls Bosch's painting in the Prado entitled "*Meester snijt die keye ras Myne name is lubbert das,*" or "The Cure of Folly." See Tolnay, *Hieronymus Bosch* (Baden-Baden, 1965), pp. 54–55 and 335–36; D. Roggen, "*J. Bosch.*"

In the sixteenth century "*een kei in het hoofd hebben*" (to have a pebble in the head) meant to be mad, and "to have an operation for the pebble" meant to be cured of one's madness. In our opinion Bruegel is satirizing the folly of the world—indeed, the very height of folly: allowing oneself to be taken in by the promise to cure madness by excision of the pebble.

The title "The Dean of Renaix" is derived from a handwritten owner's notation on one of the few surviving prints. See Bastelaer, No. 192.

The text in the scroll attached to the curtain is difficult to decipher. Bastelaer reads it as "*T'HUIS VA[N] [N]ERI or NAERHEYT?*" "*THVIS VA NE*" is clear, but the ending of the last word is practically illegible. Van Gills suggests "*THVIS VAN NEMESIS*"; J.G. de Brouwere (in "*De Deken van Ronse*") "*THUIS VAN NERING*" (The House of Trade)—a reading which certainly fits what is going on in the shop.

The theory that this is also an illustration of the seven deadly sins (see De Brouwere) is not completely convincing, but it may be provisionally accepted, since all those who lead a vicious life are called *sotten en sottinekens* (fools, male and female). *Cf.*, for example, *Een schoon liedekens Boeck*, p. 245.

Lebeer (No. 83) thinks the engraver made a poor copy of Bruegel's drawing.

131 "*Patientia.*" Brussels, Bibliothèque royale, Print Collection. Bastelaer, No. 124. Lebeer, No. 25. Legend: "*Patientia est malorvm qvae avt infervntvr avt accidvnt, cvm aeqvanimitate perlatio. Lact. Inst. Lib. 5.*"

Some details seem to refer to vices, especially licentiousness and gluttony. The symbolic meaning of other details is obscure. For the significance of the crown, the jug and the *spreeuwpotten* (starling jars) see Cat. No. 13 and 30.

132 "The Last Judgment." Vienna, Albertina. Bastelaer, No. 121. Lebeer, No. 25. The drawing has the following legend: "*Compt ghy gebenedyde myns vaeders hier | En gaet ghy vermaledyde in dat eeuwighe vier.*" On the engraving this is preceded by the Latin version: "*Venite Benedicti Patris mei in Regnvm aeternvm | Ite maledicti Patris mei in ignem sempiternvm.*"

This engraving may belong to the series of "The Seven Deadly Sins" (Note 129).

133 "Wedding Dance." Brussels, Bibliothèque royale. Print Collection. The engraving is undated. Bastelaer says: "According to H. Hymans, copies exist dated 1558. This composition must not be confused with the '*Festin de noces rustiques,*' an etching made by Pieter van der Borght in 1559, which bears the signature and address of Barthélémy de Momper" (*Les Estampes*, No. 210, Note 1*).* Thus the only evidence for the date 1558 is a reported statement by Hymans. Hulin de Loo has pointed out (pp. 315–17) that this engraving and the "Wedding Dance" painted in 1566 (Cat. No. 32) are compositionally similar. Lebeer (No. 61) suggests the date 1566.

The engraving has an inset with the following verse: "*Locht op speelman ende latet wel dueren, | Soo langh als de lul ghaet en den rommel vermach: |*

"The Witch of Mallegem." Engraving. See Note 136.

Doet lijse wel dapper haer billen rueren, | Want ten is vrij met haer gheen bruijloft, alden dach. || Nu hebbelijck hannen danst soomen plach ... | Ick luijster na de pijp' en ghy mist den voete: | Maer ons bruijt neemt nu | van dansen verdrach, | Trouwens, tis oock best, want sij gaet vol en soete"—a call to the minstrel to keep the fun going, for it's not every day that there's a wedding to celebrate. The bride is not dancing, "and that is all for the best," says the last line, tongue in cheek, "for she walks full and sweetly." In other words, she is pregnant. Grossmann (*The Paintings*, p. 201) thinks it is probably wrong to interpret these peasant dance scenes as genre pictures without deeper meaning, and the legend seems to support his feeling that they carry a didactic message. See De Jongh, *Zinne- en Minnebeelden.*

In the background relatives and friends are arriving with wedding presents. We recognize a cradle, a saltbox, plates, a spoon, a spit, fire tongs, a three-legged stool, and a distaff. See Weyns. See also Cat. No. 35.

Many paintings based on this composition exist. See Glück, *The Large Bruegel Book*, No. 56.

134 "Twelve Proverbs." Antwerp, Mayer van den Bergh Museum. (Overall size: 29 by 38³/₈ inches.) See J. de Coo, "*Twaalf spreuken.*" Accepted by others as an authentic Bruegel, Grossmann, however, omits it from his catalog. Signature and date are partly effaced and cannot be

definitively deciphered. The montage was certainly not executed in Bruegel's studio.

The work consists of twelve medallions set in an inlaid panel. The medallions were certainly made on a lathe, suggesting that they were originally platelike panels with ornate borders which were later sawed or planed off for mounting. The montage is thought to date from the seventeenth century or possibly the sixteenth. H. D. L. Vervliet dates the inscriptions "shortly after 1560" on the basis of the form of certain capital letters (*"De Twaalf spreekwoorden"*). Several of the medallions are mounted slightly crooked.

135 "Skating Outside Saint George's Gate." United States; Private collection. The drawing is dated and signed but has no legend. An inscription at the top of the second state engraving reads: "*Lvbricitas vitae hvmanae. La lubricité de la vie humaine. De slibberachtigheyt van s menschen leven*" (The slipperiness [uncertainty] of human life). Above the gate are the words "*Porta S. Georgii Antverpiae 1553.*" This date does not coincide with the one on the drawing, which Münz dates 1559 and Glück 1558.

See Bastelaer and Hulin de Loo, pp. 64–66; Bastelaer, No. 205, where the subject is identified; Glück, *The Large Bruegel Book*, No. 78.

Note the child's sled made of a jawbone and propelled by a pronged stick and the man who seems to be playing ice hockey. *Cf.* "Winter

Landscape with Skaters and a Bird Trap," Cat. No. 28.

The second state engraving also has three lines of verse: "*Soo rijdtmen op het ijs t'Antwerpen voor de stadt | D'een herwaerts, d'ander gins, begaept van alle sijen | D'een stronckelt genen valt, die houdt hem recht en prat | Ay leert hier aen dit beeldt, hoe wij ter wereldt rijen | En slibb'ren onsen wegh, d'een mal en d'ander wijs | Op dees verganckhijkheijt veel brooser als het ijs.*" Lebeer is certainly right in saying that "what Bruegel was aiming at was to immortalize, through his own forceful rhythm, the vivid, picturesque character of a scene which inspired so many painters." However, we should not forget that Bruegel's contemporaries never missed a chance to moralize.

136 "The Witch of Mallegem." Brussels, Bibliothèque royale, Print Collection. Bastelaer, Nos. 193 and 28. Legend: "*Ghy lieden van Mallegem wilt nu wel syn gesint | Ick Vrou Hexe wil hier oock wel worden bemint | Om v te genesen ben ick gecomen hier | Tuwen dienste met myn onder meesterssen fier | Compt vry den meesten met den minsten sonder verbeyen | Hebdy de wesp int hooft, oft loteren v de keyen.*" The witch is addressing the people: "People of Mallegem, be of good cheer. I, Mistress Witch, want to be welcome here. I have come to cure you and be of service to you, together with my underlings. Come, all of you, great and small, without delay, if you have a wasp in the head or if the pebbles rattle in it [*i.e.*, if you are mad]."

The text of the diploma, obviously a gibberish of Latin and Dutch, is almost illegible, except for the signature "Jan Kernakel." Under the table sits a man with a padlock on his mouth and a fool's bauble up his sleeve. He is holding up what look like ordinary pebbles. This is probably an allusion to trickery. The expression "*de aap komt uit de mouw*" (the monkey comes out of the sleeve) is still used in modern Dutch to denote that someone's true intentions are being concealed.

In Bruegel's engravings, as in the work of Hieronymus Bosch, we constantly come across an object whose symbolic meaning has never been explained: the partly broken-out eggshell. In the texts this is sometimes referred to as a *vuyl ei*, a rotten egg. Bastelaer and Hulin de Loo (p. 94) believe that it symbolizes the inscrutable, but this seems questionable. Is it somehow associated with foolishness? Here it is probably meant to sum up —in a nutshell or an eggshell—what is being "hatched out" in the scene as a whole. Bastelaer and Hulin de Loo are probably right in associating the beans in the lower right corner with the foolishness of the people coming to the witch to be healed. *Cf.*, for instance, the song in *Een schoon liedekens Boeck* (pp. 245–47) entitled *"Vanden boonkens."* A sixteenth-century German proverb says: "When beans are in flower, there's no lack of fools," and the French say: *"Les fèves sont en fleur, les fous en vigueur"* (the beans are in flower and the fools in full vigor) or *"fèves fleuries temps de folies"* (beans in flower, the season for follies). See F. A. Stoett, No. 199.

Weyns thinks the animal's hoof stuck in the man's cap is a goat's hoof worn as an amulet.

137 "The Festival of Fools." Brussels, Bibliothèque royale, Print Collection. Bastelaer, No. 195; Lebeer, No. 29. Legend: *"Ghij Sottebollen, die met ijdelheyt ghequelt syt, | Compt al ter banen, die lust hebt om rollen, | Al wordet déen syn eere en dander tgelt quyt | De weerelt die vrijft de grootste Sottebollen | Men vint Sottebols, onder elcke nacie, | Al en draghen sij geen sotscappen op haeren cop | Die int dansen hebben, al sulken gracie, | Dat hunnen Sottebol, drayt, ghelyck eenen top | De vuijlste Sottebols, lappent al duer de billen. | Dan sijnder, die d'een dander, metten nuese vatten, | De sulck, vercoopt trompen, en dander brillen, | Daer sy veel, Sottebollen, mede verschatten | Al synder Sottebols, die haer wijsselijck draghen | En van Sottebollen, den rechten sin smaken | Om dat sij in hun selfs sotheijt hebben behaghen | Sal hueren Sottebol alderbest de pin raken."*

The word *"bol"* means "ball," "globe," or, in an extended sense, "head." The engraving and legend center on the word *"zottebol"* (literally, "fool's head"). The legend calls on all madmen to come and play ball. Fools are to be found everywhere—and they don't always wear a foolscap. Some of them are drunkards; others "lead each other by the nose" (*cf.* Cat. No. 6, proverb 44); others sell trumpets and spectacles (*cf.* Notes 128 and 159). But there are also some fools who behave decently. They have recognized the true nature of folly and are content with their condition. Their ball hits the target.

In Bruegel's day the pursuit of folly was actually a way of life for many people. Erasmus of Rotterdam's *Praise of Folly* is an exemplary treatment of a theme so popular as to be almost commonplace. The court had its fools, as did every school of rhetoric. (See E. van Even.) In 1551 the town of Bois-le-Duc paid twelve guilders to Langh Claesken for traveling expenses to the Festival of Fools held in Brussels in July. In 1563 a medal was struck in honor of Jan Walravens, also known as Meester Oomken, with the inscription: *"Maistre Oomken Prince Coronne Des Doctevrs A Quatre Oreilles Aet. 56."* See F. Lyna and Van Eeghem.

138 "The Kermess of Saint George." Brussels, Bibliothèque royale, Print Collection. Bastelaer,

"The Festival of Fools." Engraving. See Note 137.

No. 207; Lebeer, No. 52. The engraving has no legend. On the banner is a scroll with the inscription: *"Laet die boeren haer kermis houuen"* (Let the peasants have their kermess—or "to each his own"). Hulin de Loo (p. 383) mentions an engraving by Pieter van der Borght published in Antwerp in the same year, 1559, with a legend to the effect that drunkards have a fine time at a kermess because they can brawl and fight and get drunk to their heart's content: *"De dronckarts verblijen hem in sulcken feesten | Kijven en vichten en dronken drincken als beesten | Te kermissen de [te?] ghaenne tsy mans oft vrouwen | Daer ome laet de boeren haer kermisse houwen."* This legend occurs again on a contemporary engraving of the same subject. Bruegel's engraving probably has a moralistic overtone too. Early seventeenth-century prints reflect a similar attitude. See, for instance, "Boeren Geselschap" in Bredero's *Boertigh, Amoreus en Aendachtigh Groot Liedtboeck* (1622). See also Note 140.

The wine jug hanging on the wall of The Crown, the tavern at the right, shows that wine is served there. Many of the details are of great documentary value in the study of Brabantine folklore: the bow and arrows on the banner, the stage supported by barrels, the ball and hoop game, the triangular pennant in the pilgrim's cap, the pageant of Saint George and the Dragon, and especially the sword dance. See Weyns and J. Gessler.

139 Small Landscapes of Brabant and Campine. Bibliothèque royale, Print Collection. To quote Bastelaer (No. 35): "These little landscapes were published several times in different sets. The number and type of prints in a set varied, since substitutions were often made.... Bruegel's name is never mentioned; his authorship is first revealed in a copy or in another series of engravings from the same sketches issued by J. C. Visscher [in Amsterdam in 1612]."

First set: *"Mvltifariarvm casvlarvm rurivmque lineamenta cvriose ad vivum expressa. Vele ende seer fraeye ghelegentheden van diuerssche Dorphuysingen, Hoeuen, Velden, Straten, ende dyer ghelijcken, met alderhande Beestkens verciert. Al te samen gheconterfeyt naer dleuen, ende meest rontom Antwerpen gheleghen sijnde. Nu eerst nieuwe ghedruct ende wt laten gaen by Hieronymus Cock, 1559, Cum gratia et priuilegio Regis."* (Bastelaer, No. 19, has a reproduction of the title sheet.)

Second set: *"Praediorvm villarvm et rvsticarvm icones elegantissimae ad vivvm in aere deformatae. Libro secundo, 1561. Hieronymvs Cock excvdebat cvm gratia et privilegio."* (Title sheet reproduced in Bastelaer, No. 33.)

Visscher's edition is entitled: *"Regiunculae et villae aliquot ducatus Brabantiae, a P. Breugelio, delineatae, et in pictorum gratiam, a Nicolao Joannis Piscatore excusae et in lucem editae., Amstelodami 1612."*

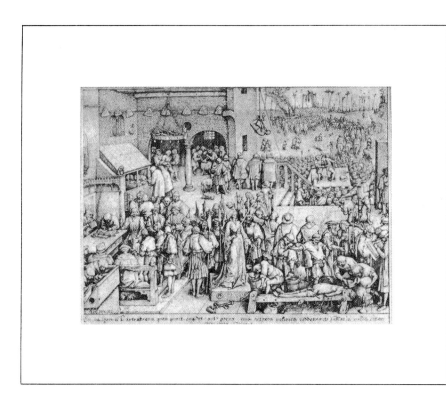

"Justitia." Pen drawing. Brussels, Bibliothèque royale, Print Collection. See Note 141.

"Fides." Pen drawing. Amsterdam, Rijksmuseum, Print Collection. See Note 141.

140 "The Kermess of Hoboken." Formerly London, Oppenheimer Collection. The drawing has no legend. In reproduction (Münz, plate 138) the banner inscription is practically illegible except for the word *"hoboken,"* but the inscription in the engraving: *"Dit is de Gulde van hoboken"* (This is the Guild of Hoboken [a village near Antwerp]) is obviously different. The engraving (Bastelaer, No. 208) has the following legend: *"Die boeren verblijen hun in sulken feesten | Te dansen springhen en dronckendrincken als beesten | Sij moeten die kermissen onderhouwen | Al souwen sij vasten en steruen van kauwen | Bartolomeus de mumpere Excud."* This is so similar to the legend on Pieter van der Borght's 1559 engraving (Note 138) that they might well have been written by the same person.

Lebeer challenges the authenticity of the drawing *(Miscellanea L. van Puyvelde,* Brussels, 1949). Cf. Glück, *The Large Bruegel Book,* No. 79. See also Note 141 and Cat. No. 30.

141 "The Seven Virtues." Except for *"Fortitudo"* all the drawings have a legend in Latin, which is repeated (with minor orthographical variations) on the engravings:

"Fides." Amsterdam, Rijksmuseum. *"Fides maxime a nobis conseruanda est praecipue in religionem, quia deus prior et potentior est quam homo."*

"Spes." Berlin, Kupferstichkabinett. *"Iucundissima est spei persuasio et vite imprimis Necessaria inter tot aerumnas peneq. intolerabilis."*

"Charitas." Rotterdam, Boymans-van Beuningen Museum. *"Speres tibi accidere quod alteri accidit ita denum excitaberis ad opem ferendam si sumpseris eius animum qui opem tunc in malis constitutus implorat."*

"Iustitia." Brussels, Bibliothèque royale, Print Collection. *"Scopus legis est aut ut eum quem punit emendet, aut poena eius ceteros meliores reddet aut sublatis malis ceteri securiores viuant."*

"Prvdencia." Brussels, Musées royaux des Beaux-Arts. *"Si prudens esse cupis in futurum prospectum ostende et quae possunt contingere animo tuo cuncta propone."*

"Fortytvdo." Rotterdam, Boymans-van Beuningen Museum. The legend (?) on the drawing is written in illegible characters. The legend on the engraving reads: *"Animum vincere, iracvndiam cohibere caeteraq. vitia et affectvs cohibere vera fortitudo est."*

"Temperancia." Rotterdam, Boymans-van Beuningen Museum. The inscription is in mirror image: *"Videndum ut nec voluptati dediti prodigi et luxuriosi appareamus, nec auara tenacitati sordidi aut obscuri existamus."*

The engraving of "Christ in Limbo" (Note 142) may belong to this set. For an analysis of the whole series see Van Gelder and Borms, also Lebeer, Nos. 31–37.

Commentary on "The Seven Virtues" is diverse. Tolnay's interpretation of several of the scenes (in *Pierre Bruegel l'Ancien*) is hard to reconcile with their traditional Christian imagery. It is therefore important to note that the legends are quite in keeping with iconographical tradition. Perhaps the satirical tone of some of the scenes is due to Bruegel's realism, which irrepressibly brings out the characteristic behavior of all his models.

Bruegel has depicted all these allegorical subjects except "*Fortitudo*" in an everyday setting. Once again many of the details are of great interest: the sickle with a notched blade, the wooden spade tipped with iron, the bread basket, the tub chair, the leather fire buckets, the hook attached to an extension pole for pulling out burning thatch, the skittle-shaped saltbox, etc. See Weyns and T. Theuwissen. "*Iustitia*" might be called an encyclopedia of contemporary law enforcement. See J.G. de Brouwere, *De Gerechtigheid*.

142 "Christ in Limbo". Vienna, Albertina. The legend on the drawing reads: "*Toblite o porte capita vestea attolimine fores sempiterne et ingredietur Rex ille gloriosus.*" It was copied on the engraving (Bastelaer, No. 115; Lebeer, No. 38). Van Gelder and Borms (p. 105) suggest that the date 1561 may be a later addition.

143 The Landjuweel was a national theatre contest held by the *Rederijkerskamer*, or schools of rhetoric—a tradition which still survives today. The Landjuweel of August 3, 1561, in which fourteen schools of rhetoric participated, was an especially successful one. The set subject was: "*Wat den mensch aldermeest tot conste verwect*" (What makes man most responsive to art?). The texts were published in 1562: "*Spelen van sinne vol scoone moralisacien vvtleggingen ende bediedenissen op alle loeflijcke consten vvaer inne men claerlijck in eenen spieghel/Figuerlijck... mach aenschouwen hoe nootsakelijck ende dienstelijck die selue consten allen menschen zijn. Ghespeelt met octroy der Con. Ma. binnen der stadt van Andtwerpen op d'Lant Juweel by die veerthien cameren van Retorijcken die hen daer ghepresenteert hebben den derden dach Augusti int Jaer ons Heeren M.D.LXJ. Op die Questie vvat den mensch aldermeest tot conste vervvect... Tot Antwerpen by M. Willem Siluius / Drucker der Con. Ma. An. M.CCCCC.LXJJ.*"

The pages are not numbered. These texts are of great value in increasing our understanding of the milieu in which Bruegel's art achieved such popularity. See Van Even.

"The Poor Kitchen." Engraving. See Note 146.

"The Rich Kitchen." Engraving. See Note 146.

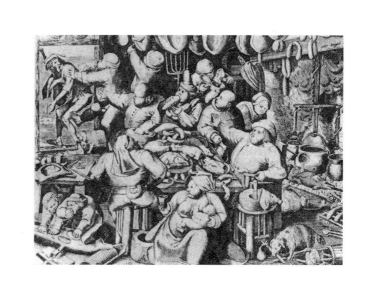

144 "Towers and Gates of Amsterdam." Three drawings, one in the Boston Museum of Fine Arts, two in the Besançon Musée des Beaux-Arts. None of the drawings has a legend. See C. P. van Eeghen, "*Poorten en Torens van Amsterdam*" in *Algemeen Handelsblad*, December 3, 1935; Münz, Nos. 46–48.

145 "The Blind Men." Berlin, Kupferstich-kabinett. There is no doubt about the middle figure, but are the others really blind? Despite the title by which this drawing is generally known, its meaning is obscure.

146 "The Poor Kitchen" and "The Rich Kitchen." Brussels, Bibliothèque royale, Print Collection. These engravings of a subject which probably dates back to an earlier age were re-published several times. See Bastelaer, Nos. 154 to 163; Lebeer, Nos. 55, 56. The engraver seems to have made some mistakes in copying the French legends: "*On [=ou] Maigre-os le pot mouue, est [?] vu [=un] pouure Conuiue | Pomre [pour ce], a Grasse-cuisine iraij, tant que ie viue || Daer magherman die pot roert is een arm ghasterije | dus loop ick nae de vette Cuecken met herten blije.*" "*Hors dici Maigre-dos a eune' hideuse mine | Tu nas que' faire ici Car cest Grasse-Cuisine || Vuech magherman uan hier hoe hongherich ghij siet | Tis hier al uette Cuecken ghi en dient hier niet.*"

The expression "*daer roert magherman de pot*" (there Bare Bones stirs the pot) is a common metaphor for frugal living in sixteenth-century literature.

We should not be tempted to read into these prints an attack on social injustice. We know from a satirical play that Bare Bones was the father of Saint Reynuyt (Note 71) and that his mother was Vrou Lorts. In Middle Dutch "*lortsen*" means "to be dishonest." The same text tells us that Vrou Lorts lost her virtue in the cowshed (*Geneuchlijcke dichten*, p. 114).

The figure of Bare Bones in this print is strongly reminiscent of the Alchemist (Note 86).

Weyns gives additional information on some of the domestic articles: the *bakermat*, a sort of cradle for nurse and infant, the ladle and roasting pan, the kettles hanging from the iron frame in the hearth, the candle basket, the spit, the grater, the mortar, the cauldron, the oil lamp, the round table *(rondeel)*, and the three-legged stool *(driestal)*. These two prints also tell us something about the simple food of the poor: mussels, turnips and bread, as well as the type of dishes served at feasts: roast goose, suckling pig and pork, ham and sausages. See Grauls, *Volkstaal*.

147 "The Pilgrimage of the Epileptics to the Bridge of Sint-Jans-Molenbeek." Vienna, Albertina. "*Vertooninge Hoe de Pelgerimmen, op S. Iansdagh, buyten Brussel, tot Meulebeeck danssen moeten; ende als sy over dese Brugh gedanst hebben, ofte gedwongen werden op dese volgende maniere, dan schijnen sy, voor een Iaer, van de vallende Sieckte, genesen te zijn. Voor aen gaen dese Speellieden ofte Moeselaers, speelende op Sack-pijpen; daer nae volgen de Pelgrims, die met stercke Huyslieden gevat worden, seer ongaerne tegen haren wil (gelijck in de tweede ende derde volghende Figuere vertoont wert) som krijtende en roepende; maer komende ontrent de Brugge, soo keerense haer om, ende gebruycken groot tegenweer; maer gevat zijnde, werden over de Brugge geheft ende gedragen; over zijnde sitten neder als vermoeyt wesende: ende dan komen de Huyslieden van dier plaets, haer lavende, en wat warms in-gevende: ende is soo dit werck voleyndt. Seer aerdigh uyt-gebeelt door den uytnemenden konstigen Schilder Pieter Breugel. Gesneden ende gedruckt ten Huyse van Henricus Hondius, in 's Graven-Hage, 1642.*" Bastelaer, No. 222; Lebeer, Nos. 91–93.

This drawing (Münz, No. A55) with an inscription and the signature "bruegel.m.ccccc.lxiiij" (*i.e.,* 1564) is now believed to be a copy, probably by Pieter Bruegel the Younger.

Although these drawings of Bruegel's are known to us only through the engravings made after them by Hondius, they are of great documentary value. Bruegel, who had just moved to Brussels, had been an eyewitness of the extraordinary pilgrimage of epileptic women to Molenbeek-Saint-Jean. Every year on Midsummer Day these women had to cross the bridge in order to be cured, at least for the coming year.

148 Ship Series. Brussels, Bibliothèque royale, Print Collection. Lebeer (Nos. 41–50) discusses the number of prints in this series (ten, eleven, twelve or thirteen) and dates them between 1561 and 1562. See also F. Smekens, J. van Beylen and O. Buyssens.

149. "The Fall of the Magician Hermogenes." Amsterdam, Rijksmuseum. The drawing (Münz, No. 150) has no legend. The engraving made from it has the inscription: "*Idem impetravit a Deo vt magvs a demonibvs discerperetvr.*" The other engraving of this subject has the legend: "*Divvs Iacobvs diabolicis praestigiis ante magvm sistitvr.*" See Bastelaer, Nos. 117, 118; Lebeer, Nos. 57, 58. The subject comes from the *Legenda aurea* of Jacobus de Voragine.

150 "Spring." Vienna, Albertina. This drawing (Münz, No. 151) is inscribed: "*de lenten. Mert April Meij*" (spring. March, April, May). It prob-

ably belongs to a series of "The Seasons" completed after Bruegel's death by Hans Bol. We do not know whether Bol worked from Bruegel's sketches or not. See Lebeer, No. 77.

Because of its date this drawing is related to the famous paintings of "The Months," one of which is missing. But there is no reason to assume that this is a preliminary sketch for the missing picture, since it is compositionally quite different from the paintings. On the other hand it certainly has features in common with the drawing and engraving of "Summer" dated 1568 (Note 160).

151 "The Calumny of Apelles." London, British Museum. This drawing (Münz, App. 8) was discovered in 1959. See Note 17.

152 "The Parable of the Wise and Foolish Virgins." Brussels, Bibliothèque royale, Print Collection. The engraving is undated. No drawing for it is known, so any tentative date must be based on stylistic evidence. Lebeer (No. 39) proposes 1560–61. The legend reads: "*Date nobis de oleo vestro, qvia lampades nostra extingvntvr | Neqvaqvam, neqvando non svfficiat nobis et vobis math. 25.*" The inscription on the scroll says: "*Ecce sponsus uenit exit obùiam ei.*" On the staircase are the words "*Non noui uos.*" See Bastelaer, No. 123.

The illustrations of articles used in spinning are of great interest to folklorists. See Weyns.

153 "The Parable of the Good Shepherd." Brussels, Bibliothèque royale, Print Collection. On the engraving is the legend: "*Hic tvto stabvlate viri, svccedite tectis; | me pastore ovivm, ianva laxa patet | Qvid latera, avt cvlmen perrvmpitis? Ista lvporvm | Atqve fvrvm lex est, qvos mea cavla fvgit.*" Bastelaer, No. 122; Glück, *The Large Bruegel Book*, No. 80; Lebeer, No. 59. Note the bellwether in the right foreground.

We see no reason to read any political implications into this picture. Van Vaernewijck (Vol. III, p. 213) records an edict of January 12, 1567 (*i.e.,* 1568), directing town dwellers and villagers to protect their "shepherds," who are constantly threatened by bands of dissidents. According to these official documents, the authorities feared that the shepherds (the priests) might be forced to abandon their defenseless flocks (their parishioners) to the wolves. In another passage Van Vaernewijck castigates the priest of Hazebrouck for neglecting his duties as a good shepherd. Obviously Bruegel's print can be interpreted in line with these texts, but we must bear in mind that the engraving is earlier than the edict.

154 "The Painter and the Connoisseur." Vienna, Albertina. Münz, No. 126. Four old copies of this

drawing exist, of varying quality. It is not surprising that this sketch of an artist who obviously takes a slightly sardonic view of his patron, the connoisseur, and the public in general should have been taken for a self-portrait. Attractive as this theory is, especially when we look at the drawing in the context of Bruegel's work as a whole, there is little positive evidence to support it. See Stridbeck, *Bruegelstudien*, pp. 15–42; Tolnay, *"Le Peintre et l'Amateur."*

155   "The Marriage of Mopsus and Nissa." New York, Metropolitan Museum. The drawing is glued to a wood block on which some cutting has already been done. The engraving based on the drawing, made by Pierre van der Heyden in 1570 (Bastelaer, No. 216, Lebeer, Nos. 79, 80) has the following legend: *"Mopso Nisa datvr, qvid non; speremvs amantes."* Pursuing a suggestion by M. J. G. Boekenoogen, Grossmann interprets the subject, which occurs again in "The Fight Between Carnival and Lent" (Cat. No. 7), as the proverbial *"vuile bruid,"* the dirty bride or the slut *(The Paintings*, pp. 190–91). See Bastelaer and Hulin de Loo, p. 105; Bastelaer, No. 215.

156   "The Masquerade of Ourson and Valentine." Brussels, Bibliothèque royale, Print Collection. The drawing for this woodcut was probably one of a pair, a counterpart of "The Wedding of Mopsus and Nissa" (Note 155). The subject is taken from a chapbook which first appeared in Lyons in 1489 and was republished many times, though there was no Dutch edition until 1640, some seventy years after Bruegel's death. The subject occurs again in "The Fight Between Carnival and Lent" (Cat. No. 7). See Bastelaer and Hulin de Loo, p. 105; Bastelaer, No. 215; Lebeer, No. 60.

157   "Hunting the Wild Hare." Brussels, Bibliothèque royale, Print Collection. This is the only surviving print that can be identified as Bruegel's own work. Bastelaer, No. 1; Lebeer, No. 63.

158   F. Goedthals, *"Les proverbes anciens flamengs et françois correspondants de sentence les vns aux autres colligés & ordonnés par M. François Goedthals. A Anvers. De l'Imprimerie de Christofle Plantin. M.D.LXVIII. Avec Privilège."* In his dedication to the "grand Baillif de Gand" Plantin refers to the author as a citizen of Ghent. This little work is invaluable for an understanding of Bruegel's illustrations of proverbs.

159   "Twelve Flemish Proverbs." Amsterdam' Rijksmuseum and Brussels, Bibliothèque royale. Each medallion is surrounded by a border which

"The Calumny of Apelles." Pen drawing. London, British Museum. See Notes 151 and 17.

"Summer." Pen drawing. Hamburg, Kunsthalle. See Note 160.

carries a legend explaining what it symbolizes or the saying it illustrates. Bastelaer, Nos. 167–86; Lavalleye, plates 151–62; Lebeer, Nos. 65–76. Grauls rightly points out ("*Ter verklaring*," pp. 151–53 and 155–56) that Bastelaer misinterprets the meaning of two of the prints: the one with the misleading caption "*Tout mercier vante sa marchandise*" (every peddler praises his own wares [Bast. No. 175]) and the one entitled "*Le mercier sans soin*" (the careless peddler [Bast. 183]). Lavalleye corrects these false titles. According to the legends, the first print depicts the quack whose wares are "nets, trumpets and flutes." In the second Bruegel seems to be ridiculing the trickster tricked: in this case a man who thought he had married a rich wife only to find that he has been deceived.

160 "Summer." Hamburg, Kunsthalle. Münz, No. 152. This drawing belongs to the series of "The Seasons" (Note 150). For an analysis of this masterful drawing, see Vanbeselaere, p. 88; Bastelaer, No. 202; Lebeer, No. 78.

161 "The Beekeepers." Berlin, Kupferstich-kabinett. Münz, No. 154. According to the in-scription, the drawing illustrates the proverb "*dye den nest weet dye weeten dyen Roft dy heeten*" (he who knows where the nest is has the knowledge; he who robs it has the nest. *Cf.* Cat. No. 39). Even assuming that the inscription was added in Bruegel's time—and several scholars dispute this— this particular proverb does not seem to offer an entirely satisfactory explanation. Is there not a closer analogy in another proverb found on con-temporary engravings: "*Die honing wil eten moet lijden dat hem de bijen steken*" (anyone who wants to eat honey must risk being stung)?

162 "The Drunkard Shoved into the Pigsty." Brussels, Bibliothèque royale, Print Collection. Bastelaer and Hulin de Loo, p. 252; Bastelaer, No. 164; Lebeer, No. 64.

163 According to Van Mander, Bruegel adopted from Jan de Hollander (Jan van Amstel) a method of using the reflective effect of the white ground color of his panel: "*de manier van al swadderende op de Penneelen oft doecken de gronden mede te laten spelen | het welck Brueghel seer eyghentlijck nae volghde*" (*Schilderboeck*, ed. of 1604, p. 215). Such laboratory analysis of Bruegel's work as has been undertaken confirms what Van Mander says. Bruegel's color technique is simple: often he uses a single layer of paint, occasionally two. In some cases he has used a ground of lead white. The following pigments have been identified: lead white, azurite, ochre, bone black, smalt, madder lake, and cinnabar. The mixtures he used are simple ones of two or—rarely—three pigments. For instance, he makes green out of azurite, ochre and sometimes bone black.

Bruegel's technique of painting is on the whole close to the standard Netherlandish technique of his time, but his application of it was masterful. See Cat. No. 44.

164 Glück (*The Large Bruegel Book*) and Gross-mann (*The Paintings*) seem to have been the first to mention data obtained from X-ray photo-graphs, but their books contain no reproductions.

Little has been published on Bruegel's painting technique. De Coo touches on it in his article on the "Twelve Proverbs," but the authenticity of the work he is discussing is doubtful.

A theoretical plan for laboratory analysis of Bruegel's work was published in the journal *Vlaanderen*, 103, January–February, 1969.

THE PAINTINGS OF PIETER BRUEGEL

"Landscape with the Fall of Icarus"

Ovid tells the dramatic story of the fall of Icarus in Book VIII of his *Metamorphoses*, mentioning the fisherman, the shepherd and the peasant who go quietly about their work and fail to see the soaring Icarus plunge into the sea:

74

Far off, far down, some fisherman is watching / As the rod dips and trembles over the water, / Some shepherd rests his weight upon his crook, / Some plowman on the handles of the plowshare, / And all look up, in absolute amazement,/ At those air borne above …

And the boy /

Thought *This is wonderful!* and left his father, / Soared higher, higher, drawn to the vast heaven, / Nearer the sun, and the wax that held the wings / Melted in that fierce heat, and the bare arms / Beat up and down in air, and lacking oarage / Took hold of nothing. *Father!* he cried, and *Father!* / Until the blue sea hushed him, the dark water / Men call the Icarian now. And Daedalus, / Father no more, called "Icarus, where are you! /Where are you, Icarus? Tell me where to find you!" / And saw the wings on the waves …

(Ovid, *Metamorphoses*, translated by Rolfe Humphries, Bloomington, 1961, pp. 188-89.)

Bruegel's presentation of the scene is calm and static. The terrifying depth of Icarus' fall is brought out by the terraced foreground, where the plowman is cutting his furrows. On the mirror-smooth sea Bruegel has set a ship with bellying sails, imperturbably following its course, although Icarus has just plunged headlong into the water close by. The picture's deeper theme is presented quietly and metaphorically. The multilevel exposition shows that Bruegel was no stranger to Humanistic thought. The message—a warning against flying too high—would have been quite familiar to his contemporaries.

75   Catalog No. 3. Plates pp. 74–81.

"Every figure is linked to the central happening in a particular way. As our eye follows the throng of people in the left half of the picture from foreground to background, we see that this receding movement is accompanied by a progressive lowering of excitement over the event occurring in the foreground. Here Bruegel shows his understanding of the psychology of a crowd stirred by a happening. The event—the adoration of the kings—is communicated from foreground to background through individual figures and groups. The various groups all reflect a different mood, and here too there is a certain heightening of intensity. In the foreground, around the kneeling king in the ermine mantle, the amazement of the spectators expresses itself chiefly in the gesture of hands and arms raised in wonder or in prayer. Farther back in the crowd the astonishment decreases and finally yields to an indeterminate, almost passive waiting."

GOTTHARD JEDLICKA

82

"The Adoration of the Kings"

This unsigned and undated tempera painting has suffered great damage over the years, but perhaps its poor condition actually adds to its special charm. The texture of the canvas is clearly visible. A seemingly endless throng is crowding in from two directions. Facial expressions have been painted with particular care. The principal group—the Virgin and Child—is small and understated. Behind them stands Saint Joseph, looking on. Against an empty background we see the traditional ox and ass, the latter tossing its head and baring its teeth as it neighs uncannily.

83   Catalog No. 4. Plates pp. 82–85.

"Landscape with the Parable of the Sower"

There had been important landscape painters before Bruegel—Joachim Patenier and his pupil Herri met de Bles, for instance—and Bruegel borrowed from them. A characteristic of his landscape is that man and his activities are linked with nature and at the same time shown in conflict with it. Here a broad river landscape opens into a deep bay. In the foreground of this land of promise a sower is scattering his seed. This is not an incidental detail: the picture illustrates the parable of the sower recounted in Luke 8:5–15:

> A sower went out to sow his seed: and as he sowed, some fell by the wayside; and it was trodden down, and the
> fowls of the air devoured it. And some fell upon a rock; and as soon as it was sprung up, it withered away, because
> it lacked moisture. And some fell among thorns; and the thorns sprang up with it, and choked it. And other fell on

good ground, and sprang up, and bore fruit a hundredfold. And when he had said these things, he cried, He that hath ears to hear, let him hear.

And his disciples asked him, saying, What might this parable be?

And he said, Unto you it is given to know the mysteries of the kingdom of God: but to others in parables; that seeing they might not see, and hearing they might not understand. Now the parable is this: The seed is the word of God. Those by the wayside are they that hear; then cometh the devil, and taketh away the word out of their hearts, lest they should believe and be saved. They on the rock are they, which, when they hear, receive the word with joy; and these have no root, which for a while believe, and in time of temptation fall away. And that which fell among thorns are they, which, when they have heard, go forth, and are choked with cares and riches and pleasures of this life, and bring no fruit to perfection. But that on the good ground are they, which in an honest and good heart, having heard the word, keep it, and bring forth fruit with patience.

87   Catalog No. 5. Plates pp. 86–87.

"The Netherlandish Proverbs"

Nearly a hundred Netherlandish proverbs are cataloged in this picture, which used to be known as "The Blue Cloak" or "The Folly of the World." A setting of buildings, hills, river, and plain is filled with innumerable groups of figures, all illustrating a proverb or saying. On the wall of the house at the left "the world turned upside down" immediately catches the eye, stating the theme of the whole picture.

Catalog No. 6. Plates pp. 88–101.

"On his panel depicting Netherlandish proverbs Bruegel has compiled an encyclopedia of the proverbial wisdom of his people."

WILHELM FRAENGER

He who wants to make his way through the world has to squirm.

95

"At that time—on March 25, 1568—the Duke of Alba issued an order to all officers and men who were quartered in houses of good repute to stop taking girls of easy virtue home with them and thus make an end of the nuisance. Many people thought the order had been issued only because Easter was approaching; thereafter the merrymaking would go on as before. And so a flaxen beard is stuck on our Lord and Saviour. But the soldiers refuted this allegation and said the order they had received was very strict."

MARCUS VAN VAERNEWIJCK

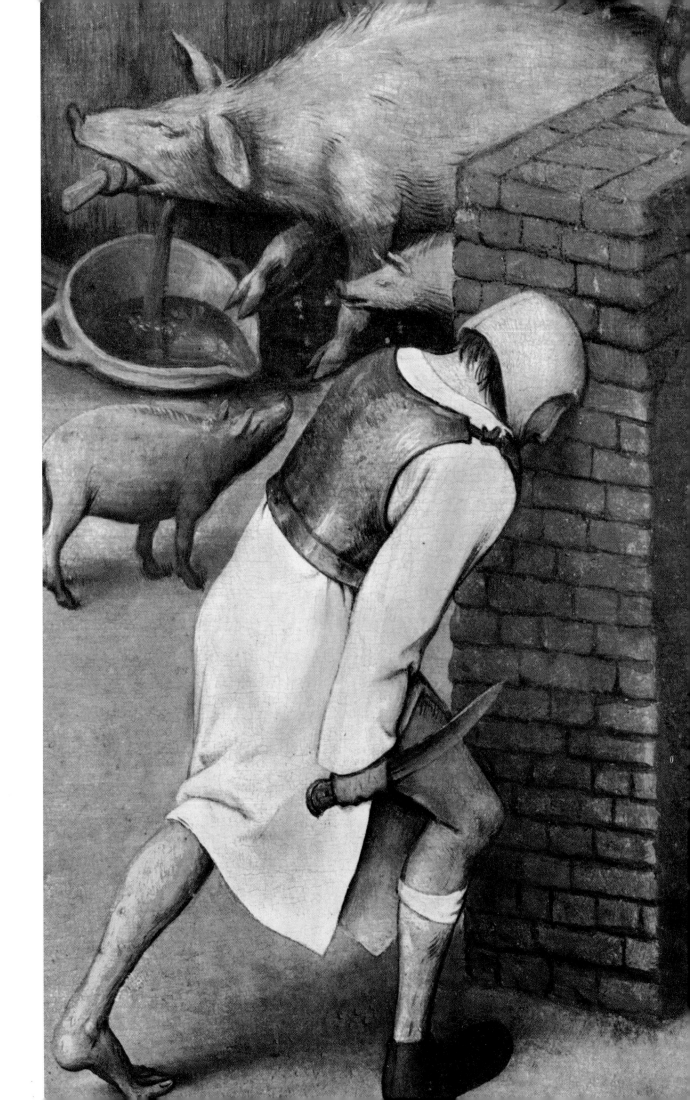

"The Fight Between Carnival and Lent"

The underlying principle of the composition is antithesis. Carnival has its citadel in the Blue Ship tavern on the left, while the followers of austere Lent come streaming out of the church at the right. The contrast is delightfully exploited. Carnival is personified by a rotund Prince of Carnival riding on an enormous barrel on runners, which is being pushed along by his retinue. The Carnival fools are dressed in bizarre costumes draped with strings of eggs, waffles or fritters. One of their duties is to make a racket with an extraordinary assortment of instruments. In the background Carnival plays such as *The Story of Ourson and Valentine* and *The Marriage of Mopsus and Nissa* are

being performed. The boisterous fun spreads through the little town from street to street; even the cripples seem to be affected by it. The scene around gaunt, grim Lent is the opposite. Lent is a scrawny old woman sitting on a straight wooden chair on a creaking platform, which is being pulled along by a friar and a nun. The weapon she holds is a long baker's paddle with two herrings on it. She wears an old beehive on her head; at her feet are meager Lenten foods. Her retinue is made up of good little girls and boys, poor people, pillars of the church and society, and almsgivers. Beside the fish tank her Lenten fare is being prepared.

The confrontation recalls traditional humorous debates in which each participant states his case and the spectator is left to decide whose side he favors.

Catalog No. 7. Plates pp. 102–5.

"Children's Games"

In this picture a whole town has been given over to the children as a playground. Some eighty-four games have been identified, most of them—playing with dolls, for instance—still popular today. We see children blowing bubbles, dressing up, swinging, turning somersaults and cartwheels, riding hobbyhorses, rolling hoops, throwing knives, playing mounted tug-of-war, leapfrog and kick-the-pot, walking on stilts, climbing, wrestling, playing hide-and-seek and follow-the-leader, doing acrobatics, playing with tops, paddling, and swimming. We are struck by the serious expressions of these gnomelike figures, many of whom are imitating adult activities such as wedding

processions or christenings. In his typical metaphorical fashion Bruegel is calling attention to the strangeness and perversity of human ways. Van Vaernewijck said that "children are like monkeys: they want to imitate everything," and this was a widely held view of the child's nature. To quote Jacob Cats: "The world and all its activity is but

a children's game." This picture is probably connected with the "ages of man" theme; Bruegel may have planned a whole set of pictures like the "Series of the Months."

Catalog No. 8. Plates pp. 106–9.

"The Triumph of Death"

Bruegel often pointed out the follies of the world, although he recognized that all his warnings were in vain. Here, in this powerful *memento mori*, his vision achieves its most splendid and terrible expression. This world of sinners and fools who heed no warnings has been overrun by Death, but he is no longer the figure with the scythe of the traditional Dance of Death. Now the entire cosmos, doomed to destruction, teams with death and dead bodies. Death breaks through the face of the clock to point out how late it is. His armies are on the march; his knights pass the final judgment, and his hosts carry it out. In his myriad forms he is everywhere, accompanied by his cartloads of skulls and bones. No one is spared: neither king nor cardinal nor mother with child. Even the dead seem doomed to suffer death. Corpses struggle in the river. The air is full of pestilence and fire. Here and there a cross reaches toward the sky, but it can no longer offer any refuge. Much more numerous are the gallows and the torture wheels. Even far out at sea catastrophes are occurring. At the edge of the picture, removed from the turmoil, stands a festive table, now abandoned. The fool is trying to creep under it. A valiant young man draws his sword to defend himself. Two lovers lean back, absorbed in their song, but behind them too Death strikes up his music.

Catalog No. 14. Plates pp. 110–35.

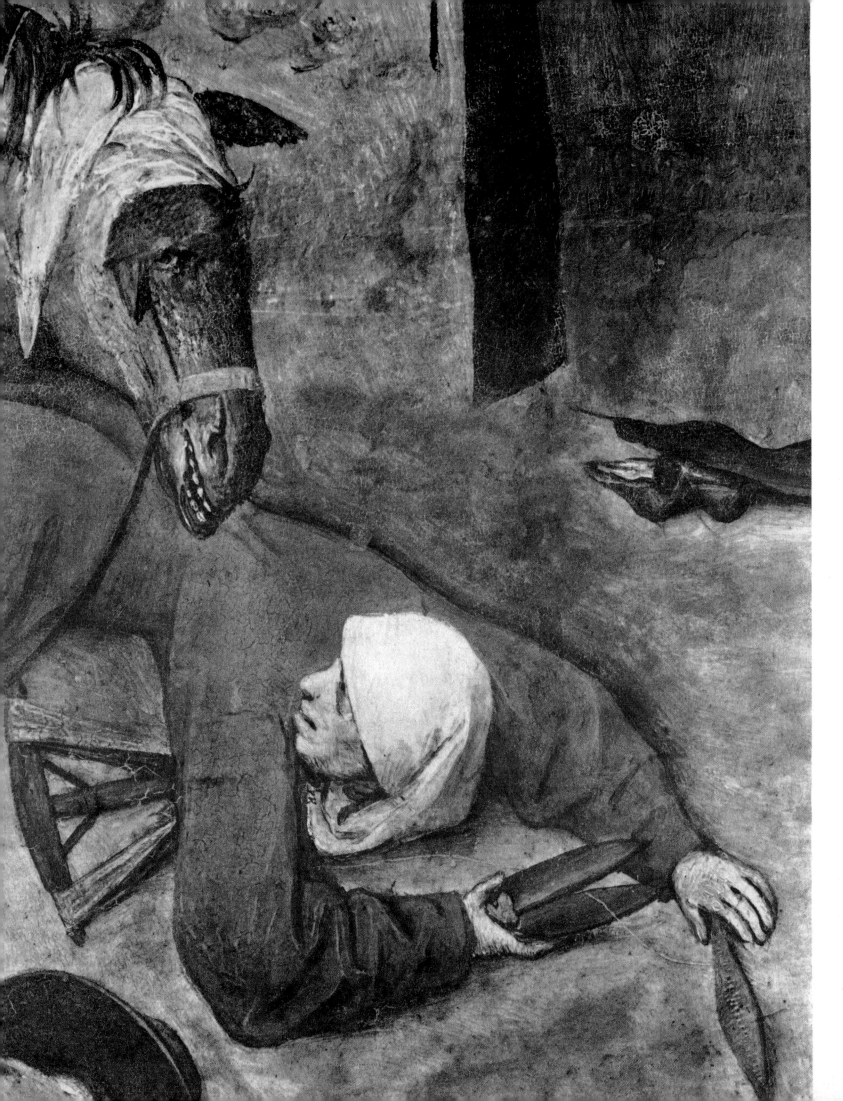

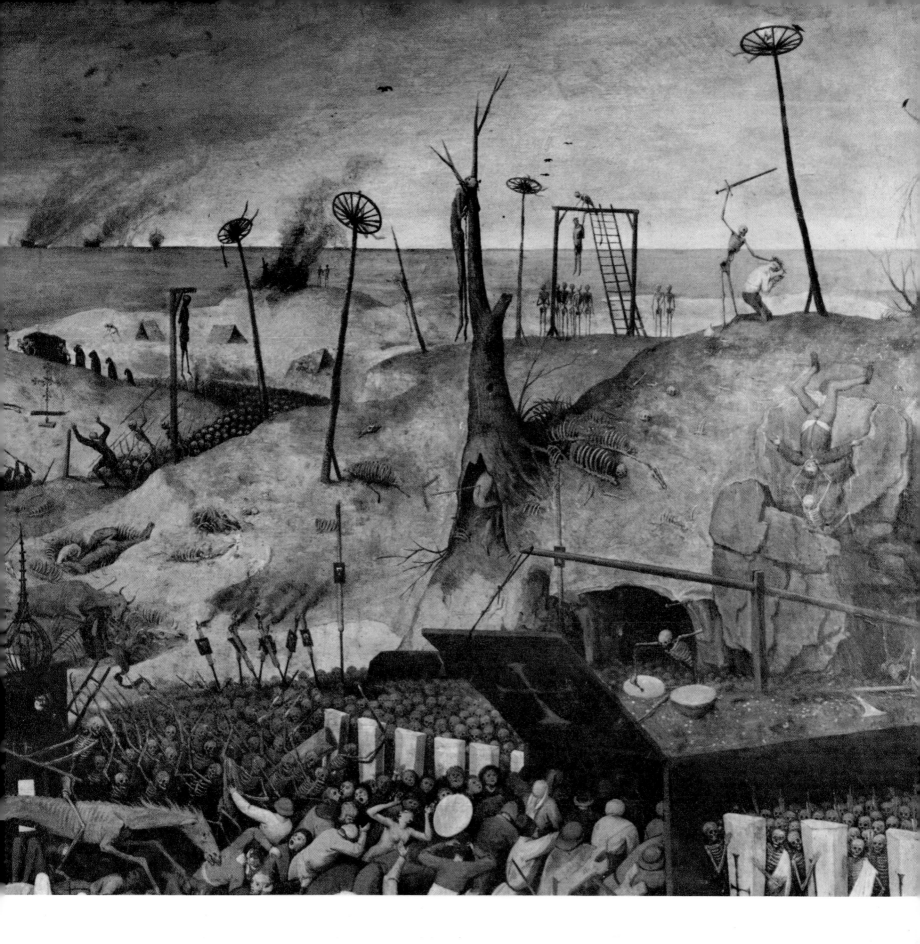

"The Resurrection of Christ"
Catalog No. 11. Plates pp. 136–37.   136

"The Fall of the Rebel Angels"

The Brussels "Fall of the Angels" stands in a great pictorial tradition. Its intricate composition was anticipated by late Gothic painters and engravers like Martin Schongauer. Such compositions offered infinite scope for ornamental traceries of tangled bodies and virtuoso displays of demons, monsters and bizarre imaginative creations, and for this reason were as attractive to the artist as to his audience. Hieronymus

138

Bosch also painted extraordinarily forceful visions of this kind, and a comparison of the two artists reveals both Pieter Bruegel's capacities and his limits. As Lampsonius asked rhetorically: "Who may be this other Jeroon Bos, who came in this world again, who pictures to us the fantastic conceptions of his own master again, who is most able with the brush, who is even surpassing his master?"

The subject of "The Fall of the Angels" is pride punished—an admonition to humility—and it can be argued that Bruegel's "realistic" treatment of detail diverts attention from the deeper meaning of this divine punishment. Our curiosity leads us to examine minutely all the cryptic details of the picture, and we come to understand what Van Mander meant when he said that Bruegel "made many weird scenes and drolleries, for which reason he was often called Peter the Droll."

Catalog No. 12. Plates pp. 138–51.

141

145

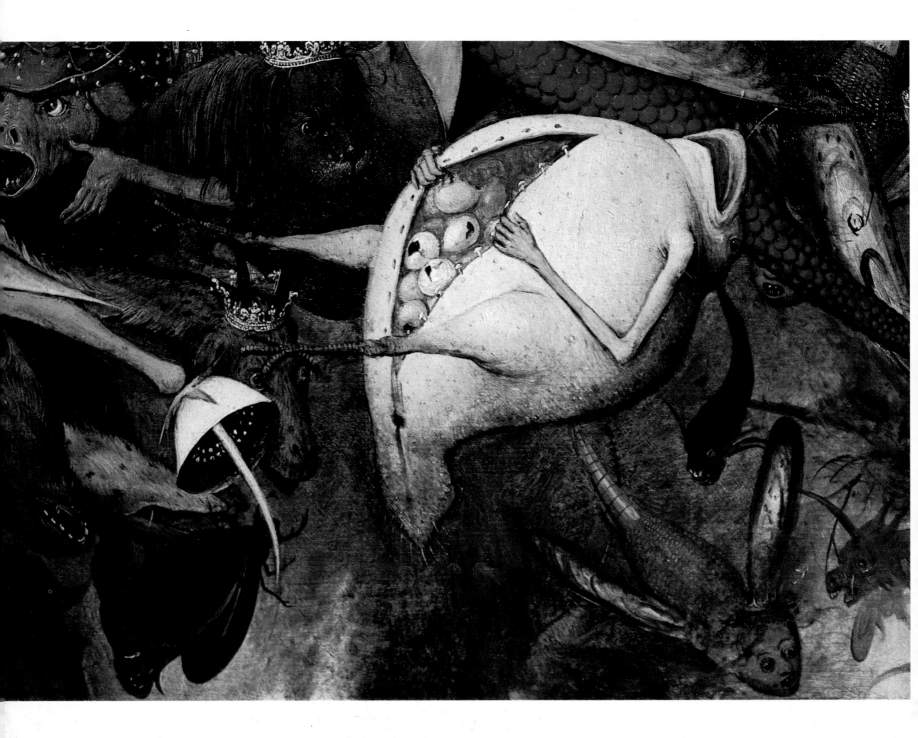

"Dulle Griet" sometimes called "Mad Meg"

This is one of the most puzzling of Pieter Bruegel's pictures and has been interpreted in many different ways. Its meaning may well have been far more obvious to Bruegel's contemporaries and to whoever commissioned the painting than it is to us. Possibly it is based on some lost literary model. Even Van Mander seems to shake his head in some bewilderment when he speaks of this picture: "... a *Dulle Griet*, who is stealing something to take to Hell, and who wears a vacant stare and is strangely dressed." This gaunt, belligerent, toothless old woman stands in the foreground. She seems to belong to the same tribe of rawboned women as "Lent" (Plate p. 105) and she looks anything but appealing.

Bruegel is not trying to depict the Renaissance conception of the beautiful warlike Amazon and her train. Rather—and this is often true—he is following popular tradition, heightening or exaggerating it through his own forceful vision. The fierce old woman has dressed herself in a helmet and armor and carries a striking set of attributes which she has obviously stolen. Her big pan, her basket and her apron are full of loot: goblets, plates of precious metal, rings—valuables which might well have come from church treasuries. But the basket this aggressive woman carries over her arm also contains everyday objects—an earthenware pitcher and a long-handled frying pan. Under her arm she clutches a treasure chest. Her right hand clasps a shining sword with which she is about to charge the menacing jaws of Hell. Behind her

152

is a small-scale mob of equally belligerent women, who are overthrowing, clubbing and tying up all kinds of horrible demons. This violent horde is preparing to storm a tumbledown house on the roof of which crouches a figure engaged in ladling money out of his backside—a symbol of profligacy. On his back is a "ship of fools." Weird phantoms and will-o'-the-wisps, whose counterparts exist only in the apocalyptic visions of Hieronymus Bosch, rage and tumble around them in a wild dance. The meaning of this figure representing the antithesis of charming femininity is obscure.

153   Catalog No. 13. Plates pp. 152–77.

154

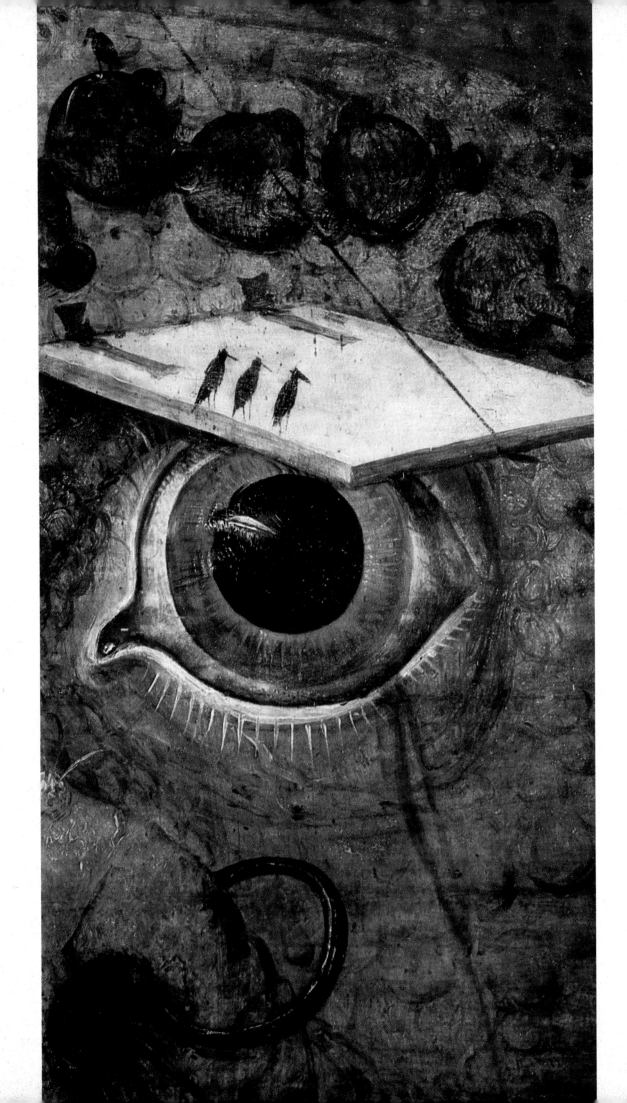

162

"Two Monkeys"

This little painting is remarkably appealing. The subject is simple: two monkeys chained in an arched opening in a wall. In the distance behind them a subtly suggestive view of the port of Antwerp. Birds in midair. On the lower left of the window ledge the inscription "BRVEGEL MDLXII." On the right empty nutshells. The exotic animals are beautifully characterized: their shivering, crouching posture, their disconsolate apathy as they stare out upon a shadowy freedom. The picture is certainly unusual for its time, and many interpretations have been proposed. Presumably Bruegel had an opportunity to make life studies of these animals, which must have come by ship from Africa. They may even have belonged to him. Perhaps he combined two studies of one animal in one composition. Since the notion of art for art's sake was unknown to Bruegel, this picture, like so many others, probably has some symbolic meaning. Our eye is caught by the dreamy vision of the prosperous city of Antwerp filling the horizon, and we know that Bruegel left Antwerp soon after he painted this picture. Perhaps the monkey had some kind of

evil-averting significance. In the Middle Ages the ape, as a caricature of covetous man, was a common symbol for the devil. Whether we regard this sensitive picture as a study from nature exemplifying Bruegel's acute observation or a symbolic presentation, its subtle painterly charm places it among his most appealing creations.

Catalog No. 15. Plate p. 179.

"The Suicide of Saul" or

"The Battle on Mount Gilboa"

180

Bruegel has chosen a mountain landscape as the dramatic setting of Saul's suicide. The turmoil of the battle is rendered almost in miniature, like a battle of insects. The victorious army of the Philistines winds in from the right. Saul is hidden away in the left foreground. He and his armor-bearer are falling on their own swords rather than yielding to their pursuers. "Now the Philistines fought against Israel: and the men of Israel fled from before the Philistines, and fell down slain in mount Gilboa. And the Philistines followed hard upon Saul and upon his sons; and the Philistines slew Jonathan, and Abinadab, and Melchishua, Saul's sons. And the battle went sore against Saul,

and the archers hit him; and he was sore wounded of the archers. Then said Saul unto his armor-bearer, Draw thy sword, and thrust me through therewith; lest these uncircumcised come and thrust me through, and abuse me. But his armor-bearer would not; for he was sore afraid. Therefore Saul took a sword and fell upon it. And when his armor-bearer saw that Saul was dead, he fell likewise upon his sword, and died with him. So Saul died, and his three sons, and his armor-bearer" (I Samuel 31:1–6). The symbolic theme of the picture is pride punished.

181   Catalog No. 10. Plates pp. 180–81.

Bruegel himself saw and sketched Naples and its gulf during his visit to Italy is uncertain, but he must at least have had realistic *vedute* of the city to work from. The contrast between the distant harbor, the cloudy sky and the rippled sea dotted with all kinds of ships is most appealing. Like tiny toys, the distant ships move in to attack. Some are enveloped in little puffs of gunsmoke; here and there two are engaged in close combat. The whole panoramic scene has the ceremonial character of a precisely planned maneuver. In the right half of the picture are several of the swift little galleys used by the Turks, suggesting that this is a naval battle between Christian and Turkish fleets.

Catalog No. 9. Plates pp. 182–89.

"View of Naples" sometimes called "The Sea Battle"

Pieter Bruegel lived during the age of world discovery. Every day new broadsheets appeared telling of the discovery of some mysterious new land of fabulous riches across the sea. These voyages of exploration demanded great fleets of oceangoing ships, and Bruegel must have had ample opportunity to study ships of every conceivable type in the roadstead of Antwerp. A nation of seagoing people living along its coast would naturally be interested in anything to do with shipping, and we know that *Marinen*—seascapes and paintings of ships—were extremely popular in the seventeenth-century Netherlands. Some painters specialized exclusively in this genre. For Bruegel it was just one subject among others, yet his perceptive vision made him an important forerunner of the *Marinen* genre. Whether

"The Tower of Babel"

sometimes called

"The Small Tower of Babel"

Bruegel made three paintings of this subject, which must have fascinated him and his patron. This version is certainly an echo of his visit to Rome: the lower tiers of the gigantic circular building recall the Colosseum. In this tower reaching skyward into the clouds Bruegel has combined an almost infinite variety of architectural forms, endless variations on the archway theme. At the lower right we see a minutely observed harbor and docks, of which Bruegel must surely have made preliminary studies. Here, as in all his pictures, we marvel at the unique blending of faithfully observed realistic details, for which he relied on preliminary sketches, into an imaginative total vision.

Even this subject has its moralistic aspect: The Babylonian tower symbolized pride punished—a reminder of the fruitlessness of human endeavors undertaken without God's blessing. It could also symbolize sectarians and feuding groups whose quarreling leads to neglect of the greater common purpose.

Catalog No. 17. Plates pp. 190–95.

193

"The Tower of Babel"

Van Mander mentioned in 1604 that two versions of Bruegel's Babylonian tower were in the possession of Emperor Rudolph II, who had a great weakness for mannerist compositions. This is one of them; the other is probably the smaller picture in Rotterdam (Catalog No. 17. plate p. 191). Here the gigantic tower looks more unfinished; in

196

places it is even in ruins. The surroundings are painted with great care. In the right foreground is a harbor, and to the left a densely clustering old Netherlandish town, its proud patrician houses, churches and walls painted as delicately as a miniature. In the foreground King Nimrod and his retinue are inspecting the building yard to check on the progress of the tower.

Catalog No. 16. Plates pp. 196–97.

"Christ and the Woman Taken in Adultery"

"And the scribes and Pharisees brought unto him a woman taken in adultery; and when they had set her in the midst, they said unto him, Master, this woman was taken in adultery, in the very act. Now Moses in the law commanded us, that such should be stoned: but what sayest thou? This they said, tempting him, that they might have to accuse him. But Jesus stooped down, and with his finger wrote on the ground, as though he heard them not. So when they continued asking him, he lifted up himself, and said unto them, He that is without sin among you, let him first cast a stone at her. And again he stooped down, and wrote on the ground. And they which heard it, being convicted by their own conscience, went out one by one, beginning at the eldest, even unto the last" (John 8:3–9).

Catalog No. 29. Plate p. 198.

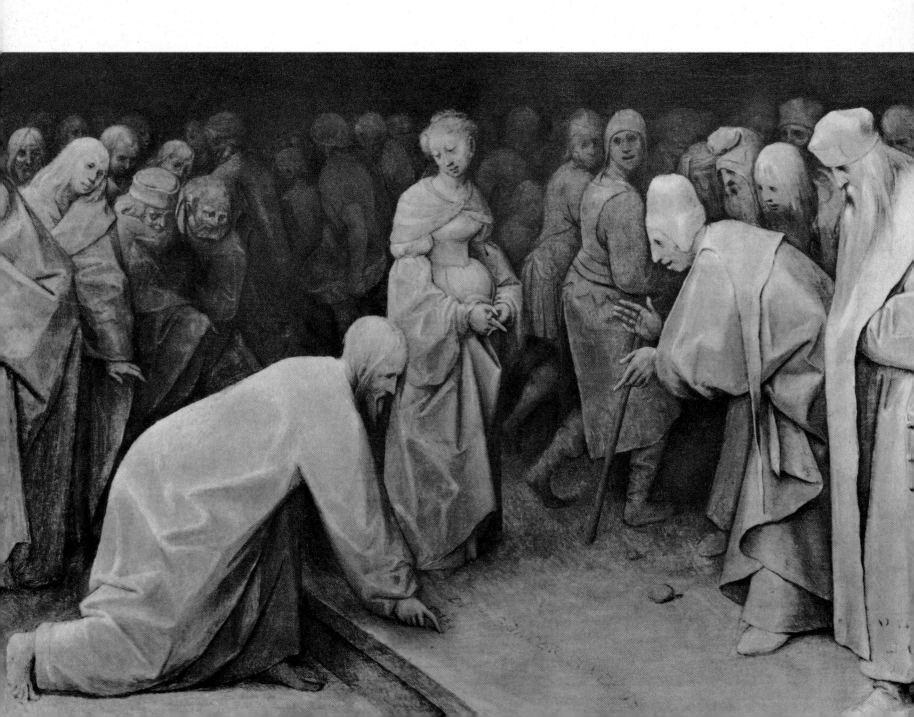

"The Flight into Egypt"

In Bruegel's time landscape as such, without figures, that is to say, without edifying Biblical or mythological scenes, hardly existed. Bruegel obviously had a strong interest in pure landscape, and we feel that in this painting the Virgin and Child riding on the donkey and led by Joseph on their flight into Egypt were almost an afterthought. The landscape is probably based on studies from his Italian sketchbook—perhaps of some lake in northern Italy. The contrast between the wild, rugged mountains and the vast open view gives the composition a feeling of vitality. The travelers have left behind the serene country we glimpse in the distance. The hard road ahead leads into the dark uncertainty of the abyss.

Catalog No. 18. Plate p. 199.

Christ carrying the cross was a subject which would have inevitably attracted a tireless observer of human nature like Pieter Bruegel. He painted two versions of it, "always with a few drolleries in them somewhere," as Van Mander tells us. By "drolleries" Van Mander means scenes like the one where Simon of Cyrene's wife is wildly trying to prevent her husband from picking up the cross after Christ has fallen under its weight (plate p. 206). We should bear in mind that in popular passion plays the tragedy was traditionally relieved by burlesque.

The endless procession to Calvary is skillfully composed. Riders in red tunics make a colorful leitmotiv which helps us follow what is going on. In the right foreground is a conventional rendering of the group of mourning women. Some of the figures are borrowed from fifteenth-century Flemish painting. We note the harmonious drawing, the nobility of gesture and the discipline and restraint of the women's grief. The attitude of the common people is in strong contrast: Their faces express nothing but listless indifference and fainthearted impotence. We are shocked by the general air of resignation and by the inevitability of what is about to occur.

Catalog No. 20. Plates pp. 200–11.

The devout spectator with folded hands at the extreme right may be a self-portrait.

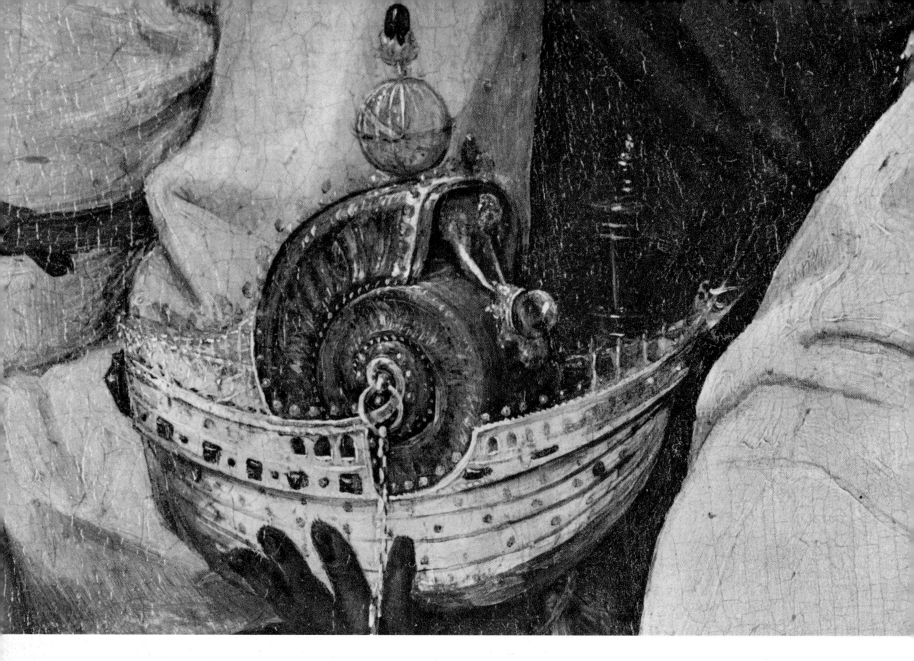

"The Adoration of the Kings"

At the center of this Adoration sits the Mother with her Child, heavy almost to the point of clumsiness and enveloped in draperies. Two of the kings bow before her, weighed down by their ornate robes, awkward and ill at ease in their act of homage, looking more like dressed-up commoners than high-born rulers. To the right is a mysterious Moor whose costume stems from the inexhaustible imagination of Hieronymus Bosch. He bears a costly gift in the form of a bizarre ship fashioned by a goldsmith. Joseph, the honest carpenter, is forced to listen to the whisperings of some stranger while the sacred act is performed. At the extreme right stand two men, probably Pharisees. One of them wears spectacles—perhaps because, having eyes, he sees not. This powerful scene is played out under the massive beams of the stable roof. To the left, heads of armed men crowd densely into the picture.

Catalog No. 19. Plates pp. 212–17.

216

"... the freeze began nine days before Christmas and lasted until the Feast of Saint Matthew. ... It was very cold, so few people were to be seen in the streets, but the young men who are tough and unafraid enjoyed themselves all day long on the ice."

DANIEL VAN OESBROECK

"Winter Landscape with Skaters and a Bird Trap"

While Bruegel often questions man and his handiwork, the purity and beauty of his landscapes are beyond question. Nature—Creation as it existed before man brought sin into the world—has its own laws and its own measure: the seasons. Pieter Bruegel stands at the beginning of a long winter landscape tradition which was to be continued by the Dutch painters of the seventeenth century. This picture falls into two scenes of activity in an atmospheric setting. On the left, people are disporting themselves on the frozen river. Under a bare tree on the right, birds are innocently pecking at food set out for them under a board which is actually a bird trap. In the midst of this snow-covered world danger threatens the unwary. From one minute to the next the carefree birds may be killed; the happy skaters are in equal danger. They symbolize the *lubricitas vitae*, the uncertainty of existence. Other pictures with contemporary legends support this interpretation.

219   Catalog No. 28. Plates pp. 218–23.

224

"Haymaking"

Bruegel's painting of summer is pervaded by the joy of living. The peasants are working hard to bring in the hay. To the right, others are carrying baskets brimming with fruit and vegetables down to the valley. Three girl harvesters are coming up to lend a hand, rakes on their shoulders. The man with the scythe on the extreme left, the ephemeral summer flowers, the poppies along the path, are a quiet reminder to the wise that everything must perish. Since the seasons were often associated with the ages of man, there is an implied warning that in the time of ripeness one must also be mindful of the harvest. Ever since classical antiquity carefree rural life has held an appeal for the city dweller. In this tradition of poetically transfigured country life, Pieter Bruegel is an important figure.

225   Catalog No. 22. Plates pp. 224–37.

"If the peasant did not provide the raw materials, neither spinners nor weavers nor masons nor carpenters nor cabinetmakers nor bakers nor brewers nor physicians nor clerks could carry on their trades."

"Everyone laughs at the peasant and makes fun of him and even thinks him stupid; they make this judgment out of ignorance."

"Day in and day out the good farmer feeds provinces, castles and towns."

228

232

236

"The Hunters in the Snow"

Bruegel conveys the dark, frozen atmosphere of this winter landscape with tremendous intensity. The snow-covered slope in the foreground drops steeply down to the valley. The pack of hounds, worn out with hunting, sniff the familiar track leading toward home. Winter holds everything in its spell. We no longer ask whether this consummately realized impression of winter holds a deeper hidden meaning.

Catalog No. 25. Plates pp. 238–39.

"The Gloomy Day"

This is a calendar picture. The figures on the right display allusions to Carnival and perhaps suggest that it depicts the months of January and February.

Bruegel's subject here is not the somber gloom of autumn but the time of year when a stirring begins in the ground. The ice is breaking up; the flooding rivers flow in a mighty tide toward the sea. Something within man is striving to break out too; he is ready to play pranks on winter and drive it out for good. The peasants are engaged in pruning away dead wood to make room for new growth.

Catalog No. 26. Plates pp. 240–41.

"The Return of the Herd"

This picture represents autumn. The cattle are being driven down from the high mountain pastures. The men feel cold; they have put on their warm clothing; it will soon snow. The fallow season of the year is beginning. Even the wedge-shaped herd, trotting gently downhill, is painted in autumn colors.

The occasion is obviously not just the daily return of the herd at sunset, but its more momentous yearly return from the mountain pastures. Bruegel had probably encountered this custom, unknown in his own sea-level country, when he was traveling in the Alps.

Catalog No. 24. Plates pp. 242–43.

"The Corn Harvest"

While the mood of "Haymaking" is carefree and almost playful, this picture shows more laborious work in progress. To the left the reapers are cutting the corn. A boy carrying a full pitcher approaches along a narrow pathway. Under a tree to the right the hardworking peasants are taking a rest, leaning on sheaves and enjoying the refreshments they have brought along. Big as their appetites are, the loaves of bread about to be sliced up are bigger.

244

Sour milk spooned out of a rough bowl or drunk straight from the jug tastes delicious. Summertime is harvesttime. Prosperous farms hug the gentle slopes. In the distance a dreamy little town beckons. Behind the trees we catch a glimpse of a church. All seems to be well in this blessed country world of summertime.

Catalog No. 23. Plates pp. 244–47.

247

"The Massacre of the Innocents"   Catalog No. 27. Plates pp. 248–49.

"The Numbering of the People at Bethlehem"

Pieter Bruegel was always making studies from life to be used in his scenes of everyday activities, and this accounts for their remarkably lifelike freshness. This splendid winter picture is a good example. At the left a crowd has gathered around a shabby country tavern to be counted and registered. The Virgin, wrapped in a cloak and riding on a donkey, and Joseph, leading the animals, are just arriving. Village life goes on as usual despite the emperor's momentous decree. A pig is being slaughtered; a poor man is bringing home a load of kindling from the woods; children play on the ice. There is no end to the variations of minutely observed detail. Scrawny chickens peck the snow in search of a grain of corn. Men carrying heavy loads trudge through the snow or pick their way across the ice. In the background a crowd has collected around a fire or an improvised tavern. Boys are having a snowball fight. Carts and wagon wheels stand idle, half covered with snow, waiting for better times when they will be needed again.

Catalog No. 30. Plates pp. 250–67.

251

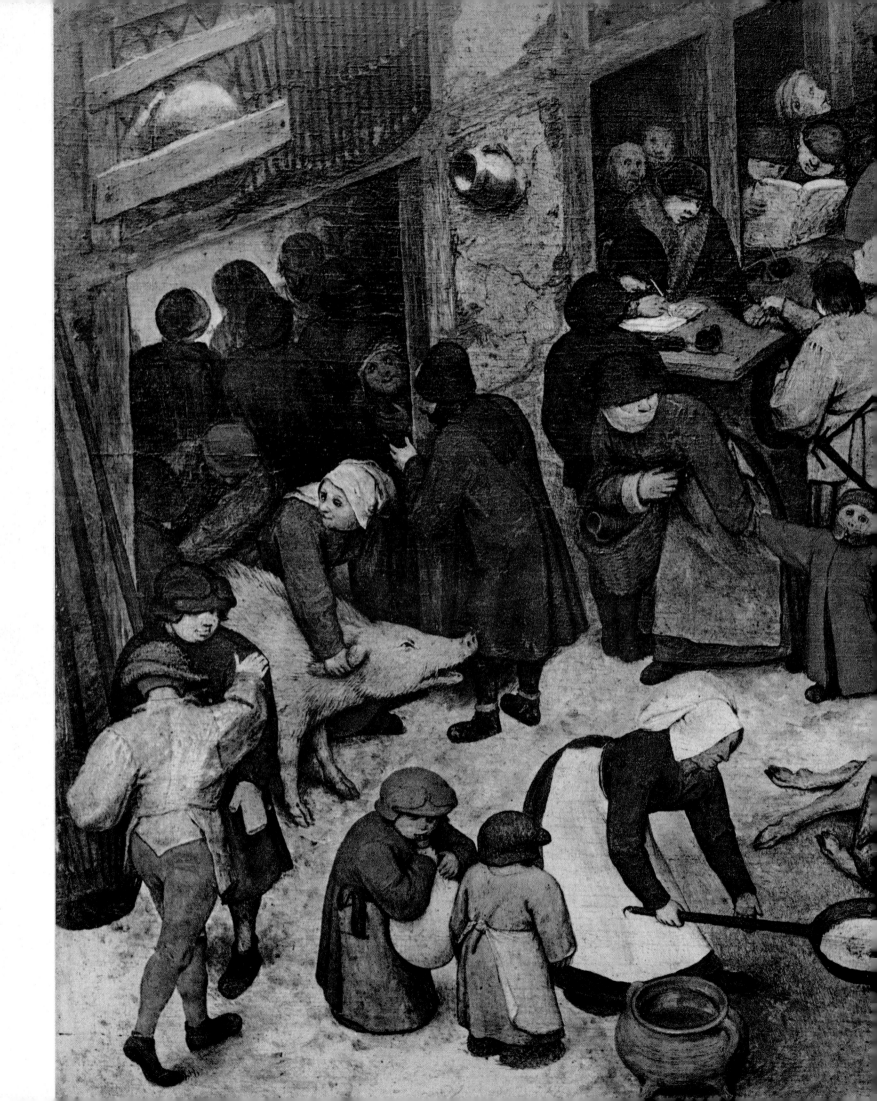

264

267

"The Sermon of Saint John the Baptist"

A great crowd has assembled in the open air to listen to the ascetic's exhortations to repent and change their lives. Some faces show rapt attention, others bewilderment and doubt. Here again the painter dresses the Biblical scene in the costume of his own time, thus creating a powerful sense of actuality. We know that in Bruegel's day the common people were urgently seeking a faith they could believe in. Innumerable preachers held clandestine outdoor services known as *hagepreken*. Van Vaernewijck tells us that the people to be seen there were "chiefly common folk, people who led dissolute lives ... but to tell the truth, there were also men of good reputation who led blameless lives. One would never have believed it possible that such people would attend the sermons."

Catalog No. 31. Plates pp. 268–70.

"The Wedding Dance in the Open Air"

"With this Franckert, Bruegel often went on trips among the peasants, to their weddings and fairs. The two dressed like peasants, brought presents like the other guests, and acted as if they belonged to the families or acquaintances of the bride or of the groom," writes Van Mander.

Pieter Bruegel certainly knew his countrymen inside out. The merry villagers at this peasant wedding are obliquely seen from above. The couples in the foreground, some quick-footed, some clumsy, are dancing a lively round. The noisy merrymaking fills the shady village green. Off in the background things are quieter. Bruegel's *naer het leven* sketches were an inexhaustible source of material for scenes like this.

271   Catalog No. 32. Plates pp. 271–73.

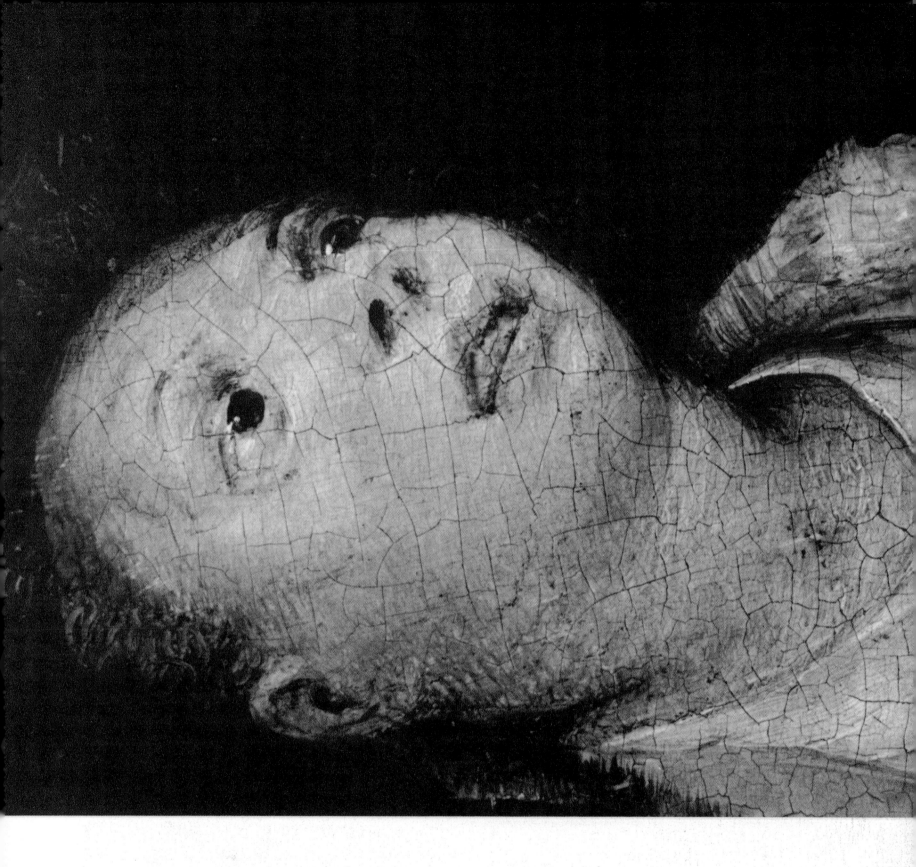

"The Land of Cockaigne"

While this dense scene appeals to us as a splendid illustration of a legend, it also offers a warning against dissolute living, for "idleness is the root of all evil." The warning is meant for three important classes of people: peasants, clerks, and soldiers. We see representatives of all three exposed to the temptations of this delightful land of plenty.

275   Catalog No. 37. Plates pp. 274–77.

"The Adoration of the Kings in the Snow"

"Now when Jesus was born in Bethlehem of Judea in the days of Herod the king, behold, there came wise men from the east to Jerusalem, saying, Where is he that is born King of the Jews? for we have seen his star in the east, and are come to worship him. When Herod the king had heard these things, he was troubled, and all Jerusalem with him. And when he had gathered all the chief priests and scribes of the people together, he demanded of them where Christ should be born. And they said unto him, In Bethlehem of Judea; for thus it is written by the prophet, And thou Bethlehem, in the land of Juda, art not the least among the princes of Juda: for out of thee shall come a Governor, that shall rule my people Israel. Then Herod, when he had privily called the wise men, inquired of them diligently what time the star appeared. And he sent them to Bethlehem, and said, Go and search diligently for the young child; and when ye have found him, bring me word again, that I may come and worship him also. When they had heard the king, they departed; and, lo, the star, which they saw in the east, went before them, till it came and stood over where the young child was. When they saw the star, they rejoiced with exceedingly great joy. And when they were come into the house, they saw the young child with Mary his mother, and fell down, and worshipped him: and when they had opened their treasures, they presented unto him gifts; gold, and frankincense, and myrrh. And being warned of God in a dream that they should not return to Herod, they departed into their own country another way" (Matthew 2: 1–12).

In this Adoration we recognize many features from other winter scenes by Bruegel. Here he actually depicts a heavy snowfall through the naïve—and to the modern viewer charming—technique of scattering white flakes over the finished picture. This heightens the feeling of spontaneous movement. So far as we know, no one had ever painted a snowstorm before.

Catalog No. 33. Plates pp. 279–89.

284

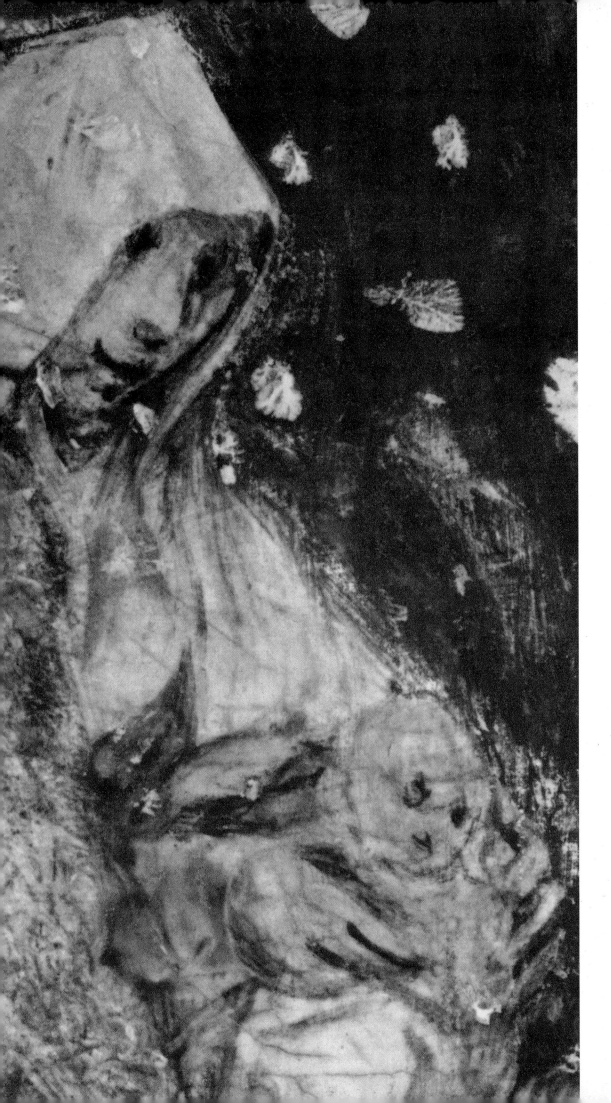

"The Conversion of Saint Paul"

This picture again recalls Bruegel's own crossing of the Alps. In a mountain landscape of steep rock faces and southern conifers, a procession winds along a narrow track. There is some confusion, for people, including knights in full armor, on foot and on horseback, are crowding in from above and from the ravine below. Riders, horses, costumes, and harnesses are carefully and lovingly painted. As the eye follows the rich detail of the procession it suddenly perceives in its midst a tiny figure lying on the ground. This is Saul being converted. "And as he journeyed, he came near Damascus: and suddenly there shined round about him a light from heaven: And he fell to the earth, and heard a voice saying unto him, Saul, Saul, why persecutest thou me? And he said, Who art thou, Lord? And the Lord said, I am Jesus whom thou persecutest: it is hard for thee to kick against the pricks" (Acts 9: 3–5).

In a period of religious strife, internal dissent, sudden conversions, and changes of faith, the Saul-Paul story was timely. Moreover, it offered scope for all kinds of political allusions. In 1567, the year Bruegel painted this picture, the Duke of Alba and his Spanish troops were crossing the Alps of Savoy on their march into the Netherlands. There was still some hope that the duke might be converted to a policy of tolerance. Everywhere the uneasy people sought portents and miracles that could be taken as omens. Van Vaernewijck tells us, for example, that when Count Egmont suffered a fall from his horse, there was much murmuring and "many wanted to make a Paul of him for everyone construed the matter in his own way."

Catalog No. 34. Plates pp. 290–93.

291

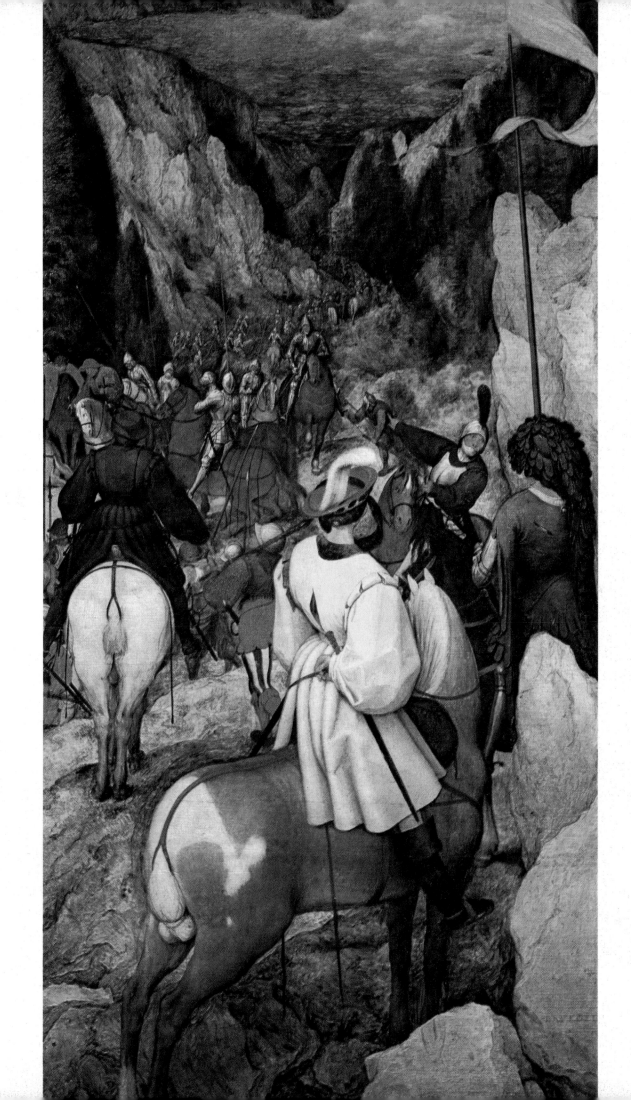

293

"The Peasant Wedding" sometimes called "The Wedding Banquet"

This is one of Bruegel's most popular paintings. Its spontaneity and directness make an immediate appeal. The country folk invited to the festivities are seated around a wide table; their behavior is restrained and solemn rather than noisy. The board is by no means groaning with delicacies; the course being served seems to consist of mush served in flat earthenware dishes. The two servingmen in the foreground are using a door to carry in the plates. Everything in the picture looks solid and sturdy. In the center sits the bride with downcast eyes and folded hands. Above her hangs the bridal crown. Music is provided by two bagpipers. It is uncertain which figure is the bridegroom—possibly the man in the left foreground pouring wine into earthenware pitchers. In the rear to the left a colorful crowd of curious onlookers is crowding through the open door.

We do not know whether this is simply a picture of a peasant celebration or whether it holds a deeper meaning. A hint of such significance can be seen in the gentleman and the monk engaged in serious conversation to the right of the table, next to a man who looks much like Erasmus. Another conspicuous figure is the child in the foreground sitting on the floor and concentrating on cleaning out his bowl with his finger. He is weighed down by a huge cap coming down over his eyes, which is trimmed with a peacock feather—a symbol of earthly transitoriness. The possibility that this picture has a symbolic meaning is not to be dismissed. Old mystical texts compare man's soul with a bride joyfully and confidently awaiting her lord and master. The soul can partake in the wedding only if it holds aloof from earthly joys. According to this tradition, the picture could be read as a warning against excess and gluttony which threaten the soul's salvation.

Catalog No. 35. Plates pp. 294–97.

"The Peasant Dance"
sometimes called
"The Kermess"

"Yes, my darling, in a
corner behind the tent I
asked you if you would
share your life with me
until death, and I gave
you a *pfefferkuchen*. And
before we parted, we ate
a piece of it."
"They play the fiddle, the
bagpipes and the flute, but
before the boys break up
they draw their knives."
BREDEROO
Catalog No. 36.
Plates pp. 298–301.

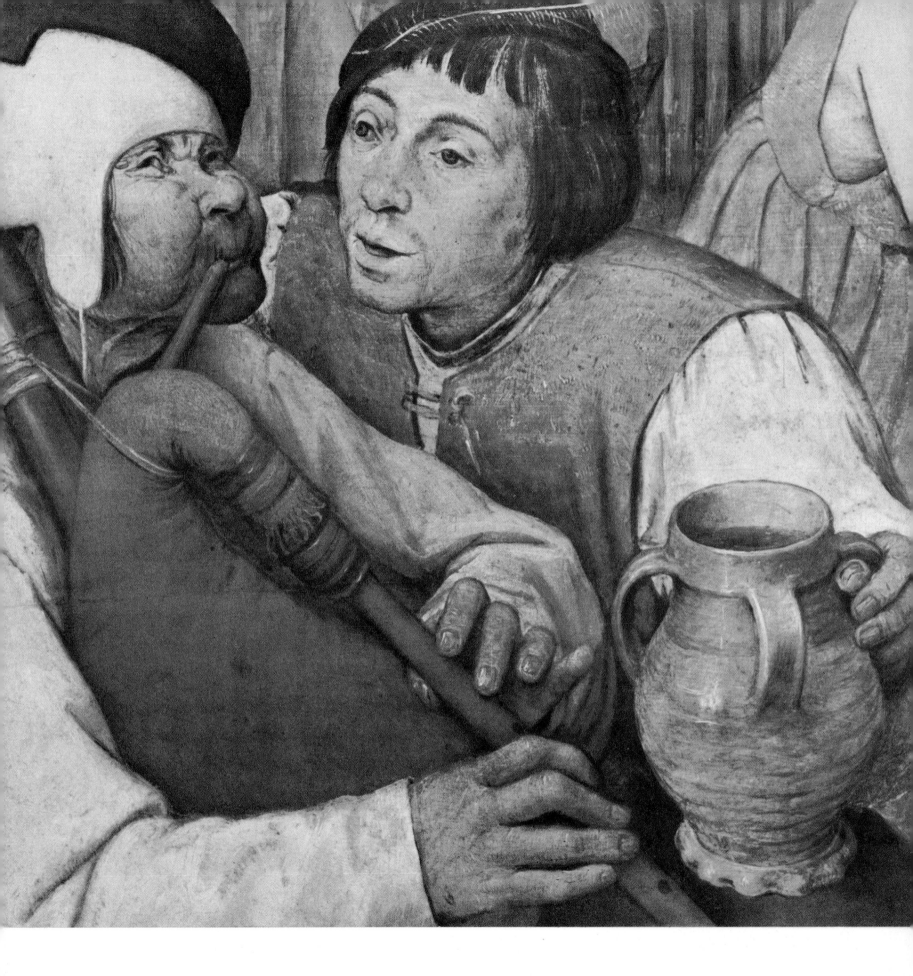

301

Om dat de Werelt is soe ongetru
Daer om gha ic in den ru

"The Misanthrope" or "The Perfidy of the World"   "Because the world is so faithless, I wear mourning."   Catalog No. 40. Plates pp. 302–3.

"The Parable
of the Blind"

Christ's symbolic words "And if the blind lead the blind, both shall fall into the ditch" (Matthew 15:14) were known to everybody. The saying was used proverbially in speaking of stupidity and hopeless situations. Bruegel has discarded everything conventional in this portrayal of six blind men whose sight is totally extinguished, whose faculty of perception is gone. The atmosphere is oppressive. Far and wide no help is near—no one who might see, rescue and counsel them. The inevitability of their fall is terrible to see. The leader with the stick has already stumbled backward into the swampy mire, half crushing his musical instrument, a hurdy-gurdy which almost seems to be pulling a face at him. The second man trips and falls on top of him. The others follow, walking unsteadily on tiptoe. Around them in the foreground is nothing to hold onto, just a shifting, sandy bank and withered scrub—a mere caricature of a tree.

The picture offers no sympathy but only a warning. Blindness is shown as an irremediable state of the soul, the stigma of a corrupt world. We who look at the picture are not blind like the men it depicts, and we are admonished not to act like them, putting blind trust in blind leaders.

Catalog No. 42. Plates pp. 304–13.

308

309

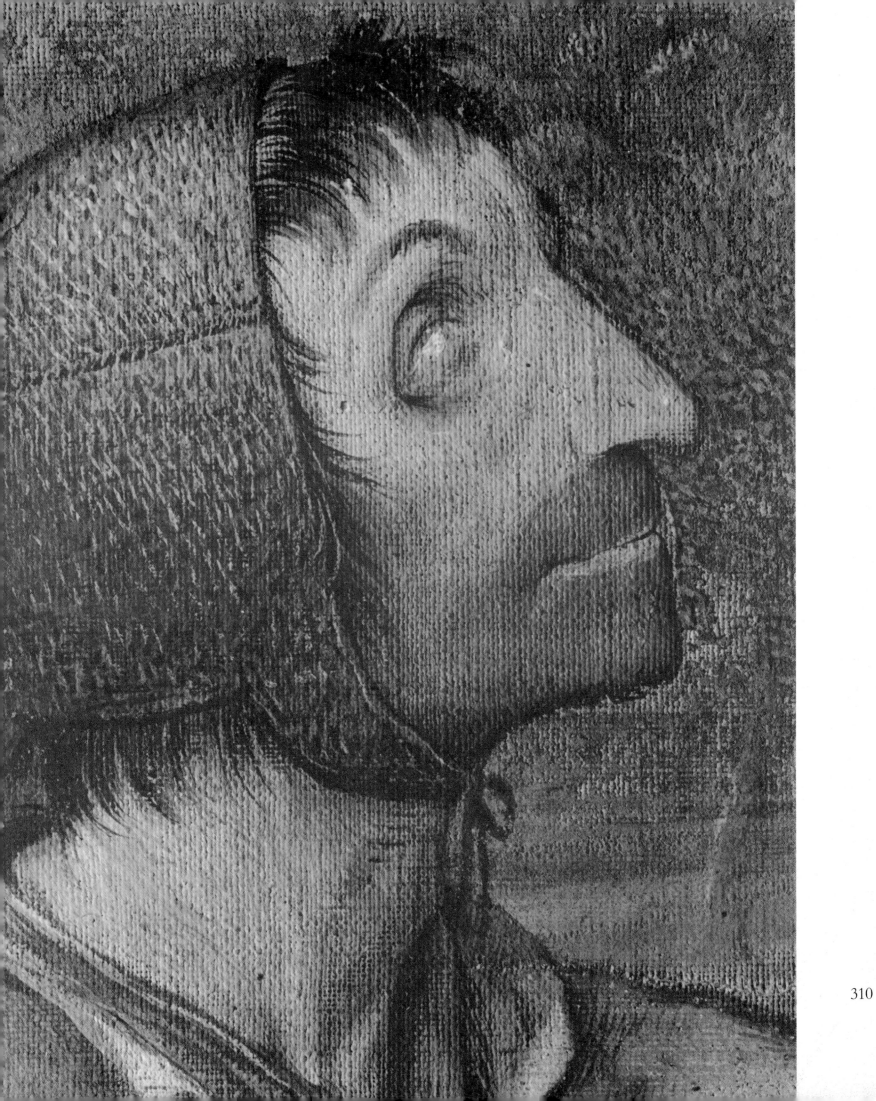

312

"The Magpie on the Gallows"

"In his will he left his wife a picture of 'A Magpie on a Gallows'. By the magpie, he meant the gossips whom he delivered to the gallows," says Van Mander. If we are to believe the imaginative biographer, this picture represents Bruegel's personal legacy. In that case it would seem that the independent-minded painter had reason to fear what vicious tongues might say. We are also told that when he was dying he told his wife to burn a number of his drawings. Recalling the political situation in the Netherlands toward the end of Pieter Bruegel's life, we readily understand such a mistrustful attitude. There was general intolerance for other people's fundamental views. There was persecution. Uncertainty and distorted values prevailed. A critical, observant mind like Bruegel's must have often marveled at the topsy-turvy, corrupt world he lived in. Again and again we find him shaking his head over the folly of the world with a smile which could express either benevolence or secret despair.

"The Magpie on the Gallows" is probably Bruegel's last landscape, and somehow it has a tenuous quality, a lightness we do not find in his earlier paintings. The trees are almost exaggeratedly slender and delicate; the distance is transfigured in a soft haze.

In the foreground something strange is going on. We see an empty gallows with a magpie perched on it. Below it stands a roughly hewn cross. High-spirited peasants are coming up the path leading to the gallows. Some of them caper about to the music of the bagpipes in a heavy-footed dance, enjoying themselves in their own stolid way. Bystanders wave to them. In the extreme left corner a man is defecating. No one seems to be paying any heed to the menacing gallows or to be aware of the paradisiac landscape, whose meaningful order is perhaps the final expression of Bruegel's sense of nature. This soulful landscape still communicates its essence.

Catalog No. 43. Plates pp. 314–27.

"The Cripples" sometimes called "The Beggars"

The meaning of this picture of five cripples grouped together yet all irritably heading in different directions has not yet been plausibly explained. With their crutches and wooden stumps, their shapeless headgear and extraordinary clothes trimmed with foxtails, they epitomize misery itself.

   Catalog No. 41. Plate p. 329.

   "Head of an Old Peasant Woman"   Catalog No. 38. Plate p. 328.

"The Peasant and the Bird Nester"

The plundered bird's nest probably symbolizes the proverb "He who knows where the nest is has the knowledge; he who robs it has the nest."

Catalog No. 39. Plates pp. 330–31.

"... whales or great sea monsters can destroy the ships with their heavy bodies. They crush them with their tail or swamp them with so much water that they sink. How can they be tricked? As soon as they are sighted, casks and barrels are thrown overboard, and they play with them. In the meantime the helmsman can hold his course, and the ship escapes with all aboard. Do you not agree that the Privy Council is much more sagacious than the common man or the many others who want to effect changes through force?"

MARCUS VAN VAERNEWIJCK

"The Storm at Sea"

This magnificent, tempestuous seascape is one of the last paintings Pieter Bruegel made. Ships with sails stretched to bursting are tossed on a dirty, weirdly lighted sea. The waves, shaped like fish heads, drive like arrows. Far away in the background to the left is land and the outline of a church. Looking more closely, we see a barrel floating in the sea behind the ship in the center. Behind it lurks a whalelike monster with gaping jaws. Bruegel was not merely painting a stormy sea; the picture contains a moral which his contemporaries would have been quick to recognize. It symbolizes unflinching single-mindedness.

Catalog No. 44. Plates pp. 332–35.

In 1581 a contemporary of Bruegel, the Spaniard Juan de Boria, wrote this maxim: "Do not seek yourself outside yourself ... The farther one proceeds in self-knowledge, the closer he comes to the knowledge of God ... Thus everyone must seek himself within himself if he is to find himself, because it is impossible for a man to find and know himself if he dissipates himself and strays outside himself. This is symbolized by the snail ... And the greater a man's realization of this, the higher he will raise himself toward knowledge of the unfathomable treasure of God's omniscience and wisdom, in which knowledge man's true happiness primarily resides." An appropriate symbol of De Boria's maxim would be the golden ship bearing the snail shell of self-knowledge on which rests a cosmic armillary globe—the most precious gift that can be offered to the newborn babe.

Catalog No. 19. Plate p. 212.

It may be useful to recall the names of some of the outstanding artists who died during the first half of the sixteenth century: Giorgione, 1510; Bramante, 1514; Leonardo da Vinci, 1519; Raphael, 1520; Albrecht Dürer, 1528; Jan Gossaert (or Mabuse), 1533; Correggio and Lucas van

	Biographical Data and Historical Events	Drawings	Prints	Paintings
1550	Bruegel collaborates on altarpiece of Malines Glovers' Guild (after August 30).[31],[32] Death of P. Coeck (December). First edition of Vasari's *Lives*.[44]			Altarpiece of the Malines Glovers' Guild, exterior of side panels (now lost).[32]
1551	Bruegel becomes a free master in Antwerp and is entered in the *Liggeren*, the membership rolls of the Guild of Saint Luke.[34]			
1552		"River Valley with Mountain in Background" (Rhone valley?). Dated: 1552. (Signature controversial.) "Mountain Landscape with Italian-Style Cloister." Signed: brueghel 1552.		
1553	Bruegel in Rome. P. Coeck's *Moeurs et fachons de faire des Turcz*[65] published posthumously. Persecution of Protestants in England by Mary Tudor (Bloody Mary). Death of Rabelais (probably early in April) and Lucas Cranach the Elder.	["The Ripa Grande in Rome." Inscribed *a rypa*. Signed: brùegel.[121]] "Landscape with Walled Town." Signed: p. brueghel 1553. "Landscape with River and Mountains." Dated: 1553. "Alpine Landscape." Signed: 1553 BRVEGHEL. "Landscape with Town and Saint Jerome." Signed: .553. BRVEGHEL "View of Waltersspurg." Inscribed: Waltersspurg. (1553–54?) "The Large Rhine Landscape." Signed: P. BRVEGHEL.	"River Landscape with the Rape of Psyche by Mercury."[123] Signed: Petrus Bruegel fec. Romae Aº 1553. "River Landscape with the Fall of Icarus."[123] Signed: Petrus Bruegel fec. Romae Aº 1553. 1553–57: Series of twelve large "Landscapes"[124] and a single large "Alpine Landscape."[124] Signatures: BRVEGHEL, brueghel, bruegel, brughel.	["Landscape with Sailing Boats and a Burning Town." Unsigned and undated.] Cat. No.1. "Landscape with Christ Appearing to the Apostles at the Sea of Tiberias." Signed: P. BRVEGHEL 1553. Cat. No.2.

Leyden, 1534; Erasmus, 1536; Albrecht Altdorfer, 1538; Barend van Orley, 1542; Hans Holbein the Younger, 1543.

Bruegel's famous contemporaries included: Michelangelo, Titian, Paolo Veronese, Tintoretto, El Greco, Giovanni da Bologna, Jacopo da Ponte (or Bassano), Montaigne, Mercator, Tycho Brahe, Pieter Pourbus, Anthonis Mor, Frans and Cornelis Floris, Guillaume Dufay, Johannes Ockegem, Gilles Binchois.

Works in brackets are of questioned authenticity.

	Biographical Data and Historical Events	Drawings	Prints	Paintings
1554		"Large Landscape with Trees, a Church" (and Watermill). Signed: .ruegel 1554. "Mountain Ravine."	See 1553.	
1555	Formal abdication of Emperor Charles V (October 25). Palestrina's *Missa papae Marcelli.* Prophecies of Nostradamus.	Signed: ..ueghel ..55.[124]	See 1553.	["Landscape with the Fall of Icarus."] Cat. No. 3.
1556	Brueghel works in Antwerp, making drawings for Hieronymus Cock's engraving workshop, "The Four Winds."	"The Ass at School."[125] Signed: brueghel 1556. "Big Fish Eat Little Fish."[126] Signed: 1556 brueghel. "The Temptation of Saint Anthony."[127] Signed: Brùeghel 1556 (controversial). "*Avaritia*"—Covetousness.[129] Signed: brueghel 1556.	"The Ass at School."[125] (1556–57) "Big Fish Eat Little Fish."[126] (1556–57) "The Temptation of Saint Anthony."[127] (1556–57) "The Sleeping Peddler Robbed by Monkeys."[128] (1556–57? The second state engraving is signed: 1562, BRVEGHEL INVE). "*Avaritia*"—Covetousness.[129] (1556–57).	["The Adoration of the Kings."] Cat. No. 4.
1557	Battle of Saint-Quentin (August 10). Michel Coxcie copies for Philip II. Van Eyck's "Adoration of the nystic Lamb" altarpiece in Ghent	"*Ira*"—Anger.[129] Signed: brueghel 1557. "*Desidia*"—Sloth.[129] Signed: brueghel 1557. "*Superbia*"—Pride.[129] Signed: brueghel 1557. "*Gula*"—Gluttony.[129] Signed: brùeghel 1557. "*Invidia*"—Envy.[129] Signed: brùeghel 1557. "*Luxuria*"—Lust.[129] Signed: brùeghel 1557.	"*Ira*"—Anger.[129] "*Desidia*"—Sloth.[129] "*Superbia*"—Pride.[129] "*Gula*"—Gluttony.[129] "*Invidia*"—Envy. "*Luxuria*"—Lust.[129] "The Excision of the Stone of Madness" or "The Dean of Renaix."[130] Signed: BRVEGEL INVEN 1557. "*Patientia*"—Patience.[131] Signed: 1557 Brueghel Inuent. See 1553.	"Landscape with the Parable of the Sower." Cat. No. 5. Signed: ..VEGHEL .557.

339

	Biographical Data and Historical Events	Drawings	Prints	Paintings
1558	Death of Charles V (September 21) and Mary Tudor (November 17).	"The Last Judgment."[132] Signed: brueghel 1558. "*Elck*"—"Everyman."[79] Signed: brùeghel 1558. "The Alchemist."[86] Signed: BRVEGHEL 1558	"The Last Judgment."[132] "*Elck.*"—"Everyman."[79] "The Alchemist."[86] "Wedding Dance." Signed: P. BRVEGEL INVENT.[133]	["Twelve Proverbs." Signed: BRVEGHEL 1..8 (effaced).[134]]
1559	Treaty of Cateau-Cambrésis (April 3). Philip II orders the Council of Brabant to enforce his edicts rigorously (Letter dated Ghent, August 8). Sails from Vlissingen on August 25. Three farces prosecuted in Brussels.[108] Death of Henry II of France.	"Skating Outside Saint George's Gate."[135] Signed: brueghel 1559. "Rocky Landscape with Castle and River Valley." Signed: P. BRVEGEL 1559. "Sea Landscape with Rocky Island and an Italian-Style Cloister; with the Holy Family in the Foreground." Signed: brùegel f. "The Kermess of Hoboken."[140] Signed: 1559 BRVEGEL. "*Fides*"—Faith.[141] Signed: BRVEGEL 1559. "*Spes*"—Hope.[141] Signed: BRVEGEL 1559. "*Caritas*"—Charity.[141] Signed: BRVEGEL 1559. "*Justitia*"—Justice.[141] Signed: 1559 BRVEGEL. "*Prudentia*"—Prudence.[141] Signed: BRVEGEL 1559.	"Skating Outside Saint George's Gate."[135] The date 1553 is thought to be incorrect. "The Witch of Mallegem."[136] Signed: P. brueghel inventor— H. Cock excud. cum privilegio 1559. "The Festival of Fools."[137] Signed: P. Brueghel Inuentor. "The Kermess of Saint George."[138] Signed: BRVEGEL INVENTOR. [Small Brabant and Campine landscapes.[139]] "The Kermess of Hoboken."[140] "*Fides*"—Faith.[141] (1559–60) "*Spes*"—Hope.[141] (1559–60) "*Caritas*"—Charity.[141] (1559–60) "*Justitia*"—Justice.[141] (1559–60) "*Prudentia*"—Prudence.[141] (1559–60)	"The Netherlandish Proverbs." Cat. No. 6. Signed: BRVEGEL 1559. "The Fight Between Carnival and Lent." Cat. No. 7. Signed: BRVEGEL 1559.
1560	Edict restricting freedom to perform farces, morality plays and pantomimes.[107] Antoine Perrennot Granvelle (1517–86) elected Bishop of Malines. Birth of Annibale Caracci. Death of Philipp Melanchthon.	"*Fortitudo*"—Fortitude.[141] Signed: BRVEGEL 1560. "*Temperantia*"—Temperance.[141] Signed: BRVEGEL 1560. "The Small Landscapes." A series of eleven landscapes, ten of which are signed: P. BRVEGEL 1560.	"*Fortitudo*"—Fortitude.[141] "*Temperantia*"—Temperance.[141]	"Children's Games." Cat. No. 8. Signed: BRVEGEL 1560.

	Biographical Data and Historical Events	Drawings	Prints	Paintings
1561	Bruegel mentioned in a letter from Scipio Fabius to Ortelius.[45] Landjuweel in Antwerp.[143] Building of new Antwerp city hall begins. Birth of Luis de Gongora and Francis Bacon. Death of Lancelot Blondeel.	"Christ in Limbo."[142] Signed: BRVEGEL 1561. Six small "Landscapes" Signed: (P.) BRVEGEL 1561 —Bruegel 1561—bruegel 1561.	"Christ in Limbo."[142] "Sea Battle in the Straits of Messina."[37] Signed: M.D. lxi Bruegel Inven. "River Landscape with Castle." Signed: Bruegel in. 1561. [Continuation of the Brabant and Campine landscapes.[139]]	
1562	Bruegel's visit to Amsterdam (?). Birth of Lope de Vega and Jan Pietersz. Sweelinck. Rabelais' *L'Isle sonnante*.[115] Massacre of Wassy (March 1).	"Towers and Gates of a Town" (Amsterdam!)[144] Three drawings. Signed: bruegel 1562—P. BRVEGEL 1562—P. BRVEGEL 1562. Two "Landscapes." Signed: bruegel 1562. "The Blind Men."[145] Signed: bruegel 1562. "The Resurrection of Christ." Cat. No. 11. Signed: BRVEVEGEL	"The Resurrection of Christ." Cat. No. 11.	["View of Naples" sometimes called "The Sea Battle."] Cat. No. 9. "The Suicide of Saul" or "The Battle on Mount Gilboa." Cat. No. 10. Signed: Saul. XXXI CAPIT BRVEGEL M.CCCCC.LXII. (Possibly 1563 or 1565?) "The Fall of the Rebel Angels." Cat. No. 12. Signed: M.D.LXII BRVEGEL. *Dulle Griet* sometimes called "Mad Meg." (1562?) Cat. No. 13. "The Triumph of Death." (1562?) Cat. No. 14 "Two Monkeys." Cat. No. 15. Signed: BRVEGEL MDLXII.
1563	Bruegel and Mayken Coeck married in Notre Dame de la Chapelle, Brussels.[43] Bruegel settles in Brussels. Ambroise Paré's treatises on surgery published. Council of Trent ends. Building of Escorial begins.		"The Battle Between the Money Banks and the Strongboxes."[83] Signed: P. Bruegel Inuet. "The Poor Kitchen."[146] Signed: brueghel inue 1563. "The Rich Kitchen."[146] Signed: pieter brueghel inue 1563.	"The Tower of Babel." Cat. No. 16. Signed: BRVEGEL FE. M.CCCCCLXIII. "The Tower of Babel" sometimes called "The Small Tower of Babel." (Rotterdam). Cat. No. 17. "The Flight into Egypt." Cat. No. 18. Signed: BRVEGEL MDLXIII. See also 1562.

341

	Biographical Data and Historical Events	Drawings	Prints	Paintings
1564	Birth of Bruegel's son, Pieter (Helsche [Hell] Brueghel or Pieter Bruegel the Younger).[18] Cardinal Granvelle leaves the Netherlands (March 12). Shakespeare and Galileo born. Death of Calvin, Michelangelo and Vesalius. Rabelais' *Cinquième et dernier Livre* published.	"The Fall of the Magician Hermogenes."[149] Signed: BRVEGEL MDXLIIII. (This date is an error on Bruegel's part; it should read MDLXIIII.)	"The Fall of the Magician Hermogenes."[149] (published in 1565). Series of five engravings: "The Epileptic Women of Molenbeek."[147] (published in 1642). Series of thirteen(!) engravings of ships,[148] one dated 1565 "The Death of the Virgin" (published in 1574).	"The Procession to Calvary." Cat. No. 20. Signed: BRVEGEL MD.LXIIII. "The Adoration of the Kings." Cat. No. 19. Signed: BRVEGEL MDLXIIII. "The Death of the Virgin." Cat. No. 21. Signed: BRVEGEL ... (the year is effaced and practically illegible).
1565	Bruegel again mentioned in a letter from Scipio Fabius to Ortelius.[45] Antwerp city hall finished.	"Spring."[150] Signed: MD.LXV BRVEGEL. "The Calumny of Apelles."[151] Signed: P. BRVEGEL M.D.LXV. "The Painter and the Connoisseur"[154] (said to be a self-portrait [1565?]). Signed (controversial): BRVEGEL.	"Spring."[150] Dated 1570. "Saint James and the Magician Hermogenes."[149] Signed: 1565 Bruegel inuent. "The Parable of the Wise and Foolish Virgins."[152] Signed: BRVEGEL INV. (1565?) "The Parable of the Good Shepherd."[153] Signed: BRVEGEL IN:VEN: 1565. "Christ and the Woman Taken in Adultery." Cat. No. 29. (Engraving 1579)	"Haymaking." Cat. No. 22. (apocryphal signature removed) "The Corn Harvest." Cat. 23. Signed: BRVEGEL ..LXV. "The Return of the Herd." Cat. No. 24. Signed: BRVEGEL MDLXV. "The Hunters in the Snow." Cat. No. 25. Signed: BRVEGEL MD.LXV. "The Gloomy Day." Cat. 26. Signed: BRVEGEL [MDLX]V. "The Massacre of the Innocents." Cat. No. 27. "Winter Landscape with Skaters and a Bird Trap." Cat. No. 28. Signed: BRVEGEL M.D.LXV. "Christ and the Woman Taken in Adultery." Cat. No. 29. Signed: BRVEGEL M.D.LXV.
1566	On February 21 Nicolas Jongelinck deeds his art collection, including sixteen Bruegels, to the city of Antwerp as security.[47, 48] Second edition of Copernicus' *De Revolutionibus orbium coelestium*. Iconoclasts' Revolt (August 10 to end of August).	"*De vuile Bruid* (The Dirty Bride)" or "The Marriage of Mopsus and Nissa."[155]	"*De vuile Bruid*" or "The Marriage of Mopsus and Nissa."[155] Signed: 1570 Bruegel inuentor. "The Masquerade of Ourson and Valentine."[156] Signed: 1566 BRVEGEL. "Hunting the Wild Hare."[157] Signed: BRVEGEL 1566.	"The Numbering of the People at Bethlehem." Cat. No. 30. Signed: [BRVEGEL 1566.] "The Sermon of Saint John the Baptist." Cat. No. 31. Signed: BRVEGEL MD.LXVI. "The Wedding Dance in the Open Air." Cat. No. 32. Dated: M.DLXVI.

	Biographical Data and Historical Events	Drawings	Prints	Paintings
1567	Bruegel mentioned in Guicciardini's *Descrittione*.[23] Duke of Alba enters Brussels (August 22). Birth of Claudio Monteverdi.		"The Land of Cockaigne." Cat. No. 37. (1568–69).	"The Adoration of the Kings in the Snow." Cat. No. 33. Signed: BRVEGEL MDLXVII (date almost illegible). "The Conversion of Saint Paul." Cat. No. 34. Signed: BRVEGEL M.D.LXVII. "The Peasant Wedding" sometimes called "The Wedding Banquet." Cat. No. 35. "The Peasant Dance" sometimes called "The Kermess." Cat. No. 36. Signed: BRVEGEL. "The Land of Cockaigne." Cat. No. 37. Signed: M.DLXVII BRVEGEL.
1568	Birth of Bruegel's son, Jan (Velvet Breughel).[20] Bruegel mentioned in the second edition of Vasari's *Lives*.[44] Goedthals' *Les proverbes anciens*.[158] Execution of Count Egmont and Count Hoorn in Brussels (June 5). Death of Jean Goujon.	"Summer."[160] Signed: BRVEGEL MD.LXVIII. "The Beekeepers."[161] Signed: BRVEGEL MDLXV (date incomplete, probably 1568).	"Twelve Flemish Proverbs."[159] (1568–69?) "Summer."[160] "The Drunkard Shoved into the Pigsty."[162] Signed: P. BREUGHEL invent. (1568–69?)	"Head of an Old Peasant Woman." Cat. No. 38. "The Peasant and the Bird Nester." Cat. No. 39. Signed: BRVEGEL MD.LXVIII (signature and date have been overpainted). "The Cripples" sometimes called "The Beggars." Cat. No. 41. Signed: BRVEGEL M.D.LXVIII. "The Misanthrope" or "The Perfidy of the World." Cat. No. 40. Signed: BRVEGEL 1568 (controversial). "The Parable of the Blind." Cat. No. 42. Signed: BRVEGEL M.D.LXVIII. "The Magpie on the Gallows." Cat. No. 43. Signed: BRVEGEL 1568.
1569	Bruegel's death, probably on September 5.			"The Storm at Sea." Cat. No. 44.

BIBLIOGRAPHY

The literature on Bruegel, his work and the many problems it poses is extensive, and this bibliography makes no claim to completeness. Biographical reference works, museum and exhibition catalogs, and works on art history in general and Netherlands painting in particular are mentioned only in exceptional cases.

Antwerpens Gouden Eeuw. Kunst en kultuur ten tijde van Plantin. Antwerp, 1955.

ARPINO, G., and BIANCONI, P., *L'opera completa di Bruegel.* Milan, 1967.

Atti del II Congresso di Studi umanistici. Rome, 1952.

AUNER, M., "*Pieter Bruegel, Umrisse eines Lebensbildes.*" *Jahrbuch der kunsthistorischen Sammlungen in Wien,* 52 (1956), pp. 51–122.

BAIE, E., *Le Siècle des Gueux.* Six vols. (1937–53).

BALDASS L. VON, "*Die niederländische Landschaftsmalerei von Patinir bis Bruegel.*" *Jahrbuch der kunsthistorischen Sammlungen in Wien,* XXXIV, 4 (1918), pp. 111–57.

———, "*Les Paysanneries de Pierre Bruegel.*" *Les Arts plastiques* (1948), pp. 471–84.

BARKER, V., *Peter Bruegel the Elder.* New York, 1926; London, 1927.

BARNOUW, A., *The Fantasy of Pieter Bruegel.* New York, 1947.

BAUDELAIRE, C., "*Quelques caricaturistes étrangers.*" *Le Présent* (October 15, 1857), *L'Artiste* (September 26, 1858).

———, *Curiosités Esthétiques.* Paris, 1868; ed. of J. Crépet, Paris, 1923, p. 445.

BAX, D., *Ontcijfering van Jeroen Bosch.* The Hague, 1949.

BENESCH, O., *The Art of the Renaissance in Northern Europe; Its Relation to the Contemporary Spiritual and Intellectual Movements.* Cambridge, Massachusetts, 1945; London, 1965.

BERGSTRÖM, I., "*The Iconological Origins of 'Spes' by P. Bruegel the Elder.*" *Nederlands Kunsthistorisch Jaarboek* (1956), pp. 53–63.

BERNARD, C., *Pierre Breughel l'Ancien.* Brussels, 1908.

BERTOLOTTI, D., *Giulio Clovio principe dei miniatori.* Modena, 1882.

BOSSUS, C., "*En cherchant où est né Pierre Bruegel.*" *Les Arts* (October 17, 1947), p. 3.

———, "*Sur la date de naissance de Bruegel le Vieux.*" *Gazette des Beaux-Arts* (February, 1953), pp. 124–26.

BOSTRÖM, K., "*Das Sprichwort vom Vogelnest.*" *Konsthistorisk Tidskrift,* XVIII (1949), pp. 77–89.

———, "*Ar 'Stormen' verklingen en Bruegel?*" *Konsthistorisk Tidskrift,* XX (1951), pp. 1–9 and XXIV (1955), pp. 34–37.

BRION, M., *Bruegel.* Paris, 1936.

Bruegel, Catalog of the Exhibition, Musées royaux des Beaux-Arts, Brussels, 1969.

BURCHARD, L., and TERVARENT, G. DE, "*Bruegel's Parable of the Whale and the Tub.*" *Burlington Magazine,* XCI (1949), p. 224.

BUYSSENS, O., "*De schepen bij Pieter Bruegel de Oude; proeve van identificatie.*" *Mededelingen der Academie van Marine van België,* VIII (1954), pp. 159–91.

CALMANN, G., "*The Picture of Nobody.*" *Journal of the Warburg Institute* (January–June 1960), pp. 60–104.

CASTELLI, E., *Il demoniaco nell' arte.* Milan, Firenze, 1952. (French ed., Paris, 1958.)

CLAESSENS, B., *Aimer Brueghel.* Brussels, 1963.

———, and ROUSSEAU, J., *Notre Brueghel.* Antwerp, 1969.

COENEN, J., *Pieter Bruegel de Oude.* Maaseik, 1924.

———, "*Waar werd Pieter Bruegel geboren?*" *Het Oude Land van Loon,* IX (1954), pp. 56–61.

COHEN, G., *Histoire de la mise en scène au moyen âge.* Paris, 1906.

COLIN, P., *Pierre Bruegel le Vieux.* Paris, 1936.

COMBE, J., "*Jérôme Bosch dans l'art de Pierre Bruegel.*" *Les Arts plastiques* 11–12 (1948), pp. 435–46.

COREMANS, "*L'Archiduc Ernest, sa cour et ses dépenses d'après les comptes de Blaise Hütter son secrétaire intime et premier valet de chambre.*" *Bulletin de la Commission royale d'Histoire,* XIII (1847), pp. 85–147.

COX, T., *Pieter Bruegel.* London, 1951.

CRUCY, F., *Les Bruegel.* Paris, 1928.

CUVELIER, J., *Les dénombrements de Foyers en Brabant (XIVe–XVIe siècle).* Brussels, 1912.

DEBLAERE, A., "*Erasmus, Bruegel en de humanistische visie.*" *Vlaanderen,* 103 (January–February, 1969), pp. 12–20.

DE COCK, A., and TEIRLINCK, L., *Kinderspel en kinderlust in Zuid-Nederland.* 1902–5.

DE COO, J., "*Twaalf spreuken op borden van Pieter Bruegel de Oude.*" *Bulletin des Musées royaux des Beaux-Arts de Belgique.* Brussels (1965), pp. 83–104.

DEDEKIND(US), F., *Friedrich Dedekinds Grobianus verdeutscht von Kaspar Scheidt.* Reprint of the first edition of 1551, Halle (Saale), 1882.

DE JONGH, E., *Zinne- en Minnebeelden in de schilderkunst van de zeventiende eeuw.* Nederlandse Stichting Openbaar Kunstbezit en Openbaar Kunstbezit in Vlaanderen, 1967.

DE KEYSER, P., "*Rhetoricale toelichting bij het Hooi en den Hooiwagen.*" *Gentsche Bijdragen tot de Kunstgeschiedenis,* VI (1939–40), pp. 127–33.

DELEVOY, R.-L., *Bruegel.* Paris, 1953; London, 1953.

———, *Bruegel: Etude historique et critique.* Geneva, 1959.

DE MAEYER, M., *Albrecht en Isabella en de schilderkunst.* Brussels, 1955.

DE MEYER, M., *De volks- en kinderprent in de Nederlanden.* 1962.

DE MEYERE, V., *De Kinderspelen van Pieter Bruegel den Oude verklaard.* Antwerp, 1941.

———, and BAEKELMANS, L., *Het Boek der Rabauwen en Naaktridders. Bijdragen tot de studie van het volksleven der 16de en 17de eeuwen.* Antwerp, 1914.

DE MONT, P., *Peter Brueghel der Ältere.* Berlin, 1904.

———, "*De Genesis van de Kunst van P. Bruegel den Oude.*" *Elsevier's geillustreerd maandschrift* (1913), pp. 1–24, 139–62.

DEMORIANE, H., "*Bruegel et son fils.*" *Connaissance des arts,* 192 (February, 1968), pp. 94–101.

DENUCÉ, J., "*De Insolvente Boedelskamer, X, Familie de Bruyne.*" *Antwerpsch Archievenblad* (1928), pp. 195–207.

———, *Bronnen voor de Geschiedenis van de Vlaamsche Kunst. I, Kunstuitvoer in de 17de Eeuw te Antwerpen. De Firma Forchoudt; II, De Konstkamers van Antwerpen in de 16de en 17de Eeuwen. Inventarissen van kunstverzamelingen.* Antwerp, 1931–32. *III, Brieven en documenten betreffende Jan Breughel I en II.* Antwerp, 1934.

DE PAUW–DE VEEN, L., *Hieronymus Cock.* Brussels, 1970.

DE POTTER, F., and BORRE, P., *Geschiedenis der Rederijkerskamer van Veurne*. Ghent, 1870.

Der Fielen, Rabauwen oft der Schalcken Vocabulaer, ooc de beueysde manieren der bedeleeren oft bedelerssen, daer menich mensche deur bedrogen wort. … Ghedruct Thantwerpen by Jan de Laet in die Rape, Anno M.D.LXIIJ. See DE MEYERE and BAEKELMANS.

DVOŘÁK, M., *Pieter Bruegel der Ältere*. Vienna, 1921. Republished in *Kunstgeschichte als Geistesgeschichte*. Munich (1924), pp. 219–57. Second ed., 1928.

———, *Pierre Bruegel l'Ancien (37 chromophototypographies d'après ses principales œuvres à Vienne avec une introduction dans son art.)* Translated from the German by E. Klarwill. Vienna, 1931.

———, *Pieter Brueghel, Flämisches Volksleben*. Berlin, 1935.

———, *Die Gemälde Peter Bruegels des Älteren*. Vienna, 1941.

Een schoon liedekens Boeck inden welcken ghy invinden sult Veelderhande liedekens. Oude en nyeuwe. Om droefheyt en de melancolie te verdrijuen … tot Jan Roulans, 1541. See HELLINGA.

EHRENBERG, R., *Das Zeitalter der Fugger, Geldkapital und Kreditverkehr im 16. Jahrhundert*. Jena, 1896. French ed.: *Le siècle des Fugger*, Paris, 1955.

ENKLAAR, D. T., *Varende Luyden*. Assen, 1937. Second ed., 1956.

FAGGIN, G., *Brueghel*. Verona, 1953.

FEBVRE, L., *Le problème de l'incroyance au XVIe siècle. La religion de Rabelais*. Paris, 1947.

———, *Au cœur religieux du XVIe siècle*. Paris, 1957.

FEINBLATT, E., *Pieter Bruegel the Elder. Exhibition of Prints and Drawings*. Los Angeles County Museum, 1961.

FIERENS, P., *Bruegel l'Ancien*. Paris, Brussels, 1942.

———, *Bruegel the Elder*. London, Paris, 1946.

———, *Le fantastique dans l'art flamand*. Brussels, 1947.

———, "Sur la 'Tempête' de Bruegel." *Miscellanea J. Gessler*. Vol. I (1948), pp. 483–90.

———, *Peter Bruegel, sa vie, son œuvre, son temps*. Paris, 1949.

FRAENGER, W., *Der Bauern-Bruegel und das deutsche Sprichwort*. Erlenbach-Zurich, 1923.

———, "Die Fette und Magere Küche Pieter Bruegels." *Bildende Kunst* (1957), pp. 234–36.

FRANCIS, J., *Brueghel contre les pouvoirs*. Brussels, 1969.

FRIEDLÄNDER, M.-J., "Bruegels Schlaraffenland." *Zeitschrift für bildende Kunst* (1919), p. 74.

———, *Pieter Bruegel der Ältere*. Berlin, 1904. Second ed., 1921.

———, *Von Eyck bis Bruegel*. Berlin, 1915. Second ed., 1921.

———, "Pieter Bruegel." *Die Altniederländische Malerei*, XIV (Leiden, 1937).

FRYNS, M., *Pierre Brueghel l'Ancien*. Brussels, 1964.

GASCOIGNE, B., *World Theatre*. London, 1968.

GEISBERG, M., *Der Deutsche Einblatt-Holzschnitt in der ersten Hälfte des 16. Jh.* Munich, 1930.

GENAILLE, R., *Pierre Bruegel l'Ancien*. Paris, 1953.

GERARD, J., *Breughel le Vieux, toujours jeune*. Brussels, 1969.

GLÜCK, G., *Peter Bruegels des Älteren Gemälde im Kunsthistorischen Hofmuseum zu Wien*. Brussels, 1910. Introductory text reprinted in *Aus drei Jahrhunderten Europäischer Malerei*. Vienna, 1933.

— — —, "A Newly Discovered Painting by Brueghel the Elder." *Burlington Magazine*, LVI, 327 (June, 1930), pp. 284–86.

———, "Die Darstellung des Karnevals und der Fasten von Bosch und Brueghel." *Gedenkboek A. Vermeylen*. Antwerp, 1932.

———, "Über einige Landschaftsgemälde Peter Bruegels des Älteren." *Jahrbuch der kunsthistorischen Sammlungen in Wien*, N.F. IX (1935), pp. 151–65.

———, "Peter Brueghels des Älteren 'Kleiner Turmbau zu Babel.'" *Jahrbuch der kunsthistorischen Sammlungen in Wien*, N.F. X (1936).

— — — Hence M. DVOŘÁK), *Die Gemälde Peter Bruegels des Älteren*. Vienna, 1941.

— — —, "Bruegel the Elder and Classical Antiquity." *The Art Quarterly* (1943), pp. 167–86.

———, "Le paysage avec la Fuite en Egypte de Pierre Bruegel le Vieux." *Les Arts plastiques* 11–12 (1948), pp. 447–54.

———, *The Large Bruegel Book*. Vienna, 1952. (English edition of *Das grosse Bruegel-Werk*. Vienna, 1951. Third ed., 1955.)

GOEDTHALS. See Note 158.

GORIS, J. A., *Les colonies marchandes méridionales à Anvers de 1488 à 1567*. Louvain, 1925.

GOSSART, E., *L'établissement du régime espagnol dans les Pays-Bas et l'insurrection*. Brussels, 1905.

GRAULS, J., *De spreekwoorden van Pieter Bruegel den Oude verklaard*. Antwerp, 1938.

———, "Uit Bruegels Spreekwoorden." *Annuaire des Musées royaux des Beaux-Arts de Belgique*, II (Brussels, 1939), pp. 91–107.

———, "Ter verklaring van Bosch en Bruegel." *Gentsche Bijdragen tot de Kunstgeschiedenis*, VI (1939–40), pp. 139–60.

———, *Volkstaal en volksleven in het werk van P. Bruegel*. Antwerp, Amsterdam, 1957.

———, "Het spreekwoordenschilderij van Sebastiaan Vrancx." *Bulletin des Musées royaux des Beaux-Arts de Belgique* 3–4 (Brussels, 1960), pp. 107–64.

GROSSMANN, F., "Bruegel's 'Woman Taken in Adultery' and Other Grisailles." *Burlington Magazine*, XCIV (1952), pp. 218–29.

— — —, "The Drawings of Pieter Bruegel the Elder in the Museum Boymans." *Bulletin Museum Boymans-van Beuningen*, Rotterdam, V (July, 1954).

———, *Bruegel, The Paintings*. London, 1955. (Dutch ed., Utrecht, 1956; Italian ed., Milan, 1956.)

— — —, "New Light on Bruegel, I. Documents and Additions to the Oeuvre; Problems of Form." *Burlington Magazine*, CI, 678–79 (September-October, 1959), pp. 341–46.

———, "Bruegels Verhältnis zu Raffael und zur Raffael-Nachfolge." *Festschrift Kurt Badt*. Berlin, 1961.

GUICCIARDINI. See Note 23.

HAENDCKE, B., "Der Bauer in der Deutschen Malerei von ca. 1470 bis ca. 1550." *Repertorium für Kunstwissenschaft* (November, 1912).

HARREBOMÉE, P. J., *Spreekwoordenboek der Nederlandsche Taal*. Utrecht, 1858–70.

HAUSENSTEIN, W., *Der Bauern-Bruegel*. Munich, Leipzig, 1910. Second ed., 1920.

HAUSER, H., *La modernité de XVIe siècle*. Paris, 1930. Reprinted in *Cahier des Annales*, 21 (1963).

HELLINGA, W. G., *Een Schoon Liedekens-Boeck*. The Hague, 1941. Second ed., 1968.

HESSEL, J. H., *Abrahami Ortelii Epistolae*. Cambridge, 1887.

HILLS, J., *Das Kinderspielbild von Pieter Bruegel d. Ä. (1560). Eine volkskundliche Untersuchung.* Veröffentlichungen des Österreichischen Museums für Volkskunde, Vienna, 1957.

HYMANS, H., *"Pierre Breughel le Vieux."* Gazette des Beaux-Arts, III (1890), pp. 361–75; IV (1891), pp. 361–73; V (1891), pp. 20–40. Reprinted in *Oeuvres*, III, Brussels, 1920.

JACOBS-HAVENITH, L., *"Dulle Griet de Bruegel l'Ancien."* Revue catholique des idées et des faits, XV, 6 (1936), pp. 13–17.

JÄNICKE, T., *Pieter Bruegel. Weisheit und Torheit. Die verborgene Botschaft im Werk des Meisters.* Berlin, 1952.

JANS, A., *"Enkele grepen uit de kerkelijke wetgeving ten tijde van Pieter Bruegel."* Jaarboek, Museum voor Schone Kunsten Antwerpen (1969), pp. 105–112.

JEDLICKA, G., *Pieter Bruegel. Der Maler in seiner Zeit.* Erlenbach-Zurich, 1938. Second ed., 1947.

———, *Die Blinden von Pieter Brueghel.* Ratlingen, 1953.

KLEIN, H. A., *Graphic Worlds of Peter Bruegel the Elder.* New York, 1963.

KNIPPING, J. B., *Pieter Bruegel de Oude.* Amsterdam, 1945.

———, *Pieter Bruegel de Oude: De val der opstandige Engelen.* Leiden, 1949.

KREUZBERG, C., *"Zur Seesturm-Allegorie Bruegels."* Deutsches Jahrbuch für Volkskunde, VI (1960), pp. 33–49.

LAVALLEYE, J., *Pieter Bruegel the Elder and Lucas van Leyden. The Complete Engravings, Etchings, and Woodcuts.* London, 1967. (French ed., Paris, 1966; German ed., Vienna, 1966.)

LEBEER, L., *"De Blauwe Huyck."* Gentsche Bijdragen tot de Kunstgeschiedenis, VI (1939–40), pp. 161–229.

———, *"Nog enkele wetenswaardigheden in verband met Pieter Brueghel den Oude."* Gentsche Bijdragen tot de Kunstgeschiedenis, IX (1943), pp. 217–36.

———, *"Le Pays de Cocagne (Het Luilekkerland)."* Bulletin des Musées royaux des Beaux-Arts de Belgique (Brussels, 1955), pp. 199–214.

———, *Bruegel. Le Stampe.* Florence, 1967.

———, *Les Estampes de Pierre Bruegel.* Brussels, 1969.

LECLERC, A., *Bruegel the Elder.* London, 1950.

LEDERER, J., *"Les mendiants de Bruegel."* Mélanges historiques Et. de Cauwenberghe (Louvain, 1961).

LESCURE, P. DE, *"Notes sur Breughel et l'art romanesque."* Les Arts plastiques 11–12 (1948), pp. 495–99.

LIEBAERS, H., *"Pieter Bruegel de Oude, Brabander en wereldburger."* Brabant, 5 (1969), pp. 18–32.

LINFERT, C., *"Die Vermummung, eine Figuration der Angst und der Lüge in Bildern von Bosch, Bruegel und Max Beckmann."* Atti del II Congresso di Studi umanistici (Rome, 1952), pp. 263–68.

LOMAZZO, G. P., *Trattato della Pittura, Scultura e Architettura.* Milan, 1585.

LOOSJES, J., *De invloed der Rederijkers.* Utrecht, 1909.

LUGT, F., *"Pieter Bruegel und Italien."* Festschrift für Max J. Friedländer (Leipzig, 1927), pp. 111–29.

LYNA, F., and EEGHEM, W. VAN, *De Sotslach, klucht uit ca. 1550.* Brussels, 1932.

MAETERLINCK, L., *Nederlandsche spreekwoorden handelend voorgesteld door Pieter Breughel den Oude.* Ghent, Koninklijke Vlaamsche Academie, 1903.

———, *"Pieter Breughel den Oude en de prenten van zijnen tijd."* Verslagen en mededelingen der Koninglijke Academie voor Taal- en Letterkunde (Ghent, 1903), p. 109.

———, *Le genre satirique dans la peinture flamande.* Ghent, 1903. Second ed., 1907.

MARIETTE, *"Abecedario et autres notes relatives aux arts et aux artistes."* Archives de l'Art français (1851–53).

MARIJNISSEN, R. H., *"Het wetenschappelijk onderzoek van Bruegels œuvre."* Vlaanderen, 103 (January–February, 1969), pp. 4–11.

———, *"Pieter Bruegels kleurnotities op zijn tekeningen 'nart het leûen'."* Brabant, 3 (1969), pp. 24–32.

———, *Bruegel, 16de eeuwse Brabander.* Amsterdam, Antwerp, 1969.

M[ARLIER], G., *"Pierre Bruegel l'Ancien."* Le siècle de Bruegel (Brussels, 1963), pp. 66–74.

MARLIER, G., *"Peeter Balten, copiste ou créateur?"* Bulletin des Musées royaux des Beaux-Arts de Belgique (Brussels, 1965), pp. 127–42.

———, *La Renaissance Flamande, Pierre Coeck d'Alost.* Brussels, 1966.

MÉLOTTE, G., *Études sur les vieux peintres flamands,* I, Pierre Bruegel dit le Vieux ou le Drôle. Brussels, 1864.

MENZEL, G. W., *Pieter Bruegel der Ältere.* Leipzig, 1966.

MICHEL, E., *Les Breughel.* Paris, 1892.

———, *"Pierre Bruegel le Vieux et Pieter Coecke d'Alost."* Mélanges Hulin de Loo (Brussels, 1931).

———, *Bruegel.* Paris, 1931.

———, *"Bruegel le Vieux a-t-il passé à Genève?"* Gazette des Beaux-Arts, 6e pér., XV (1936), I, pp. 105–8.

———, *"Bruegel et la critique moderne."* Gazette des Beaux-Arts, XIX (1938), I, pp. 27–46.

———, *"Bruegel ou non Bruegel."* Les Arts plastiques (1948), 11–12, pp. 460–70.

MINNAERT, P., *"Essai d'interprétation de la 'Dulle Griet' de P. Bruegel."* Apollo, XXII (1943), pp. 8–12; XXIV, p. 10.

MONBALLIEU, A., *"P. Bruegel en het altaar van de Mechelse Handschoenmakers (1551)."* Handelingen van de Koninklijke Kring voor Oudheidkunde, Letteren en Kunst van Mechelen, LXVIII (1964, 1965), pp. 92–110.

———, *"Een werk van P. Bruegel en H. Vredeman de Vries voor de tresorier Aert Molckeman."* Jaarboek, Museum voor Schone Kunsten Antwerpen (1969), pp. 113–135.

MÜNZ, L., *Bruegel. The Drawings.* Complete edition. London, 1961. (German ed., Cologne, 1962.)

MULS, J., *P. Brueghel.* Brussels, Amsterdam, 1924, 1934, 1945.

NOVOTNY, F., *"Über das 'Elementare' in der Kunstgeschichte."* Plan, I, 3 (December, 1945), pp. 174–87.

———, *Die Monatsbilder Pieter Bruegels d. Ä.* Kunstdenkmäler, Heft 4, Vienna, 1948.

PANSE, F., and SCHMIDT, H.J., *Pieter Bruegels Dulle Griet. Bildnis einer psychisch Kranken.* Leverkusen, 1967.

PFISTER, K., *Brueghel.* Leipzig, 1921.

PINDER, W., *"Zur Physiognomik des Manierismus."* Festschrift für Ludwig Klages (1932).

POPHAM, A. E., *"Pieter Bruegel and Abraham Ortelius."* Burlington Magazine, LIX (October, 1931), pp. 184–88.

RAHLENBECK, C., *Les protestants de Bruxelles.* Ghent, 1877.

Riehl, B., *Geschichte des Sittenbildes in der deutschen Kunst bis zum Tode Pieter Brueghels des Älteren.* Berlin, 1889.

Roggen, D., "*J. Bosch. Literatuur en folklore.*" *Gentsche Bijdragen tot de Kunstgeschiedenis,* VI (1939–40), pp. 107–26.

Rombouts, P., and Lerius, T. van, *De Liggeren en andere historische archieven der Antwerpsche Sint Lucasgilde onder zinspreuk "Wt ionsten versaemt."* Two vols., Antwerp, The Hague, 1864–76. Reprinted, Amsterdam, 1961.

Romdahl, A. L., "*Pieter Brueghel der Ältere und sein Kunstschaffen.*" *Jahrbuch der kunsthistorischen Sammlungen in Wien,* XXV (1905), pp. 85–169.

———, *Pieter Bruegel den äldre.* Stockholm, 1947; Oslo, 1951.

[Ronday, H. J.], *Pieter Bruegel de Oude.* The Hague, 1962.

Sacré, M., *Daniël van Oesbroeck's Rijmkroniek van Merchtem (1565).* Merchtem, 1918.

Saintenoy, P., *Les arts et les artistes à la cour de Bruxelles,* II. Brussels, 1934.

Schotel, G. D. J., *Geschiedenis der Rederijkers in Nederland.* Two vols., Amsterdam, 1862–64.

Sedlmayer, H., *Pieter Bruegel: Der Sturz der Blinden. Paradigma einer Strukturanalyse. Hefte des kunsthistorischen Seminars der Universität München,* No. 2. Munich, 1957.

———, "*Die 'Macchia' Bruegels.*" *Jahrbuch der kunsthistorischen Sammlungen in Wien,* N.F., VIII (1934), pp. 137–59.

Sée, M., Rebillon, A., and Préclin, E., *Le XVIe siècle.* Paris, 1942.

[Seilern, A.], *Flemish Paintings and Drawings at 56, Prince's Gate, London, S.W.7.* London, 1955.

Sip, J., *Pieter Brueghel d. Ä. Die Heuernte.* Prague, 1960.

Smekens, F., "*Het schip bij Pieter Bruegel de Oude: een authenticiteitscriterium?*" *Jaarboek, Museum voor Schone Kunsten Antwerpen* (1961), pp. 5–57.

Spelen van Sinne. Antwerp, 1562. See Note 143. See also E. van Even.

Spicer, J. A., "*The 'Naer het Leven' Drawings: By Pieter Bruegel or Roelandt Savery.*" *Master Drawings,* VIII, 1 (1970), pp. 3–30.

Speth-Holterhoff, S., *Les peintres flamands de cabinets d'amateurs au XVIIe siècle.* Brussels, 1957.

Stecher, J., "*La Sotie et la Sotternie flamande.*" *Bulletin de l'Académie royale de Belgique* (Brussels, 1877), p. 388.

Stechow, W., *Peter Brueghel the Elder.* New York, 1955 (French ed., 1954).

Sterck, J., "*Bruegel en de volkstaal.*" *Vlaanderen,* 103 (January–February, 1969), pp. 39–40.

Stoett, F. A., *Drie kluchten uit de zestiende eeuw.* Zutphen, 1932.

———, *Nederlandse spreekwoorden en gezegden.* Eighth ed., Zutphen, 1953.

Stridbeck, C. G., *Bruegel und der niederländische Manierismus. Ein Beitrag zur Kenntnis seines grossfigurigen Spätstils.* Stockholm, 1953.

———, "*Bruegels Fides-Darstellung. Ein Dokument seiner religiösen Gesinnung.*" *Konsthistorisk Tidskrift,* XXIII (1954).

———, *Bruegelstudien. Untersuchungen zu den ikonologischen Problemen bei Pieter Bruegel d. Ä. sowie dessen Beziehungen zum niederländischen Romanismus.* Stockholm, 1956.

———, "*Combat between Carnival and Lent.*" *Journal of the Warburg Institute* (1956), pp. 96–109.

Stubbe, A., *Bruegel en de Renaissance.* Antwerp, 1950. Second ed., Hasselt, 1964.

Sudeck, E., *Bettlerdarstellungen vom Ende des 15. Jahrhunderts bis zu Rembrandt.* Strasbourg, 1931.

Terlinden, C., "*Pierre Bruegel le Vieux et l'histoire.*" *Revue Belge d'archéologie et d'histoire de l'art,* XII (1942), 4, pp. 229–57.

Theuwissen, J., "*De localisatie van de eenstaartploeg in Vlaams België.*" *Handelingen van het XXVIe Vlaams Filologencongres.* Ghent, 1967.

———, "*Is het houtzagen afgebeeld op de 'Prudentia' van Pieter Bruegel een ironisch-satirisch tafereel?*" *Miscellanea J. Duverger* (Ghent, 1968).

Tietze-Conrat, E., "*P. Brueghels Kinderspiele.*" *Oudheidkundig Jaarboek,* II (May, 1934), p. 127.

Tolnai, K. von, "*Studien zu den Gemälden P. Bruegels d. Ä.*" *Jahrbuch der kunsthistorischen Sammlungen in Wien,* N.F., VIII (1934), pp. 105–35.

———, *Die Zeichnungen Pieter Bruegels.* Munich, 1925. Second ed., Zurich, 1952.

Tolnay, C. de, *Pierre Bruegel l'Ancien.* Two vols., Brussels, 1935.

———, "*La seconde Tour de Babel de Pierre Bruegel l'Ancien.*" *Annuaire des Musées royaux des Beaux-Arts de Belgique* (Brussels, 1938), pp. 113–21.

———, "*'Le Peintre et l'Amateur' de Pierre Bruegel le Vieux.*" *Les Arts plastiques* 11–12 (1948), 455–59.

———, "*Bruegel et l'Italie.*" *Les Arts plastiques* (August–September, 1951), pp. 121–30.

———, *The Drawings of Pieter Bruegel the Elder.* New York, London, 1952. (English edition of *Die Zeichnungen Pieter Bruegels.* [See under Tolnai].)

———, "*An unknown early panel by Pieter Bruegel the Elder.*" *Burlington Magazine,* XCVII, 629 (August, 1955), pp. 239–40.

———, "*Remarques sur quelques dessins de Bruegel l'Ancien et sur un dessin de Bosch récemment réapparus.*" *Bulletin des Musées royaux des Beaux-Arts de Belgique* 1–2 (Brussels, 1960), pp. 3–28.

Van Bastelaer, R., *Les Estampes de Peter Bruegel l'Ancien.* Brussels, 1908.

———, *L'origine et l'application du mot "Gueux" aux signataires du Compromis des Nobles.* Antwerp, 1912.

———, "*Le paysage de la Parabole des Aveugles de Pierre Bruegel.*" *Mélanges Hulin de Loo* (1931), pp. 321–25.

———, "*A propos de dessins de Bruegel.*" *Bulletin de l'Académie royale de Belgique, Classe des Beaux-Arts,* XVII (Brussels, 1935), 1–2, pp. 30–37.

———, and Hulin de Loo, G., *Peter Bruegel l'Ancien, son œuvre et son temps. Étude historique suivie des catalogues raisonnés.* Brussels, 1905–7.

Vanbeselaere, W., *Pieter Bruegel en het Nederlandsche Maniërisme.* Tielt, 1944.

———, "*Pieter Bruegel en Hugo van der Goes.*" *Gentsche Bijdragen tot de Kunstgeschiedenis,* X (1944), pp. 221–32.

———, "*Bruegeliana.*" *Dietsche Warande en Belfort* (December, 1946).

Van Beylen, J., "*De uitbeelding en de dokumentaire waarde van schepen bij enkele oude meesters.*" *Bulletin des Musées royaux des Beaux-Arts de Belgique,* X, 3–4 (Brussels, 1961), pp. 123–50.

Van Breugel, G. P. C., *Gedenkschrift wegens een schilderij van spreekwoorden door Pieter Breughel Jr (de boertige in 1623) nagelaten door Mr Joh. Enschedé in 1867 en door de erven aan de Stad Haarlem ten geschenke gegeven.* Haarlem, 1876.

347

VAN DEN BOSSCHE, L., *Breughel*. Diest, 1942.

VAN DEN DAELE, O., and VEERDEGHEM, F. VAN, *De Roode Roos. Zinnespelen en andere tooneelstukken der zestiende eeuw*. Bergen, 1899.

VAN EEGHEM, W., *Drie schandaleuse spelen (Brussel 1559) ingeleid en met de verhooren uitgegeven door ...* Antwerp, 1937.

VAN EVEN, E., *Het Landjuweel van Antwerpen in 1561*. Louvain, 1861.

VAN GELDER, J. G., "*Pieter Bruegel: 'Na(e)rt het leven' of naar 'het leven.'*" Bulletin des Musées royaux des Beaux-Arts de Belgique 1–2 (Brussels, 1960), pp. 29–36.

VAN GELDER, J. G., and BORMS, J., "*Bruegels zeven Deugden en zeven Hoofdzonden.*" Beeldende Kunst, XXV (1939), 10–11, pp. 73–106.

VAN GILS, J. B. F., *Een andere kijk op Pieter Brueghel den Ouden*. The Hague, 1940–42.

VAN LEEUWEN, F., "*Iets over het handschrift van de 'naer het leven' — tekenaar.*" Oud Holland, LXXXV (1970), pp. 25–32.

VAN LENNEP, J., "*L'Alchimie et Pierre Bruegel l'Ancien.*" Bulletin des Musées royaux des Beaux-Arts de Belgique (Brussels, 1965), pp. 105–26.

———, *Art et Alchimie*. Brussels, 1966.

VAN MANDER, C., See Note 3.

VAN OESBROECK, D., *Cleyn Memoriael*. See SACRÉ.

VAN OSTAYEN, "*P. Breugel.*" Krities Proza, II (Antwerp, 1925), pp. 124–33.

VAN PUYVELDE, L., "*Een onbekende schilderij met Vlaamsche spreuken.*" Isidoor Teirlinck Album (Louvain, 1931), pp. 293–99.

———, *Pieter Bruegel. The Dulle Griet*. London, 1945.

———, *La peinture flamande*. Brussels, 1953, 1962.

———, "*De poetische waarheid van Pieter Brueghel de Oude.*" Brabant, 3 (1969), pp. 15–23.

VAN VAERNEWIJCK, M., *Van die beroerlicke tijden in die Nederlanden en voornamelijk in Ghendt 1566–1568*, F. Vanderhaeghen, ed. Five vols. Ghent, 1872–81. French translation, Ghent, 1905–6.

VAN VLOTEN, J., *Het Nederlandsche Kluchtspel van de 14de tot de 18de eeuw*. Three vols. Haarlem, 1854.

VAN ZYPE, G., *Bruegel*, Brussels, 1926.

Veelderhande geneuchlijcke dichten, tafelspelen ende refereynen. Antwerpen, Jan van Ghelen, 1600. Maatschappij der Nederlandsche Letterkunde, Leiden, 1899.

VENTURI, L., "*Pierre Bruegel, peintre de la comédie humaine.*" Jardin des Arts, LIX (1959), pp. 668–681.

VERDEYEN, R., "*Bruegel en de dialektgeographie.*" Miscellanea J. Gessler, II (1948), pp. 1236–40.

VERMEYLEN, A., *Geschiedenis der Europeesche plastiek en schilderkunst*, III. Amsterdam, 1925, pp. 191–208.

———, "*Bruegel et l'art italien.*" Cahiers de Belgique, I (February, 1928), pp. 1–8.

———, *Pieter Brueghel, Landschappen*. Amsterdam, Antwerp, 1935.

VERVLIET, H. D. L., "*De 'Twaalf spreekwoorden' van het Museum Mayer van den Bergh. Een onderzoek naar de datum van ontstaan van de onderschriften.*" Jaarboek, Koninklijk Museum voor Schone Kunsten. Antwerp, 1945–60, pp. 73–81.

VIDEPOCHE, J., *The Elder Peter Bruegel*. New York, 1938.

VINKEN, P. J., "*De betekenis van Pieter Bruegel's Nestrover.*" Het Boek, XXXIII (1958), 4.

VLIEGHE, H., "*Overname van motieven uit het werk van Mantegna in schilderijen van Pieter Bruegel de Oude.*" Bulletin des Musées royaux des Beaux-Arts de Belgique (Brussels, 1962), pp. 277–84.

WAUTERS, A., "*La famille Breughel.*" Annales de la Societé d'Archéologie de Bruxelles, I (1887–88), pp. 7–79.

———, "*Pierre Breugel et le cardinal Granvelle.*" Académie royale de Belgique, Bulletin de la Classe des Lettres (Brussels, 1914), pp. 87–90.

WEYNS, J., "*Bruegel en het stoffelijk kultuurgoed van zijn tijd.*" Vlaanderen, 103 (January–February, 1969), pp. 24–29.

———, "*Bij Bruegel in de leer voor honderd-en-een dagelijkse dingen.*" Ons Heem, XXIII, 3, 1969. 1969.)

WINKLER, F., *Die Altniederländische Malerei*. Berlin, 1924.

WÜRTENBERGER, F., *Pieter Bruegel der Ältere und die deutsche Kunst*. Wiesbaden, 1957.

ZIMMERMANN, H., "*Quellen zur Geschichte der Kaiserlichen Haussammlung.*" Jahrbuch der kunsthistorischen Sammlungen in Wien, XXV (1905).

ZOEGE VON MANTEUFFEL, K., *Pieter Bruegels Landschaften*. Berlin, 1934.

ZUPNICK, I. L., "*The Meaning of Bruegel's 'Nobody' and 'Everyman'.*" Gazette des Beaux-Arts, LVII (Mai–June 1966), pp. 257–70.